\THE

First County Park System.

A COMPLETE HISTORY

OF THE

INCEPTION AND DEVELOPMENT OF THE ESSEX COUNTY PARKS OF NEW JERSEY.

BY

FREDERICK W. KELSEY,

Vice-President of the Original Commission.

McGrath Publishing Company

&

NATIONAL RECREATION AND PARK ASSOCIATION

WASHINGTON, D.C.

LC#77-143060
ISBN 0-8434-0444-2

CONTENTS

3

NRPA Recreation and Park Perspective Collection

edited by Dr. Diana R. Dunn
Director of Research
National Recreation and Park Association

Education through Play	Curtis, H.	$19.00
Education through Recreation	Jacks, L.	$13.00
Education by Plays and Games	Johnson, G.	$15.00
The New Leisure Challenges for the Schools	Lies, E.	$17.00
Play in Education	Lee, J.	$25.00
Play and Mental Health	Davis, J.	$15.00
Education through Recreation	Johnson, G.	$10.00
The Practical Conduct of Play	Curtis, H.	$19.00
The Play Movement	Rainwater, C.	$21.00
The Play Movement and its Significance	Curtis, H.	$19.00
Playground Technique and Playcraft	Leland, A. & L.	$17.00
American Playgrounds	Mero, E.	$17.00
Leisure in the Modern World	Burns, C.	$15.00
The Threat of Leisure	Cutten, G.	$12.00
The Normal Course of Play	NRA	$16.00
The Education of the Whole Man	Jacks, L.	$12.00
The Challenge of Leisure	Pack, A.	$14.00
Off the Job Living	Romney, G.	$15.00
A Philosophy of Play	Gulick, L.	$16.00
Europe at Play	Weir, L.	$45.00
Music in American Life	Zanzig, A.	$28.00
Music in Institutions	Van de Wall, W.	$35.00
The First County Park System	Kelsey, F.	$15.00
County Parks	NRA	$14.00
Central Park—First Annual Report	New York	$14.00
The Spirit of Youth and the City Streets	Addams, J.	$12.00
Annals March 1910	AAP&SS	$16.00
Municipalization of Play and Recreation	Fulk, J.	$10.00
Luther Halsey Gulick	Dorgan, E.	$14.00
Constructive and Preventive Philanthropy	Lee, J.	$15.00

order from:

MC GRATH PUBLISHING COMPANY
821 Fifteenth Street N.W.
Washington, D.C.

FOREWORD

PARKS and playgrounds are commanding more and more
attention. Their creation, care and maintenance have
become one of the most important of municipal functions.
The increasing interest of all classes in every urban community accentuates the movement toward better and
healthier conditions in, and contiguous to, the centers of
population. American literature on this subject has thus
far mainly considered effects rather than causes; results
instead of methods.

In this volume, the intention of the author has been to
correctly indicate, step by step, the moving forces and
potential facts in the development of an extended and
costly park system, one of the largest, and the initial county
park system of this country.

The record begins at the beginning. It deals with the
inception of the enterprise, the legislation creating it; and
reflects the smooth course of progress until the blighting
influence of special interests and of practical politics were
injected into the undertaking. Events are reflected, as by
a mirror, just as they occurred. The ten years covered by
this history indicate a period of rapid development of parks
and recreation grounds all over the country. The growth in
expenditure for park areas and attractions here are typical

of most other rapidly growing communities. The general support everywhere given by the public, and the recent awakening for better civic and municipal conditions, augur well for the future. This increasing interest in New Jersey, as elsewhere, accounts for the publication of this volume. The first publication as a serial has called forth many expressions for the history in more permanent form. The generous words of commendation received have been gratifying to the author, and have encouraged the publishers to comply with these requests.

In the concluding chapter, the experiences of other large public park undertakings, and the reasons for recommending changes in the law and in park administration here, are noted.

FIRST COUNTY PARK SYSTEM

CHAPTER I.

PLAN FOR THE ESSEX COUNTY PARKS.

THE inauguration of a great system of public improvements is often preceded by general discussion, more or less
public agitation, and sometimes by party divisions, in the
efforts to obtain the requisite legislation. This has been
not infrequently the case in the selection and acquirement
of lands for public parks, which, owing to the great cost
usually involved, becomes at once an important factor
within the community or the areas affected.

In New York the discussion over a proposed "outer park"
in 1851 resulted in a special session of the Legislature in
July of that year and the authorization made for the city
to locate the park on the East River, above Sixty-sixth
street, and including the tract then known as St. John's
Wood. Opposition to the project promptly developed, and
the property was never acquired for park uses. Two years
later, in 1853, a commission was created with authority to
locate and acquire land above Fifty-ninth street for what
is now Central Park. It was not, however, until three
years afterward that the park received its name, and not
until 1859 that the lines were extended to One Hundred
and Tenth street, and that that park, which has since been
so much to New York and to the country, was fully and
firmly established. This history of Central Park has been
repeated in many of its phases in nearly every large park
undertaking where the parks have not been acquired by
gift from individual owners.

9

Here in Essex County the commendable efforts made by
public-spirited citizens to secure a park for Newark were
actively followed for four years—from 1867 to 1871—but
without practical result, although the act of April 9, 1867,
created a preliminary commission of twenty-six members
to select and locate grounds for the purpose. From the
available records of that movement it appears that by the
selection of but one park in the northern portion of the
city, rival claims of other sections, especially from the
southern wards of the city, so complicated the situation as
to prevent further action either by the Legislature or by the
city authorities.

The dedication by the Newark Aqueduct Board in December, 1889, of the city reservoir property for park uses
was a change of record and in name only, for nothing was
done to utilize that small tract for park purposes. Its condition precluded this without some embellishment.

The interesting report of the Newark Board of Trade
committee on parks for 1892 was apparently well received.
The initiative features for carrying the project into effect
were, however, wholly lacking, and the movement did not,
therefore, reach the legislative stage. Nor did it give
opportunity for division or objection from the different
localities where the opposition had been so pronounced
against the plan for a single and similar park location as
made by the commission of 1867.

PLAN FOR ESSEX COUNTY PARKS UNIQUE.

The experience in the establishment of the Essex County
parks has been unique in the history of large public undertakings. Unlike similar enterprises, no hindrances obtained
or objections were raised. The first recommendations were
in favor of direct application and early action, and were of
comprehensive scope, hence open to attack if disfavored by
press, party or public. The reverse condition prevailed.
So smoothly and rapidly did events culminate that but
comparatively few persons not directly interested apparently appreciated the significance of the movement, or what
it meant for the future. Now that nearly twelve years

have elapsed since the inception of the enterprise, there are very many who know little as to the original plans for the acquirement and development of the parks, and many more who know even less about the causes and conditions which have led to the present status of the county park movement. This system has now cost more than $5,000,000—a fact which shows how generous the people have been in favoring the appropriations.

Many desire to know more about the formulative steps in the enterprise and the consecutive developments since. It fell to my lot to be one of those actively identified with the subject from the beginning. Requests at various times have been made that I write an account of what has occurred. With some reluctance I have acceded. To my mind the public is as fully entitled to all the available information regarding the early activities and events connected with the parks as they are to the fullest enjoyment of these pleasure grounds, purchased and improved at the taxpayers' expense.

It is, therefore, my purpose in this and in succeeding chapters to give some of the more important incidents connected with park developments in this county. As no consecutive account of the enterprise has yet been written, I shall devote some space to the inception of the movement, and to the basic principles upon which the structure of popular approval then rested; shall refer to the selection of commissioners; and shall indicate some of the more important work of the first commission, appointed July 18, 1894.

Of subsequent events, such matters will be considered, as the change in the shaping of the enterprise, from the time of the appointment of the permanent commission in 1895; how that change came to be made; the location of the parks; the contest over the parkways; the corporate influences that finally prevailed; how the original plans have been changed and enlarged at greatly increased cost; and a reflex of such other conditions as have a direct interest and potential bearing upon the subject—but always with fidelity to the facts.

In thus adhering to the line of truth, I shall reproduce here and there letters and oral statements of those officially or directly concerned, adding, in this way, the element of personal touch and a present and live interest to the record.

For a number of years prior to 1893, I had given considerable attention to the development of the larger American and European parks, and had become firmly convinced of the needs and opportunities for a park system covering the interesting and varied topography of Essex County, with Newark as the central or radiating point.

On December 6, 1893, the Board of Trade of the Oranges adopted a resolution which I had presented to the meeting, urging "that legislation may obtain at an early date that will enable the growing communities in this portion of the State to provide a suitable system of parks and parkways," and authorizing copies of the resolution sent to "His excellency, Governor Werts, also to the Senator and to the Assemblyman-elect from this district."

The resolutions were well received and favorably commented upon at the time. Very soon afterward, January 3, 1894, the first annual dinner of the board was given in the Music Hall building, Orange. Among the sixty or more guests present was President William A. Ure, of the Newark Board of Trade.

In responding to the toast, "Orange and Its Suburbs," I referred to the action that had previously been taken favoring a park system; described the wonderful views from Eagle Rock and other points on the crest of the Orange Mountain; noted that no such locations for public parks, with such views and overlooking such vast populations, were elsewhere available in this county, and brought out the desirability of immediate action. Later in the evening, in meeting then for the first time Mr. Ure, his generous and complimentary reference to my presentment of "the larger park project," as he termed it, led to the suggestion made at his office in Newark, a few days afterward, that the committees of the two boards should "get together" and see what could be done toward carrying the suggested project into practicable effect. This was soon accomplished.

In that brief conversation Mr. Ure then called my attention to the fact that the Newark board already had a special Committee on Parks; that its report two years before, although generally approved in the city, had not led to any more practical results than had the earlier efforts toward establishing a larger park; that the Park Committee and the Newark board would most willingly co-operate in any feasible plan for a much needed park system; and that anything he could do individually or in behalf of the board as president he would gladly do. Both in his bearing and conversation, he was cordial, earnest, direct and practical. Of all the men I had met since I had been a resident of Essex County, no one with whom I had up to that time discussed civic affairs had impressed me more favorably than did Mr. Ure. His evident sincerity of purpose to have something accomplished for the public good, solely for the reason that it would be for the people's interest and for civic betterment, was inspiring. The conversation was of but perhaps ten minutes' duration. It has always been a most agreeable recollection, leaving a strong impression on my mind, and, as it now comes again vividly before me, I feel impelled to pay this deserved tribute to Mr. Ure's memory.

At a meeting of the Orange board a few days after the conversation referred to, the proposition to meet with the Park Committee of Newark was explained and fully approved, and a special committee was then appointed to attend the proposed conference. This was the committee: F. W. Kelsey, chairman; Frank W. Child, E. M. Condit, J. H. Baldwin and J. S. Holmes. The committee at once took up the subject of "formulating a suitable plan," and by the time of the first meeting of the Newark and Orange committees, held at the Board of Trade rooms in Newark, on April 14, 1894, a definite and complete plan had been agreed upon.

In the meantime President Ure, who was also then pro-

prietor of The Sunday Call, had been active on lines looking
toward immediate results. On January 21, 1894, the following editorial appeared in The Call:

"The park question has been brought forward again by
the Orange people, and we hope they will keep at it. The
County of Essex is made up of cities and towns whose
people are without opportunity to get near Nature or enjoy
any open-air recreation, excepting on the public highways,
or by trespassing upon private property. There is available
for public park purposes at moderate expense the finest park
site known near any Eastern city—the slope and crown of
Orange Mountain. Delay will remove it from possible use
as a park, for it is being rapidly occupied by residences.
The appropriation of a suitable tract, at almost any point
from Maplewood west to near Montclair, is now feasible,
and it will not be so a dozen years hence."

STRONG SUPPORT FOR PROJECT.

This article indicated that at least one of the leading
county papers would favor the movement, and with the
two Board of Trade organizations actively interested in the
work, there was every encouragment that strength and enlarged influences would be rapidly added from all portions
of the county. This prediction was very soon verified, as
the sequel of events will'show.

In order to insure interest and co-operation in legislative
circles, a copy of the resolutions which had been adopted by
the Orange Board of Trade favoring a park system was
sent to Senator George W. Ketcham, then the representative of Essex County in the State Senate, to which, on
March 31, 1894, he replied:

"Your communication of the twenty-fourth instant, enclosing resolutions relative to public parks, is duly received.

"The subject is a most important one, and has my sympathy. Some weeks since the New England Society sent a
similar letter, and my suggestion was that Assemblyman

Storrs, of the district covered by these natural parks, should formulate a bill, which could be supported in both Senate and House of Assembly. If your board will suggest some particulars, naming, for example, certain areas to be set apart, I shall take great pleasure in urging the matter upon the attention of the Legislature. The time seems to be propitious for a movement of this kind. I shall be glad of any suggestions which the Orange Board of Trade may be pleased to make."

The resolutions of the New England Society had been adopted at the March (1894) meeting, and, while favorable to the park project, did not outline any definite plan of procedure. The plan was not for certain mountain areas as was evidently in Senator Ketcham's mind, but rather for a comprehensive scheme of parks and parkways for the whole county. These responses, however, indicated that the legislative coast was apparently clear for favorable action there, and, therefore, all that was needed was a concise and readily understood plan that would not only unify all interests throughout the county and districts more directly affected, but would also directly appeal to the Legislature, without the action of which no plan, even of the most attractive outline, could be carried out. With an appreciation of these underlying conditions, the Orange committee went quite exhaustively into the subject, as to how the desired results could best be accomplished.

The formulative plans and accompanying legislation of many established park systems were considered. The intent was to select the more desirable features of each, based upon practical experiences elsewhere, to simplify the most effective and practicable, and then to formulate a plan that would be in every way adaptable to the municipal, taxable and topographical conditions, and unified into one system for our "home county."

Our committee from Orange was, therefore, in a measure at least, prepared for the meeting of the joint committee on April 14, above mentioned, notices of the conference having been sent to each member of both committees April 12, 1894.

The committee from the Newark Board of Trade consisted of Messrs. Cyrus Peck, A. Q. Keasbey, J. S. Higbie, T. S. Henry, S. J. Meeker, S. S. Sargeant, E. S. Ward, J. E. Fleming, A. B. Twitchell, P. T. Quinn, Edward Schickhaus, G. W. Wiedenmayer and President William A. Ure, member ex-officio.

COUNTY PARKS' PLAN OUTLINED.

Most of the members of both committees were present at the meeting. Almost the sole topic discussed was what would be the most desirable plan for inaugurating the park movement. There was no dissenting voice as to the need of having something done, and that directly. The Orange committee, while having in mind its definite plan, stated that it would be glad to first consider any plan or suggestion from the Newark board, which represented a much larger district, and a very much larger and longer established membership. To this proposition came the response that they had no special suggestions to make at that time; that no action had been taken by them since the report of the committee of two days before; that they had understood the meeting then in session "had been called at the suggestion of the Orange committee;" and that they would therefore be glad to know what we had to suggest. As chairman of the Orange committee, I then proceeded to outline the plan as given below, stating that our committee were unanimous in favoring it; that it was, however, submitted in a tentative way, for suggestion, for improvement or amendment, or such changes as might make the plan better serve the purpose which all desired should be accomplished.

The plan as outlined was heartily approved. Its presentment in writing, and publication, was requested. A. Q. Keasbey and myself were then by resolution appointed as a sub-committee of two to prepare for prompt introduction into the Legislature a bill drawn on the lines of the plan as presented.

After the meeting I wrote out, as requested, this plan. It was in the form of a letter addressed to the chairman of Committee on Parks of the Newark Board of Trade, and was dated April 16, 1894.

As this communication and plan soon became the foundation upon which the superstructure of the movement for a county park system and the favorable legislation that soon followed rested, the letter is here given in full. It is as follows:

"Agreeable to the understanding at our meeting Saturday evening, fourteenth instant, I note below the principal features of the plan unanimously approved by all the members of both committees then present, as being the most feasible for establishing a system of parks and parkways:

"First—That action be taken by a special commission, authorized by legislative enactment applicable to Essex County.

"Second—That such commission be composed of five members appointed by the resident judge of the Supreme Court, and that an appropriation be provided by a direct charge upon the county for requisite expenses, surveys, plans, etc., the commissioners to serve without compesation.

"Third—That the commission be strictly non-partisan, its members selected for fitness, with the sole object of devising the very best scheme for a system of parks that is practicable for the entire district.

"The more we consider this plan the more simple, direct and effective it appears. It provides for immediate action. It admits of comprehensive treatment for the whole section from the Passaic River to the Second Mountain, without complications or delay incident to so many local governing bodies attempting to solve the problem. The method of appointment, free from political or speculative interference, should at once enlist the confidence and support of the community favorable to the enterprise.

BENEFITS OF A PARK SYSTEM.

"A bill, simple in its provisions, providing for the carrying out of this plan, and affecting only counties of the first class, could hardly meet with reasonable objection in the Legislature. Every one recognizes that a well-devised public park system for this great Essex County population would be not only of great benefit and value to every locality, but of immense importance to the State as well. Every home in the entire section would be more attractive and valuable; every piece of property share in the improvement; and the cost be largely or fully compensated in this way.

"Should your committee and board, upon further consideration, concur in the general plan stated, or suggest any other providing for similar results, we shall be happy to meet you again in conference at an early date with the view of arranging further details and the drafting of a bill that can be with confidence submitted to the Legislature and the people.

"Very truly yours,

"FREDERICK W. KELSEY,

"Chairman Committee of Parks and Public Improvements of the Board of Trade of the Oranges."

The plan met with immediate popular approval. The leading papers favored it. Various civic organizations passed resolutions commending it, and public-spirited citizens in different portions of the county wrote personal letters favoring its prompt adoption.

There was no longer any doubt that the time had arrived for prompt action. When Mr. Keasbey and I met soon afterward to prepare the desired legislative bill, we were entirely agreed upon all but a single point. The plan as favored by the joint committee on April 14 was to provide by legislative enactment for a permanent commission, relying upon future legislation for authority to enlarge its needed powers and to provide the requisite appropriations. This conviction, I believe, was shared by all the members present at that meeting. In preparing the bill Mr. Keasbey expressed to me the view that in law it was "inconsistent to provide by legislation for a permanent board to perform a temporary act." As the duty of the commission first appointed would be to map out and report on a plan for the park system, he contended that the term of authority and life of the commission should therefore be for a limited term only, and be provided for in the act itself. To this view I acceded, although some members of the committee felt that, owing to the uncertainties of future legislation, the provision for a permanent commission was preferable. On April 20, 1894, W. A. Ure expressed this view in a letter which I then received from him:

"Replying to yours of yesterday, I would say that the Park Commission plan you outline seems to meet all the requirements.

"As to making the commission permanent, I think that would be necessary in order to accomplish permanent benefit. At the outset, however, the joint committee, which is composed of gentlemen competent to consider the subject, might formulate a general plan to be submitted to the people of the county, the details of which, if ratified, to be afterward supervised and controlled by the commission."

In all other respects than the one limiting the time for which the commission was to be appointed, the bill was in strict accord with the plan as above outlined, and was favorably reported at the meeting of the joint committee, held at the Board of Trade rooms, Newark, the afternoon of April 25, 1894. The proposed bill was there, as drawn and without amendment, unanimously approved, and the same afternoon a copy of the bill was transmitted to Senator Ketcham at Trenton for introduction into the Legislature. The bill was accompanied by the following letter:

"We believe this bill will meet with the unanimous approval of substantially the whole county. If in your judgment the presence of representatives of our organizations will in any way tend to expedite the passage of the bill, kindly advise us by wire and we will respond promptly. A message to Frank W. Child, secretary, Orange, will reach us directly."

This letter was signed by the members of the Newark and Orange committees then present at the meeting.

Under the same date, April 25, 1894, a letter was sent to Senator Ketcham from the chairmen of the two committees, explaining that "the bill had been prepared by the joint committee on public parks of the board of trade of Newark and the Oranges;" that "it is merely the first step designed to lead to a general plan which may command public approval and accomplish great results with the aid of future legislation."

"The expenditure," the letter stated, "is limited to a small sum and the commissioners are to act without compensation. We earnestly hope that the bill may be promptly passed, so that the work of the commission may be well advanced during the coming summer."

"After much discussion and consideration of the subject," continued the letter, "we are convinced that this simple, initial step toward a great public improvement will command the general approval of the citizens of Essex County. It will not be necessary for Hudson County to adopt the plan, and, therefore, it should meet with no opposition in that quarter."

The bill as sent to Senator Ketcham was promptly introduced by him the following day, April 26, and then made its appearance as "Senate Bill No. 205." It was promptly referred to, and soon afterward reported by, the Committee on Municipal Corporations, and passed without obstruction or hardly a dissenting vote in the Senate. A like result followed in the passage of the bill in the Assembly, and on the eighth of May, within two weeks after the measure had reached the Legislature, it was approved by Governor Werts. As a result, the bill, exactly as prepared by the joint committee, had in this short time thus become "Chapter CLVI" of the Laws of 1894.

The provisions of this law, providing for a temporary commission, scarcely call for extended reference here. In brief, the presiding justice of the Supreme Court was authorized to appoint a commission of five persons for the term of two years, to "consider the advisability of laying out ample open spaces for the use of the public * * * in such county," with "authority to make maps and plans of such spaces and to collect such other information in relation thereto as the said board may deem expedient;" and "as soon as conveniently may be," to "make a report in writing of a comprehensive plan for laying out, acquiring and maintaining such open spaces."

The commission was also authorized to employ assistants, and to be reimbursed for actual traveling expenses incurred "in the discharge of their duties." The total expenditures were limited to $10,000, the payment to be provided for by the Board of Freeholders* in the usual manner.

The attitude of the public at the time of the approval of the bill had continued to grow more and more favorable. The suggestion that those identified with the enterprise had merely adapted the scheme of the metropolitan park system of Massachusetts, entirely overlooked the fact that it was merely the preliminary stages of that undertaking—the initial legislation for the first commission—which had been, in a general way, followed. The Orange committee had in the early part of that year, 1894, gone quite fully into the various phases of many of the larger park systems. It was found that the Metropolitan Park plan, embracing, as it at that time did, thirty-nine separate municipalities, and various counties about Boston, and having an entirely new and untried system of financing, was wholly unsuited to the needs of Essex County. Indeed, we had all along understood that, under the New Jersey Constitution, such a district as had been mapped out and included in the Metropolitan Parks area could not be legally laid out or established here; and that this State would not be likely, even if it

*Board of Chosen Freeholders is the official title of the county governing bodies in New Jersey.

could, to advance its credit to the various municipalities for millions of dollars, as had been done in Massachusetts, relying, as there, upon a future apportionment or assessment upon the cities and towns within the district for final reimbursements.

It was, therefore, recognized at the outset of the discussion that only the general form of the preliminary legislation in Massachusetts could be in any way advantageously used here. It had also been recognized that the movement for larger parks or park systems had taken different forms in nearly every city. New York had in 1888 expended millions of dollars in adding nearly 4,000 acres of new park lands, extending, with the great connecting parkways, from Van Cortland Park on the Hudson, to the beautiful Pelham Bay Park on Long Island Sound—all embraced in what was soon afterwards known as the park system of the Bronx.

In and about London the County Councils had at that time located and acquired, as had the authorities of Paris, vast tracts of lands for park uses, but each was then lacking, as in most other European and American urban communities, in any concerted action or comprehensive connective park system such as, I believe, was first adopted in this country in Detroit, and as was now deemed desirable for Essex County.

It was accordingly understood that the favorable legislation that had just then been so promptly obtained in our own Legislature, would not only enable the work of acquiring and developing a park system here to go readily and rapidly forward, but, under the law, a commission, "selected for fitness," would be enabled to adopt the best features of all the park systems, and by holding the enterprise on the lines so cordially approved by the Legislature, the press and the people, would retain public confidence and support, to the lasting benefit of the whole county and State.

Thus was the bark of the first county park enterprise safely launched, in smooth water, under fair skies, without a reef or ripple in view.

CHAPTER II

NOT many days after the enactment of the park law, as stated in the preceding chapter, I chanced one morning in New York to meet Senator Ketcham, and as we walked together down lower Broadway, after exchanging some congratulatory remarks over the success of the park bill in the Legislature, he said to me that he had just seen Judge Depue, and that he understood the appointment of the five commissioners was soon to be made. He then conveyed to me the message, which he said the judge had requested him to give to me, viz., that he (the judge) desired to see me with Cyrus Peck before the appointments were made. He said that he had not asked, and did not know, what object the judge had in mind.

When I learned, a day or two later, that Mr. Peck had not received any invitation for the conference direct, I wrote to Judge Depue, May 21, 1894, as follows:

"Senator Ketcham has kindly conveyed to Mr. Cyrus Peck and myself your request for further information on park matters and the suggestion that we meet you in conference. Reciprocating the confidence expressed, it will give us pleasure to meet you at such time and place as most agreeable for you to make the appointment."

The following was the response:

"11th June, '94.

"My Dear Sir—I will be glad to see you and Mr. Peck at the courthouse on Saturday morning, next, at 10 A. M.

Please bring copy of park bill with you. I will ask you to notify Mr. Peck of the appointment.

"I am now going to Trenton every day to Supreme Court, being home only in the evenings. Hope the time for the meeting will be satisfactory.

"Very truly yours,
"DAVID A. DEPUE.
"Fred. W. Kelsey, Esq."

JOINT COMMITTEE ACTS.

Before this letter was written, a meeting of the joint committee on parks was held at the Newark Board of Trade rooms on the afternoon of June 6. At this meeting resolutions were adopted, "expressing the sense of the meeting that a letter be sent Judge Depue requesting at as early a date as agreeable the appointment of the commission, as provided by recent act of the Legislature;" Also, that

"The chairman of the Newark and Orange committees be requested to present in person to Judge Depue a certified copy of the act, together with the letter signed by the full membership of each committee."

In accordance with these resolutions, the letter was then prepared and was as follows:

"Newark, June 6, 1894.
"Hon. David A. Depue, Justice of the Supreme Court.

"Dear Sir—We, the undersigned members of the committees on public parks of the boards of trade of Newark and Orange, who have been active in preparing the bill for the appointment of boards of county commissioners, a certified copy of which accompanies this letter, beg to request that you may, at as early a date as agreeable, appoint the commission as provided in said act. We have further resolved that this letter and copy of this act be presented to your honor by the chairmen of our respective committees.

"CYRUS PECK, chairman Newark committee.
"FRED. W. KELSEY, chairman Orange committee.
"S. J. Meeker, Edward Schickhaus, J. H. Baldwin,

James E. Fleming, William A. Ure, president Newark
Board of Trade; James S. Holmes, president Board of
Trade of the Oranges; F. W. Child, A. Q. Keasbey."

The judge was advised of this action the following day,
June 7, but the letter and copy of the act were retained
to present to him "in person," as called for in the resolution of the committee and as requested in his note of June
11, for an appointment.

Judge Depue received us in his private room at the courthouse on the morning of June 18, according to appointment. He said:

"Gentlemen, I sent for you because I desire to consult
with you as to the appointment of the fifth commissioner.
Four of the appointees I have already decided upon. I
have in mind the names of several men outside of Newark
whom I think well of or who have been recommended to me
as the other commissioner, but I have thought I should like
to talk with you before making a further decision.

"First," he went on, "I propose to appoint my old friend,
Edward Jackson, of Belleville. You know him, do you
not?

"Well," he continued, when we had answered him in the
negative, "I'll vouch for Ed. Jackson"—which was by common consent acceptably received; and he then said: "I am
going to appoint you, Mr. Peck, and Mr. Meeker, of the
Board of Trade committee, from Newark, and you, Mr.
Kelsey, from Orange. This leaves the fifth member from
the county at large, outside of Newark, yet to be selected."

The judge then mentioned the names of five men whom
he had in mind for the place—two from Montclair, two
from South Orange, and one from Orange. My own appointment, he said, precluded the consideration of the other
resident of Orange. The other names were then gone over.
Not one of them had been favorably considered by the members of the joint committee who had given the personnel
of the proposed commission earnest thought. When asked

our opinion, I thus stated to the judge, and explained why we believed there were others available who would better fill the requirements of the position. I explained that, in the initial stages of this large undertaking, we believed it of the utmost importance, not only that the members of the commission should possess the requisite qualifications as to competency and fitness, but also that the best results would obtain in a small board, as would be the new commission, if men were selected for congenial tastes and similar ideas of public duty.

In response to the inquiry as to whom we would suggest, two names were mentioned. One, the judge explained, he could not for local reasons consider. The other was that of George W. Bramhall. After listening to the reasons given for Mr. Bramhall's appointment as the fifth commissioner, the judge replied:

"Well, I do not know Mr. Bramhall. I never met him, but, from what has been said, I am willing to appoint him."

PARK COMMISSIONERS ANNOUNCED.

He then, from a directory on his desk, made a note of the name. Directly after this incident Mr. Peck and I withdrew. The judge came immediately into court and announced the names of the commissioners as follows: Edwin W. Jackson, of Belleville; Cyrus Peck and Stephen J. Meeker, of Newark; Frederick W. Kelsey, of Orange; and George W. Bramhall, of South Orange. His remarks in the court were brief. After referring to the application from the Board of Trade committee for the appointment of the commission and to the act authorizing the appointment, he then named the commissioners as stated in the conference, and said:

"I propose this morning to name the individuals, leaving the actual appointment until I understand whether they are willing to serve. There seems to be a great public interest in the subject pro and con, and mainly in favor of it. I have received a great many letters of advice and I may say that they governed me somewhat in the selection. The com-

missioners, while appointed, are not authorized to execute
the work. Their duties are tentative, leaving the Legislature to execute the carrying out of the scheme as future
legislation may provide.

"I think it is my duty to appoint men who are so favorable to this enterprise and so desirous that it should be
executed that they will be judicious enough to make such
recommendations as will be approved by the public, so that
the work will finally be accomplished. If I had another
commissioner to appoint, I could easily find another to fill
the place.

"The act provides that the commission employ persons,
and that it may spend a sum not exceeding $10,000, I
think. I will appoint the five men named next Saturday,
unless they should decline to serve."

Judge Depue's manner and conversation during the conference, and his remarks in open court, were indicative of
his earnest approval of the new law, of the objects sought,
and of the legal machinery provided to those ends. Considering that "fitness" for the position had already become
the corner-stone of the commission's structure, it was quite
unexpected to hear him first speak of appointing his "old
friend," without expressing any opinion as to whether he
himself believed in the appointment for reasons of especial
qualifications for the office. But there could be no reasonable doubt that the judge shared in the current sentiment
favorable to the parks. It was also plain that he was desirous of appointing a commission that would be generally acceptable, and that up to that time no pressure of political
of other scheming influences had been active in shaping
either his thought or determination in fulfilling to the best
of his ability the trust reposed in him as the sole appointing
power in naming the commission.

The public response to the announcement of appointment
of the new commission was as cordial as it was generous.
Both editorially and in the news columns, all the leading
papers within—and some without—the county were emphatic in their commendation of the project, and referred

favorably to those selected to perform the preliminary work. The Newark News editorially, on June 18, 1894, accredited Judge Depue with having "wisely sought to give every locality proper representation."

"Not in this country, if in the world," said the News at that time, "is there another place where the eye can look upon the dwelling places of so many people as may be seen on a clear day from Eagle Rock and other good points of observation on the Orange Mountain."

"The ease with which the park bill passed the House, Senate, and Governor is proof of the wisdom and .popularity of the measure," is the way The Daily Advertiser put it in an editorial of June 19; following an editorial of the day previous referring in a complimentary way to the personnel of the commission and expressing confidence that "these men will do their work faithfully and well."

At the same time the commissioners were each asked if they intended to accept the appointment and for their views for publication. Mr. Bramhall said:

"There should be a series of parks and parkways so designed that at least a part of them could be reached by walking. * * * Within the county there are many excellent locations for parks." One of the other commissioners referred to "public parks as a common possession in which the poor and the rich share, and share alike."

On June 23, 1894, Judge Depue made the formal announcement of the commission's appointment in a brief statement, again referring to the action of the Board of Trade committees, and to the act authorizing the appointment; and renaming "the commissioners—Messrs. Jackson, Peck, Kelsey, Meeker and Bramhall—to be known as the Essex County Park Commission, to hold office for the term designated in the act, and to execute all the powers, and perform all the duties, mentioned in said act."

FAVORABLE CONDITIONS.

The reader may now readily appreciate the favorable conditions under which the first park commission began the discharge of its duty on the organization of the board that same afternoon—June 23, 1894. It was with interest and enthusiasm that each of the commissioners took up the work entrusted to him. A position and condition of trust had been imposed and accepted, with the sincere desire, I believe shared in by all, to be loyal to that trust and the obligations incurred.

With the prevalent sentiment of confidence that had been extended by the public, by the Legislature, by the press and by the court, what greater incentive could be placed before a body of men than was thus placed immediately before the commission at that time? The members soon found that in the work before them they were both officially and personally congenial, and that differences in conviction were soon moulded into harmonious action for a common purpose. Such was the fact; and as I now cast a reflective view back to the efforts and results attained by that board, it occasions in my mind less surprise than ever before that this preliminary commission should have accomplished in about half a year that which it was authorized to occupy two years in doing, and that less than one-half of the available appropriation of $10,000 had been expended.

The organization of the board took place at the Board of Trade rooms, Newark. In talking with Mr. Peck prior to the board meeting, he had suggested that, as I had formulated the plan that had proven so acceptable, I should be the first president, and I was chosen temporary chairman.

The judge later sent word by his friend, Commissioner Jackson, that he desired Mr. Peck should be president. No reasons were stated. The commission was not a committee for organization under parliamentary rules, but a legally constituted body, with clearly defined duties and powers, and presumably possessing inherently the unquestionable right of providing for its own organization. As, however, Mr. Peck resided in Newark, which city represented the largest population in the county, we acquiesced. Nevertheless, we did not recognize the judge's right to interfere. I was then elected vice-president and Mr. Jackson was agreed upon as temporary secretary.

It was then agreed to employ a secretary; various committees, on by-laws, rooms, printing, etc., were selected; and the actual work of the board thus began. It was decided to have regular monthly meetings, and more frequently, as circumstances required. The requirements soon called for meetings once a week, or even more often—a policy and condition that was followed to the close of the work of the commission.

At the meeting of June 28, a series of resolutions were received from the "East Orange Park Avenue Protective Association" expressing "its approbation" of the prompt appointment of the commission, favoring additional legislation, and suggesting that the "care of certain streets and avenues leading to and through such park or parks" be placed in the hands of the new board. The resolutions also requested "the active co-operation of the said Park Commission in our efforts to preserve Park avenue for the purposes above described."

The petition was accompanied by a lengthy communication favoring "a small park or parks within the limits of each of our large cities or elsewhere in the vicinity;" a "large park or a chain of parks on or over the Orange Mountain;" and suitable approaches to the parks, "reserved as carriageways, free from trolley cars, overhead wires and anything that would detract from the character of these approaches as first-class residence streets." No reference was made to Central avenue, which was ere long to become the storm center of one of the most stubbornly fought contests between corporate greed and the forces that make for civic betterment that have yet occurred in this country.

As the commission had not at this time fairly completed its organization, and had not even taken up the subject of the proposed park locations, the communications were read and received without action.

The work of the board now went rapidly forward. Commissioner Meeker was elected treasurer. A large number of applications were received for the position of secretary. A committee of the board, after passing upon the various applicants, recommended Alonzo Church—the present secretary—and he was appointed at the meeting of July 12, 1894.

One of the first matters looking to results that was decided by the commission, was as to the desirability of getting in touch with the various governing bodies of the county. It was felt that, not only was each locality entitled to be heard regarding its preference or recommendations, but that the board would be strengthened, and in many ways assisted, by calling out the wishes and suggestions from various parts of the county. It was agreed that the most feasible and effectual way of doing this would be through a communication addressed directly to each of the local authorities and associations interested in municipal improvement. This plan was agreed upon, and on June 28, I was, by resolution of the board, requested to prepare a letter from the commission on the lines indicated. After referring to the powers conferred by the Park act, and to Judge Depue's selection of the commissioners, "two from Newark, one from Belleville, one from Orange, and one from South Orange," the letter was as follows:

THE COMMISSION'S LETTER.

"The outlining of a plan that will result in the greatest good to the greatest number, by the most direct methods and at the least cost, necessitates wide research, and the fullest suggestions as to localities and their availability. To these ends, and in the spirit indicated by the law, and the court, we invite your co-operation in according fair consideration to every portion of the district.

"That the prompt location and acquirement of a comprehensive system of parks in this county is desirable, if not imperative, for the health and prosperity of the people, appears to be generally admitted. Indeed, that this community is belated in this important public improvement is quite too apparent.

"The experience of other places demonstrates conclusively that parks are the most appreciated where most liberally provided. The more the public realize their advantage to health, to property—to say nothing of enjoyment—the more eager all classes are for park extensions and new pleasure grounds.

"With all the millions New York had previously expended for park lands and improvements, only a few years ago large areas of additional park lands were secured at an expense of some $9,000,000 or $10,000,000, and that municipality has again this year undertakings for additional parks at an authorized expenditure of several millions more.

"Philadelphia, with her city squares and beautiful Fairmount Park, is just undertaking at an estimated cost of $6,000,000, the construction of a boulevard from the new city hall direct to Fairmount Park, much of the way through a densely built up part of the city. These are only instances of the movement going on everywhere. Smaller communities like Paterson and Trenton have already parks and parkway approaches of commanding importance.

"Not one of these communities, and but few in this country or in Europe, have the natural advantages of topography, scenery, etc., that nature has already provided here in Essex County.

"Hardly another community so important has so long neglected to utilize these advantages, or so persistently failed to realize the importance of this subject.

"There are more than 300,000 people in this county, in the midst of these unusually favorable conditions, yet there are only a few acres of public park lands in the whole district.

"The whole population appears to have developed with but little regard to matters of this nature that have long ago been deemed vital in isolated cities and towns of less population and fewer resources. We believe you will concur in the conviction that existing conditions call for immediate action.

"With this view, we invite your co-operation, and would

be happy to receive from you at an early date any suggestions that occur to your honorable body as to particular
localities in your section you think could be practically acquired by gift or otherwise for park purposes, either separately or as part of a county system. We further invite any
other recommendations or objections that you may deem
of importance bearing on this question.

"Presuming you have in your vicinity lands considered
specially suited for a local park or parks, we should esteem
any suggestions as to these; also as to what proportion of
the cost of such lands and improvements you would think
equitable to be borne by your own city, or adjacent property,
or both, and what proportion, if any, by the county at large.

"Hoping we may be favored with your early reply,

"Yours very respectfully,

"ESSEX COUNTY PARK COMMISSION."

Replies were very generally received. Many were sent
promptly. All were in hearty accord with the aims and
objects of the commission. Some of the suggestions were
practical and of value; others were visionary or too elaborate. Each bore the imprint of good wishes and good will.
Mayor Lebkeucher, of Newark, was one of the first officials
to respond. He expressed the intention of co-operating
with the commission in its work and stated that he would
take up the subject with the Common Council and the
Board of Street and Water Commissioners. Mayor Gill,
of Orange, sent a similar reply.

The majority of suggestions favored the location of the
large park sites on the Orange Mountain. Montclair, East
Orange, Millburn, Bloomfield, Belleville, South Orange, and
other places were soon heard from. A number of civic associations, improvement societies, and citizens in various
localities throughout the county also responded and expressed a desire to co-operate in some way in the work of
the commission.

Indeed, the recommendations became so varied and extended as to the matter of park sites that the commissioners

began to ask themselves if the entire county was not "parkable."

While the friends of the parks were providing suggestions and recommendations, the board was looking also to broader fields of information and to the guidance of experience. At the meeting July 19, 1894, the secretary was requested to obtain the best available maps of the county; with the reports, together with such other data as might be of value to the commission, from the leading park departments of the country and from the larger cities abroad. The information thus obtained was later of great value for comparison, and in the preparation of the charter for the permanent commission.

EXECUTIVE SESSIONS OF PARK BOARD.

A resolution was also adopted at the July 19 meeting which has since remained a factor in the proceedings of the Park Board, although it long ago outlived its usefulness and therefore by sufferance remains as a relic of the past. I believe it would have been better had it never been adopted than to have encroached, as it has thus far, into a field where its purpose and workings were never intended. I may, perhaps, be pardoned for the reference to this subject here, for I drew the resolution in question and on my motion it was adopted. It provided that "the meetings of the commission be in executive session, and that the secretary furnish a report of the proceedings to the press after each meeting."

When this motion was agreed upon, every member of the commission realized that the moment our decision to locate park lands anywhere in the county was made public, there would naturally be a speculative movement attempted to forestall the future Park Board in securing the required lands at the then current prices. The matter was carefully considered, and the resolution promptly adopted for the sole and only purpose of giving any future commission the opportunity of acquiring such locations as might be needed for the parks without starting the real estate adventurers and speculators on the chase toward securing the needed acquirements first. There never was a suggestion, or a thought, which I have ever heard expressed, that favorable action on that resolution should or would have the effect of practically and permanently creating, in method of procedure, a close corporation in the transaction of public business—a method of conducting, under ordinary conditions, meetings of public officials, which I disfavored in July, 1894, as I have since the location of the parks was made public in 1896.

During the summer of 1894, the park project, so far as the commission was concerned, kept as warm as the weather. Two meetings a week were not exceptional. If not a meeting, a conference, or some other call to duty kept up an active, continuous interest. The latter part of July the commission rented the rooms at 800 Broad street, formerly occupied by Hon. Theodore Runyon—a portion of the suite since occupied by the present commission.

During August the letters of suggestion and replies to requests for reports—some from foreign countries—continued to come in. The secretary prepared, and under direction of Commissioner Bramhall, chairman of the printing committee, the board published a pamphlet on "Park Benefits" that had a friendly reception and extended distribution.

PARK SITES CAREFULLY EXAMINED.

By early September the commissioners had personally examined many of the possible park sites; had, in fact, looked over the county east of the Second Mountain quite generally. Some of the more desirable locations had been studied with care. The general plan for the park system was gradually taking shape. Expert advice was needed. Arrangements were accordingly made with five experienced landscape architects, who were to prepare plans and act in the capacity of "park making advisers" to the commission. In the engagement of Olmsted, Olmsted & Eliot, it was "with the wish and expectation that the commission obtain the personal services and report of Frederick Law Olmsted."

The request was complied with, and this was the last public work that received the attention of that great specialist in park designing. The other architects were Nathan F. Barrett, Ehrenberg & Webster, John Bogart and Gray & Blaisdell. The agreement with each was specific and well understood in advance. They were, as park experts, "turned loose in the county," figuratively speaking. Each was engaged to act entirely and wholly independent of the other. Each received a county map, upon which, after studying the topography of the whole county below the Second Mountain —the relative populations, etc., etc.—was to be marked in a way indicating the locations of such parks and connecting parkways as, in his (or their) judgment, would provide the best park system, as viewed from the standpoint of the whole county. In this view the needs and conveniences of the denser populations were to be considered. The maps, when completed and marked as indicated, were to become the property of the commission. The necessary expenses in making the investigations were to be met by the board, but the compensation was for a fixed fee, which was in each case very reasonable; for it was understood that the plans to be submitted were on the principle of competitive designs, and the architect (or firm) making the most acceptable design and report would very naturally have an advanced position for future engagement should their plans be carried out.

THE EXPERTS' PLAN.

Under this arrangement the commission received the five plans and full reports for what, in view of all the circumstances, was an exceedingly reasonable price, viz.: a total cost of but $2,372.13.

In a number of important features, their recommendations, such as the location of Branch Brook Park, Newark, the acquirement and retention of Central avenue and Park avenue as parkways, and the location of large areas for mountain parks and reservations, all agreed, and were, after careful study, found to be in full accord with the convictions of all the commissioners; and these outlines were definitely agreed upon before the close of the year. By December the plans of the board had sufficiently matured so that, on December 6, a committee of two was appointed "to wait upon John R. Emery, Esq., and consult with him about procuring his legal services for the commission," for the purpose of preparing a charter for a succeeding commission.

Thus at the close of 1894, all was yet smooth sailing. We were nearing the port of destination, and the harbor of safe condition for an attractive and most creditable county park system did not seem far beyond.

CHAPTER III.

PRELIMINARY WORK COMPLETED.

THE inspection and selection of park sites within a territory possessing the varied topography and variety of natural scenery found in Essex County was a most agreeable and interesting experience.

Three of the commissioners at this time, 1894, belonged to that numerous contingent in Northern New Jersey, who, in common parlance, "live in New York and sleep in New Jersey." They knew, from everyday experience, something of the practical workings of "the strenuous life," having passed the years of business activity under the exacting conditions imposed by close application to commercial affairs in the metropolis, yet, in common with many well-intentioned citizens of this class, they had felt some degree of interest and pride in their locality and in the county at large. It was, therefore, a pleasure for them to become better acquainted with the beauties of their own county by the personal contact and observation required in looking over possible park sites.

It is one of the unfortunate elements in all the matters pertaining to good citizenship that Essex County, and, in a greater or less degree, the entire State of New Jersey, should be deprived of the local interest of so many of her most active residents and voters, as results from so large an egress from their homes of business men and workers every day, excepting Sundays and holidays, throughout the year.

In roaming over "green fields and pastures new," all the commissioners were deeply interested in what they saw. One day they were looking at the then very unattractive

Newark reservoir (now Branch Brook Park) site; another
day found them at Millburn. Perhaps the day following
they were in the Oranges, or Montclair, or at Belleville.
Next they visited Weequahic and passed from consideration
of this mosquito-breeding and buzzing locality with unfavorable comment.

ON THE ORANGE MOUNTAIN.

But of all the experiences during the summer and
autumn of that year (1894) the days devoted to the Orange
Mountain were at once the most impressive and delightful.
As we walked on the crest of the first mountain from the
point where the mountain abruptly ends near Millburn to
the limits of the county at Northern Montclair Heights,
the beautiful and varied views were inspiring. Every new
prospect along the entire distance was a revelation.

The beauties of these diversified scenes on ideal autumnal
days can be only inadequately described. The views from
the southern points of the crest overlook plains, farms, and
occasionally a small village; or South Orange, Hilton, Irvington and the fringe of southern Newark, and an attractive section of Union County. From the central portion,
as from the cable road track above Orange Valley looking
toward Eagle Rock, Orange and East Orange, portions of
Montclair, Bloomfield and the full lines of Newark beyond,
Bergen Hill, the Brooklyn Bridge and the tall buildings of
Greater New York, all appear in view. The whole area,
save for the intercepting trees and foliage, of this vast, extended area of buildings, looks as though, of this immediate
prospect, it might be truthfully written: "All the world's
a roof." The points from the northern sections of the crest
are again more open and picturesque. Standing there, one
looks down upon the rolling country in the direction of
Brookside, and the attractive section of Franklin Township
and Nutley, and the still more picturesque central eastern
portion of Passaic County.

Over all this wonderful panorama is cast the varying
shades of sunshine, cloud, and shadow. The gray dawn of

a misty morning casts a somber aspect, which, in turn, is
transformed into brightness as the sun dispels the shadow,
and the scene changes, refulgent with the warmth and glowing tinge of light. The alternating lines of sunshine and
shadow, as the fleeting clouds pass over the landscape below,
call to mind the words of the poet, when he describes the
grandeur of nature's greater mountains, in the lines:

"The snow-capped peaks of the azure range,
Forever changing, yet never change."

From these experiences the reader may readily infer why
the first park commission favored the acquirement of liberal
areas on the Orange Mountain for parks, and may recognize the conditions that controlled such locations as were
afterward made there, and which are now a part of the
county park system.

COMMISSIONERS AS HOSTS.

In October, while the commissioners were devoting considerable time to the Orange Mountain, it occurred to me
that it might widen the scope of the enterprise to bring together a number of men, active friends of the parks, and
enlarge the acquaintance and congenial interest of some
of the earnest supporters of the movement. Accordingly I
arranged a dinner and invited a number of those interested
in the enterprise. After the commission and its guests had
spent the day of October 20 on the mountain, the evening
at the Country Club, with the entire party there, was devoted to discussing with much interest and earnestness the
pending park question.

Mayor Lebkuecher, of Newark, thought "the work of the
commission had thus far commended its recommendations
to public favor" and hoped "there would be no difficulty in
carrying out the work so auspiciously begun." Senator
Ketcham, after referring favorably to the action of the
court in the appointment of the commission, said:

"You have in this undertaking the good will of all classes
of our people. Often there are hindrances to public im-

provements, jealousies arise between communities which hamper or prevent all progress, but, in the present instance, our larger and smaller municipalities vie with each other in the desire to secure the best results from this commission." He thought "our county as a whole rivals the suburban districts of those of any in the world;" referred to the press as being "a unit for the establishment of parks and parkways;" and added that, "to set apart for public uses even a portion of these" attractive places "and bind them by a cordon of parkways, will tax the skill of the commission, but their reward will surely come."

John F. Dryden expressed regret "that Essex County, with all her resources, enterprise and wealth, should be so far behind other places in establishing suitable breathing places for public enjoyment," and, after calling attention to the needs of Newark in the matter of parks, advocated that "suitable lands for parks should be acquired now and the embellishment left mainly to the future."

Franklin Murphy was of the opinion "that what the public required and what he hoped would be accomplished was a system of parks and parkways which he, his family, and friends could enjoy now." He thought "it well to bear in mind the future, but what was wanted, were suitable parks now, and appropriate boulevards and parkways for reaching them."

Wayne Parker suggested "the immediate acquirement of waste spaces, leaving the improvements mainly to the future." Mayor Gill, of Orange, believed "that it was the consensus of opinion of all classes that the great park for the county should be located on the Orange Mountain. Frank H. Scott stated that there was "three purposes for which parks were created—health, recreation and enjoyment, and, for their attainment, three things were necessary—space, pure air and natural beauty, enhanced or supplemented by art." Wendell P. Garrison called attention to the desirability of co-operating with the State Geological Survey in considering the question of forest reservation, and to the advantages and comparatively small cost of natural reservations for park purposes. Others contended that delay would largely increase the cost of the requisite park lands. Many suggestions were made apropos of the discussion. The occasion was but another indication of the sentiment of good will and best wishes which generally prevailed at that time.

Before passing from the work of the first Park Commission, there are two or three matters that were considered and acted upon in the preparation of the charter creating the permanent commission, which it may be of interest to refer to here. There were two vital principles involved. First, as to whether the commission for establishing and maintaining the park system should be elective or appointive, and, if appointive, in what official or court or courts the appointing power should be vested. And second, should provision be made for directly assessing the cost of the lands for the parks and the improvements, or both; or should a portion of the cost, or all of the cost, be provided for by a general tax according to the ratables upon the county as a whole. It was deemed imperative to have these conditions clearly defined, and, before John R. Emery submitted the first draft of the proposed charter, on January 25, 1895, the points pro and con, as to an appointive board, had been seriously considered by the commissioners. They were unanimous in the conclusion, in consideration of the methods by which candidates for important county offices secured, or were accorded, nominations through the customary channels of party selection, that, for such a position as that of park commissioner, charged with the responsibility of locating, acquiring and developing an extended park system and the consequent expenditure of large sums of public funds, the chances might be more favorable for satisfactory results under the appointive plan than under the elective system.

THE APPOINTIVE SYSTEM.

It was recognized that the work of locating and developing a series of parks for so large an area of such diversified interests as in Essex County, would, if undertaken to the best advantage, require men especially qualified, from tastes, training and experience; and that, as the plan of having men selected because of fitness had been so well received, the continuation of a similar provision in the new charter might be equally favored by the public. It had been shown that, in many instances where the elective plan of selecting commissioners had been in vogue, the practical results had not been acceptable to the municipalities or to the other local officials, and that "practical politics" was not a desirable factor in park making, whatever might be claimed for its contributory influences in other public activities.

It was solely and only for these reasons that the commission decided for the appointive system, and not with any desire to extend the scope of a method of creating a public board, which, at least theoretically, may be criticized as contrary to the principles and prerogatives of our whole system of government. Not only were results found to have been unsatisfactory in numerous instances of elective park commissioners, but conversely in other instances—notably such examples as that of the South Park system of Chicago, where the entire control of all park matters from the inception has been vested in a commission appointed by the courts—the practical workings were found to have been satisfactory.

HOW SHOULD PARK COMMISSIONERS BE SELECTED.

To those who believe that any other than the elective plan of creating public boards for the expenditure of public funds is objectionable and un-American, it is due to say that such a plan would have been adopted in drawing up the Essex County Park act of 1895, had not the investigations then made compelled the conviction concurred in by Messrs. Emery and Coult, the able counsel of the first commission, that the appointive system was preferable here. Having determined that point, the question arose as to where the authority for making the appointments should rest. Should the Governor be charged with that office? This would mean, or might mean, possible interference in what was strictly a county affair; it would open up the field of possibilities for the exercise of political or party "influence;" and it would be open to the still further objection of a board for the county being named by the authority of an official outside the county, chosen by and representing the State at large.

Would the freeholders be likely to agree upon the right sort of a commission? Here were more serious objections still, with all the possibilities of unrestricted controversy and acute jealousy. Should one judge, or a plurality of judges, make the selection? The single court appointment was finally agreed upon, following the precedent in creating the first commission. It was this plan which was finally included in the charter and is still operative. Whether the adoption and inauguration of that plan was wise, it may be the rightful province of the public to determine. I shall refer to this subject in a later chapter. Here I will only add in passing that, before the commission of 1905 had been long in existence, circumstances developed which made it manifest that it would have been better had the plan been modified and restricted.

FINANCING PARK EXPENDITURES.

The matter as to financing the park project was at once an interesting and troublesome proposition to determine. The precedents and experiences of very many park undertakings, both in this country and in Europe, were carefully looked into. Almost every scheme of providing for the cost of park lands and the improvements was considered. They included direct assessments on contiguous property in full or in part; partial assessment on adjacent lands; and for the entire cost being provided in the general tax levy upon the whole district or municipality. Each appeared to have advantages against other more or less potent disadvantages. Direct assessments were found to have been cumbersome, costly and unsatisfactory, and in many places difficult, and not infrequently impossible, to collect. This was due to the fact that every public park, as to location, size, property environment, and other conditions determining assessable benefits on adjacent property, is a law unto itself. No two, in these respects, are alike; hence no uniform system of awarding damages and assessing benefits as obtains, for instance, in the case of municipal street openings, is possible.

This, of necessity, makes confusion and uncertainty in the legal proceedings, and gives an almost unlimited opportunity and exceedingly broad field for never-ending litigation to "those who won't pay." Then, too, as every park is different in size, topography, and the other conditions noted, the task of fixing with comparative exactness and equity the district lines within which an assessment for park benefits should be levied, becomes the more difficult the more study is given to the solution of the problem. Shall the park belt benefits extend 100 feet, 1,000 feet; or over the whole municipality or county wherein the park or parks are located? This becomes the troublesome question.

AGAINST DIRECT ASSESSMENT.

An attempted partial direct assessment for park lands on the lines as above indicated, tends to make confusion worse confounded. If the plan involves providing a portion of the cost by tax on the available ratables, on the principle that in a large park or system of parks the benefits inure to the whole community, why should not all the cost be thus provided? That is the almost invariable contention of objectors to a direct tax for special benefits.

As a matter of fact, these phases of objection to any plan of assessing benefits for the Essex County parks became so serious to the first commission that the conclusion was finally and reluctantly reached that the expense of acquiring, developing, and maintaining the parks of the system should be borne by the whole county by issuing county bonds, and through the tax levy. It was also decided that it was injudicious to attempt to provide any of the requisite

funds for the parks by direct assessment on adjoining property. The park charter was accordingly drawn on these
lines, as is these respects it at present remains.

AS TO PARKWAYS.

The precedents and conditions for providing for the cost
of the parkways were entirely different. For this purpose
existing boulevards, avenues, streets, or other public places
where rights of way had already been secured, might be
desirable in connecting the various parks into a system or
chain of parks; or new rights of way might be indispensable
for the same object. A parkway being of a definable width
similar in many respects to any other avenue or street acquirement, the application of the principle of assessing
benefits becomes a comparatively simple matter. This provision was, therefore, included in the second and sixth
sections of the park law (of 1895), and the East Orange
parkway has been laid out under the assessment-for-benefits
plan therein provided. In the method prescribed for making parkways of existing avenues or streets, there were apparently no very intricate questions to be solved.

It was deemed advisable that the future commission
should have the right, and it was provided, as it now has the
right, to appropriate for a parkway any existing highway;
but as the local municipal or county authorities already held
possession under the right of eminent domain, the proviso
(section 2 of the charter) makes it necessary to first have
"the concurrence of the Common Council or other body having authority over highways" in all cases where a larger
width of area for a parkway than the existing highway is required. The "care, custody and control" clause (the
eighteenth section), which was for so many years the bone
of contention over the efforts to make parkways of Park
and Central avenues, was intended to simplify, not to com-
plicate, the transfer and utilization of those avenues as fundamental parts of the park system.

The scramble to obtain possession of one or both of those
great county thoroughfares by the corporations for traction

uses, while not lost sight of, was not fully anticipated, as it did not seem probable that the insatiable desire for the spoils of public franchise exploitation had yet reached the point of utter disregard of public rights and a determination to push through the public property appropriation scheme at all hazards that afterward followed.

Another question which the first commission found difficult to determine was as to the amount of the appropriation that should go into the report and be provided for in the new law. Next to the matter of method in providing for the selection of the next commission, and of determining how the necessary funds for the undertaking should be obtained, this was considered of paramount importance. At first the amount suggested in our deliberations was $1,000,-000. This was soon increased by half a million. Later $2,000,000 it was deemed should be the limit.

Finally, when the different factors in the situation had been carefully gone over—the needs for a comprehensive park and parkway system adapted to, and creditable to, the whole county; the probable increased cost of future land acquirement after the parks were once established; the large expense involved in the reclamation and parklike embellishment of the "swamp" lands, such as the lower portions of the Branch Brook tract and the triangle tract in Orange; the demands that would naturally follow for enlarged parks and the inevitably unforeseen contingencies—it was finally determined that the amount should be $2,500,000.

This was with the distinct understanding, as stated in the report soon afterward issued in February, 1895, that "the amount of money which the commission feels is needed for this undertaking, $2,500,000, may seem large for practically a single investment in that direction, but it must be appreciated that it is for a system of parks in its entirety."

This was an equivocal, definite statement, and all of the members of the commission thus considered it. I believed then, as I have believed since, that it was in the nature of a trust obligation between the commission, the people, and the Legislature, and that this clearly defined obligation

rested upon the succeeding commission to carry out: Or,
failing in that, to have laid out a park "system" complete,
at least in outline, within that amount, before asking for
additional appropriation.

That the reserve policy was adopted after the organization of the permanent commission in 1895 is now well
known, and some of the reasons why the original plan,
policy, and promise were not carried out will be considered
in succeeding chapters.

It may be a matter of interest for the reader to know
that, so far as could be learned from the investigations
made in 1894-5, the Essex County Park enterprise was, and,
so far as I have since been able to learn, still is, the initial
county public park undertaking of this country. In the
legal preparation of the charter there were, for this reason,
so many novel and intricate questions involved that on
January 28, on request of the counsel, John R. Emery, it
was decided to employ Joseph Coult as associate counsel
"in the construction and provision of the bill to be presented to the Legislature."

On February 1, 1895, the draft of the bill was gone over
by the commissioners with the counsel. The recommendations that the entire financing of the undertaking be left
with the Board of Freeholders, the funds to be paid over
on requisition of the park commissioners, rather than that
an attempt should be made to create an entirely separate
system of tax levies for the parks, were agreed to, and the
finishing touches of the bill were passed upon. At the same
meeting the report to accompany the bill was considered,
corrected, and made ready for publication.

PROPOSED LAW INTRODUCED.

A few days afterward the commission received word from
Judge Depue suggesting that the report be sent to him, as
was done. A copy was also sent, with a draft of the bill, to
Senator Ketcham, who promptly introduced the measure

in the Senate. It became "Senate No. 114." The report was ordered printed at the meeting of February 4, and several thousand copies were distributed throughout the county.

About this time an effort was made to change the bill then before the Legislature so as to provide for at least six commissioners. Judge Depue favored the change. He was advised by letter as to the reasons that led to the naming of five commissioners in the bill, as "we were unanimous in the conclusion, not only upon our own judgment in view of all the circumstances, but also for the reason that experience in other places seemed to indicate that a board of five commissioners generally gives the best public service and results." The following, under date of February 13, 1895, was the reply:

"My Dear Sir—I received yours of yesterday. I have not read the proposed bill. It provides a commission, as I understand, the members of which get no compensation. I thought the number should be six for these reasons:

"First, although I hope and expect the commissioners will act in unanimity, yet if there is to be a division I thought affirmative action by a vote of 4 to 2 preferable to that of 3 to 2, a bare majority.

"Second, I thought the northwestern section of the county should be represented, say Montclair and that section, when I appointed the original commissioners, and I incline to that view with respect to the new commission.

"I have now written tersely my views. They are mere suggestions. I am not tenacious on the subject. I will be content to abide by the judgment of the commissioners.

"Very truly yours,
"DAVID A. DEPUE.

"To F. W. Kelsey, Esq."

REPLY TO JUDGE DEPUE.

My reply was as follows:

"Orange, February 26, 1895.

"Hon. David A. Depue:

"My Dear Sir—Your favor of the thirteenth instant was duly received. The suggestions therein mentioned have had thoughtful consideration.

"As to the matter of compensation to the members of the commission, there appeared but one satisfactory way of disposing of it, viz., to make the position honorary, and then rely upon the appointment of men of sufficient probity, honor and civic pride to appreciate the honor, and, in the great and lasting good and worthy repute growing out of the improvement, thereby have sufficient inducement to devote their best thought and purpose to the carrying out of the whole enterprise.

"It was felt that a small salary would sooner or later attract petty politicians incompetent to execute such a trust, and make the pressure for their appointment a burden on the appointing power, while a large salary would be open to other serious objections and tend to make the compensation the object sought, rather than the matter of pride in successful results.

"I believe that all of the commission fully concurred in this view.

"In like manner an even number has not seemed favorable for a practical working board to any of us. Four to two, as you suggest, is certainly a stronger majority than three to two; but how would it be should an even vote occur with a possible 'deadlock' lasting, as it has with some evenheaded commissions, a length of time?

"Similar commissions elsewhere for similar undertakings generally recognize a number above five as unwieldy, and the efficiency of a board reduced by a divided responsibility.

"If the right men fill such positions—those competent, faithful and loyal to the trust—there should be no division, but every vote of record undivided, and this is frequently the case with some of the higher-class commissions.

"In our board thus far, although questions have arisen upon which we have had different convictions, yet, after full consideration, all things have been harmonized so that when the ballot was taken every vote of record has stood 5 to 0.

"I do not recollect a single instance since the organization of the board in June where there has been an exception.

"A permanent commission, it would seem, should have a like result, as the ground work is now laid and some of the intricate questions already passed upon.

"The cordial public support given the commission, and its report and proposed bill (conferring, as the latter does, ample powers and a large appropriation) is, I think, owing to the fact that we have avoided local and sectional questions throughout, and have treated the county as an entirety on the lines substantially as outlined at the inception of the enterprise. It has not been the question of section, faction, or particular locality, but what was the best system which could be devised for the whole, considering topography, accessibility, convenience to population, ratables and other resources.

"In this way every section has been represented. No locality in the county, available and desirable, has been overlooked. Each section has received as careful consideration as though a member of the board were a resident of that locality.

"While Mr. Bramhall and myself were supposed to represent the Oranges, generally speaking, we have both given really more study and thought to the other portions of the county where we were less familiar and saw greater opportunities for effective parking for the county as a whole; also the entertainment given at the Country Club by myself in November was not to advance the interests of the Oranges at the expense of any other section, but solely to enlarge the acquaintance and interest and cultivate the sentiment for the enterprise in its broader sense.

"The representative element of Montclair is, I think, in accord with the work of the commission, and some of the members of the Township Committee, and others there, will co-operate with the work of the new commission as conscientiously, if not as earnestly, as though they were members of it.

"Personally, I should have been glad to have concurred in your views as to the number of commissioners, save for the reasons stated. The board, in again considering the subject since the receipt of your letter, were all of the opinion it would be better not to recommend that change in the bill.

"Senator Ketcham conferred with other of the members, and, I think, also concurred in this view. We are indebted to him for his good counsel and active interest, and he will no doubt talk with you freely about the matter.

"His approval of the suggestion of the original plan, briefly stated in the enclosed letter of April 16th last, had much to do with bringing about the present law, which was drawn in accordance with that plan by Mr. A. Q. Keasbey and myself.

"As the points mentioned in your letter of the 13th inst. have an important bearing on the new bill, I have written more at length than I otherwise should.

"Respectfully and truly yours,
"FRED. W. KELSEY."

There was apparently official anxiety in certain quarters, at least in Newark, on this question. The evening of March 4, 1895, a well-attended delegation of Newark officials met at Trenton, and agreed upon the form of a bill to amend the park bill, so as to provide for eight commissioners. The Mayors of Newark and of Orange and a representative of East Orange—all Republicans—were to be included. The other five members, according to the proposed amendment, were to be selected from Newark. Alderman William Stainsby, Chandler W. Riker, who was then city counsel of Newark, and others present at the conference favored the change. On March 7, Mr. Riker appeared officially before the commission and pleaded with much earnestness that the board should consent to the change. That view did not prevail. The scheme, which at the outset would give the park board a political complexion, was not generally approved, and, outside of a comparatively small official and political contingent, evidently received but little support. No further active effort in that direction, to my knowledge, was made.

While the bill was pending in the Senate, two of the commissioners incidentally, and almost accidentally, ascertained about the same time that the legislation providing for an appointive park commission for Hudson County a few years previous had been declared unconstitutional by the courts. The question at once arose as to how the act, then before the Legislature, could be amended so as to avoid a similar experience in Essex County. The problem was, at a special meeting of the board, immediately given to counsel to work out, and on February 18 Messrs. Emery and Coult gave three optional remedies for the apparent defect in the bill. They were:

(a) An amendment providing for the appointment of the new commission by the Governor—an elective official.

(b) To have the commission selected by or from the board of freeholders—an elective body.

(c) Apply the referendum principle and submit the measure and the question whether it should or should not become operative to the electorate of the county to determine.

LEFT TO THE PEOPLE.

The commissioners promptly decided that they would "trust the people on the issue." An amendment was at once prepared providing for a vote throughout the county at the next election, which was to occur April 9, (1895), with the ballots "For the park act" and "Against the park act." This draft of the amendment was immediately sent to Senator Ketcham, at Trenton. It was, without objection, added to the bill, and on February 26 the measure was passed in the Senate by a vote of 14 to 0. On the following day it was passed in the Assembly by a vote of 50 to 0—not a single vote having been recorded in either house against it.

The bill carried with it a direct appropriation, should it be approved by the people of the county, of $2,500,000 of public funds. This large sum was to be expended as a board of five men to be appointed by the court should determine. The conditions for raising the money were arbitrary, indeed peremptory. The disposition of the funds was unrestricted and wholly discretionary with the board when appointed. The matter of appointment, too, was left entirely within the discretion of the Supreme Court official in naming the commission.

In view of all these conditions, that such a bill should pass without objection or a negative vote, called forth much comment. It has been stated by those conversant with such matters that the passage of that bill in view of the then existing circumstances—the amount of appropriation of public moneys, etc.—was one of the most remarkable and unique pieces of State legislation which up to that time had occurred.

In Governor Werts's message of January 8, 1895, appeared a complimentary reference to the park movement in Essex County, and to the work of the commission thus far. He had also transmitted to the Legislature the commission's report after it had been sent to Judge Depue. It was, therefore, a matter of public record that he was in favor of further legislation toward the objects sought, and on March 5 he approved the second park bill, now Chapter XCL. of the laws of 1895.

The affairs of the first park commission now worked rapidly to a close. Early in April it was decided by the commission to bring the park subject as far as practicable before the people prior to the election on April 9. At the meeting of April 15 it was shown from the official canvass, as certified by the county clerk, that, in that election, the park law had been approved by a large majority. In Newark the vote was 11,853 for the bill and 9,330 against, or a majority of 2,523 in favor of it. In Orange 1,848 was reported for, to 294 against it; East Orange, 1,474 in favor of, to 305 against; Montclair, 871 for, 121 against. In other towns and boroughs the vote was equally favorable, making the majority in the county for the law 8,321.

On April 18 the appointment of the new commission was announced. Of this and of some of the conditions incident therewith, I shall treat in the next chapter.

The following day—the afternoon of April 19, 1895—the first commission met for the last time. The financial statement was then submitted and approved. The total expenditures, including architects' fees (as before stated), $2,372.13; counsel fees, $450; printing and stationery, $172.55; rent, secretary's salary, telephone, etc., and all incidentals, were $4,474.25, which amount had been received from the freeholders and the account closed. The board, by resolution, then authorized "all maps, plans, reports and other property turned over to the commissioners appointed April 18," and then adjourned sine die.

The record was made. The die was cast. The book was closed. Yet, as the people had voted for the parks and the way was at last open to secure them, the scene had shifted, and a larger book, with vastly greater possibilities, was opened.

CHAPTER IV.

As the rivulet becomes a stream, and the stream broadens into the river, the current moves on until the course is changed, or completely reversed. So the movement for the Essex County parks, from a small beginning, rapidly widened and deepened on its course, and although not directly obstructed, the current became entirely changed by the appointment of the second commission on April 18, 1895.

This commission then had everything a public board could possibly have in its favor: An extremely liberal charter, conferring ample authority, approved by almost unanimous action of the Legislature and by a large majority vote of the people of the county as well; a generous appropriation; and more, the good will and confidence of its constituency and the cordial support of public opinion throughout the State.

While the plans of the first commission were, during the early part of the year, maturing, the favorable comments and commendatory articles in the local papers were reflected in the press of other cities. The New York Tribune, Times, World, and Evening Post all had a good word for the Essex parks, during the month of January of that year, and before the new commission was appointed, had given a resume of the movement and of the friendly support extended it.

The Tribune of April 8, 1895, under the caption "A Fine Park System," dilated at length on the subject, favorable alike to the report and the bill to be voted on the following day. An editorial in the same paper gave an interesting account of "A Great Park Project in New Jersey;" described the bill; declared that "the child is born who will see this entire 150,000 square miles of Essex County a continuous city;" gave a glowing account of what "nature has done for this region" of "mountain ridges, fertile valleys and wooded slopes;" and added that "it is to be a county park system" and, "so far as we know, little opposition to the project has been developed."

The attitude of the New Jersey press had continued in laudation of the enterprise, and there appeared also a general sentiment in favor of the reappointment of the same commission that had had charge of the preliminary work in the undertaking. The Newark News of February 6, 1895, editorially referring to the report of the first commission, stated that "a good system of parks would supplement the natural attractiveness of the city and county."

And, on February 28, the same paper said: "This is a rich and populous county, and one that has a future. Before many years it will be the theatre of a greater city. Its situation destines it to a rapid and steady growth. Whatever adds to its attractiveness as a place of residence means advantage to every one of its industries, to every business enterprise carried on within its boundaries."

On February 6, The Daily Advertiser, in a lengthy editorial on "The Proposed Park System," had this to say:

"No one, of course, questions the need of a park or a system of parks in Essex County. Out of 92,000 acres in Essex County, only twenty-five acres are devoted to park purposes and uses; and as for Newark, with its population of 200,000, it is a fact that it has a smaller park acreage than any city in the United States or Europe of over 100,000 population! This in itself is a rebuke and a humiliation. * * * There is scarcely any question that the bill presented by the commission which has completed its task in one-fourth the time allotted to it, and with an expenditure of less than half the money at its disposal, will become a law. In that case, we sincerely hope that the pres-

ent commission will be reappointed to prosecute the work
so well begun."

The Newark Call of March 24, said editorially: "The
plan proposed is the best that can be devised under the circumstances.   It is a novelty in some respects, as park reserves, under county control, have not been attempted.   The
necessities of the popular conditions which prevail in Essex,
however, make the plan most desirable.   The sites for the
parks will, .in some cases at least, be in townships which
would not dream of such a reservation at their own expense,
and the county plan, in any case, will prevent conflict of
interest and secure systematic arrangement for care and
maintenance as well as location.   The scheme is, in short,
not only feasible and practical, but is probably the only one
that could be carried through."

PARK BOARD'S COURSE COMMENDED.

The Orange Chronicle, one of the most earnest exponents
of the park system cause, in an editorial February 16,
stated that "A number of improvement societies and public
boards throughout the county have passed highly complimentary resolutions relative to the work of the Board of
Park Commissioners, as shown by the report recently
published."

Even the Essex papers printed in foreign languages did
not neglect the subject.   In La Montagna of March 31, 1895,
appeared a plea "For Public Parks," in which, after referring to "the very important question the voters of Essex
County will be called upon to decide April 9," and
saying "No Italian need be told of the advantages and pleasure derived from public gardens,"
and "that the park scheme is always the poor man's
benefactor," it adds: "America is far behind the
Old World in the matter of park development, and this
county has only twenty-five acres devoted to such uses—a
less number than any other community of like population
in the world."   An interesting and evidently well-meant
statement, but quite too flattering as to the European parks

which, as a whole, do not compare favorably with the very many extensive and well-kept public parks in this country. All the papers vigorously and continuously reflected what seemed a popular public sentiment for a forward movement on the same lines and under the same management as had been the efforts thus far to obtain a park system. This view was also accentuated by the action of local associations and some of the personally disinterested friends of the parks in different parts of the county. The only discordant note which was heard out of harmony with this general acclaim favorable to the parks, and the new law for creating them, was the action of the Newark Democratic City Committee early in April, 1895, in the adoption of a resolution disfavoring the law and the appointive, instead of the elective method provided for the selection of commissioners.

Among the earnest advocates of the park system perhaps there was no one man who had been more earnest or active, or whose influence had been more effectually brought to bear in holding the enterprise on the lines as originally proposed than William A. Ure. Knowing his sincerity and interest and wishing to learn his conviction on the existing status of park matters, I wrote him April 8, the day before the election on the park bill, and, after referring to the able editorials on the park question that had appeared in The Call, and to the cordial reception of the plans and the new law by the public, expressed my appreciation of the principles which an article in The Call the day previous had indicated should govern in the selection of the new commission. I then added:

"I am glad you still favor the selection on the same principles so heartily favored at the time. If any other considerations than those of fitness are now allowed to determine the new appointments, the execution of the plans will, in my judgment, be hampered in the same proportion, and the final success of the scheme in just the same degree be imperiled. I have every confidence in Judge Depue, in his strict integrity of purpose and his loyalty to the principles of faithful administration. But it is fair to presume in a public measure like this that there may be powerful pressure brought to bear upon him at the present juncture, which the position of the real friends of the enterprise may do much to nullify or counteract. The time for naming the new commissioners is very limited, and if the efforts for place last summer, at the inception of the enterprise and before the appointment of the first commission, formulated so readily, now that the actual work is to be undertaken, speculative and corporate interests may look at the field as all the more attractive.

"The general support given the report and plans of the commission show that the great mass of people are disposed to rightly discriminate in favor of a work of great public importance undertaken on sound, correct principles; and, if the plans and policy of the present board are carried out, I believe the results will fully justify the anticipation of those who have given the subject the most thought and study.

"All this, of course, if the new bill carries. If not, we shall have more than a year yet, under the old law, to formulate new plans or present the subject in other forms. I have little doubt that the vote will be overwhelmingly in favor."

Under date of April 9, 1895, Mr. Ure's reply was as follows:

"My Dear Sir—Yours of the 8th instant received. The first person I met after reading your letter was a well known public official who brought up the park question by asking me what I thought about the appointment of new commissioners. When I told him that the present commissioners ought to be reappointed, he said there was 'no use talking to me further on that subject,' but said Messrs. Peck and Jackson did not satisfy him. This may indicate that a movement will be made to change the personnel of the present board, although I hope that any such scheme will be

frustrated. I am confident that the park bill will be in-
dorsed by the people to-day, and I am also confident that it
will require an enormous pressure to induce Judge Depue
to appoint any commissioners in place of the five he first
named, in whose ability, integrity and judgment the public,
as well as myself, have full confidence.

"Yours very truly,
"WILLIAM A. URE."

SCENE OF ACTION SHIFTED.

This correspondence is given thus fully, as it gives a clear
and correct reflex of the situation at that time.   Immediately after the county vote was found to have given a large
majority for the park bill, almost the entire field of activity
for the parks and the pressure from political and special
interests was at once transferred, and the scene of focal
action shifted to, the inner room of the court, or wherever
the judge having the appointments to make could be found.

In most instances, where large and diversified interests
are at stake and conflicting claims become a factor for adjudication, whether before a court, a legislative body or an
executive official, things are not always what they seem, and
the kaleidoscopic conditions of conclusion may be frequently
shifted almost from day to day as the see-saw of contending
influences and varying elements enter into the final disposition of the subject in hand.

The question then before the court was no exception to
this rule.   True, the judge, in announcing the new commission the morning of April 18, 1895, gave as quoted below
some of the reasons that appealed to him for making the
change against what was evidently the trend of public desire, and the conclusion left upon Mr. Ure's mind prior to
the appointment that no change would be made.   That presentment of the judge, however, gave no intimation of, nor
made the slightest reference to, some of the most important
and potential influences brought to bear upon him to make
the changes as he did.   Those influences were known to a
few at the time, but so far as I know have not yet been

publicly referred to, although the court dwelt quite at
length upon the subject. In naming the commissioners in
open court, the judge said:

"In the long service that I have had here I might say
that all of the communications put together would not occupy one-third of this bundle. It illustrates the anxiety
that the public have that, in the composition of this commission, commissioners shall be so selected that the park project
shall be considered as one that is not to be subject to fluc-
tuations arising from local feeling or local jealousies."

APPOINTMENT OF COMMISSIONERS.

Reference was then made to "more interviews on the part
of the people of this county than I have had, I may say,
during the whole of my service."

"The commissioners under the original act I appointed
on my own judgment. The commissioners' powers were
merely tentative. The commissioners have discharged their
duties in a manner that entitles them to the approval and
commendation not only of this court, but of the
community."

"There is everything in the composition and conduct of
these commissioners that makes it desirable for me to reap-
point them, and it would be my personal pleasure to com-
mend the course of these commissioners by a reappointment.
* * * But under the new act a very different condition
of affairs confronts me. This new act confers upon these
commissioners powers that I may say are extraordinary.
The amount is large, the powers of these commissioners are
very great, and, in the selection of the persons who are to
compose the commission, there are considerations to which
I must yield in the performance of a public duty. * * *
The principle on which our government is founded is that
taxation and representation shall go hand in hand. That
principle ought to govern in the execution of a public duty
which involves the creation of a debt to be paid by the taxable inhabitants of the county.

"The city of Newark pays of the county taxes about 75

per cent. It is obvious that it was the requirements of this great city which was the main object in establishing a system of public parks. It is apparent that a consideration of what the city of Newark requires, beyond the question of taxation, was a consideration which influenced the establishment of this scheme to the extent and of the magnitude that this act provides."

The court then referred to the assurances on the part of those interested in the government of Newark that, if Newark's interests were not to be provided for, "this power of selecting these commissioners would not have been conferred upon the court."

The adverse vote of Newark was next touched upon, and it was stated by the judge "that a considerable portion of this vote was due to an apprehension that in the appointment of these commissioners Newark would be subjected to taxation by persons who are not directly interested in the public affairs of the city.

CONFIDENCE IN THE BOARD.

"And I know from representations that have been made to me by gentlemen of influence in this city," continued the court, "that their votes in favor of this law were influenced by their confidence that, in the appointment of these commissioners, that which was apprehended would be obviated.

"I departed from my usual rule and asked for the appointment of six commissioners, with a view of the adjustment of representation in such a manner as to conserve the interests of the whole county. A vote of three to two would not, perhaps, be as safe as one that had the support of four of the commissioners. If I had had the lively appreciation of the condition of things that I have now I should have made the number larger yet, in order that the principle of representation and taxation should be carried out in a more perfect manner than it can by the small number of commissioners. They are not mere executive officers, but have judicial duties as well. I would not make a government of this city composed of five persons, but toward an adminis-

trative board such as the Board of Public Works, I would
pursue that course."

In reference to his being willing to continue the first
commission, the judge said: "But I am entirely satisfied
from the information I have received that that does not
conform to the wishes of the public, and that they require
as far as possible that this court, in the appointment of
these commissioners, should allow the principle that is fundamental in all government representation. These things
make it, in my judgment, absolutely essential that I should
give to the city of Newark three commissioners. When I
have done that, the readjustment of this commission is
necessary."

The resolutions of the township authorities of Montclair,
Bloomfield and West Orange were then read. They claimed
joint taxable valuations of over $25,000,000, with the com-
ment that the request justified the appointment of a commissioner from that district.

FOR CONSISTENCY.

"I have selected for the commissioner who shall represent these three townships," went on the judge, "a gentle-
man who is well known to myself, and I presume to almost
every one in this county, as a man eminently fit for this
position—Frederick M. Shepard. This appointment leaves
only one other commissioner to be selected. In the selection
of that commissioner I have felt the greatest delicacy, because a duty is imposed upon me that is not pleasant, that
of deciding between two persons, gentlemen of my own
acquaintance, who were among the most efficient of the
members of the first commission, Frederick W. Kelsey and
George W. Bramhall.

"I know that Mr. Kelsey has been actively in favor of
this project from the beginning, and, perhaps, in the inauguration and pushing through of this scheme, he has been
of great public service. If I could criticize Mr. Kelsey at
all, it would be that I might think that in an office in which
so much depends upon the judicial and conservative feat-

ures, he might, perhaps, in his zeal for the execution of this public work, allow his mind to be so influenced as not to be controlled by the question of expense.

"Mr. Bramhall I do not know. He was the only commissioner with whom I was not acquainted; but I have heard from every quarter the highest commendation of him. I know from information I have with regard to the performance of his duty in the old board that he has been one of the most efficient of the commissioners. He lives in South Orange, and I have had the same sort of representations from South Orange and Clinton townships with regard to the selection of somebody residing there that I have had from other townships. If I were left to my own inclination, and to the considerations that I have just mentioned, I would be impelled to appoint Mr. Bramhall on this board. But I propose to be consistent, not for the sake of consistency alone, but also because of the considerations which I have stated. I must regard the interests of the location which shall bear the burdens. The city of Orange, in the taxable valuations of the county, is rated at $8,290,-000. It is a city, and is one of the municipalities where the location of parks and the construction of them would probably be conserved by considering the population and the area over which it extends.

"The persons who would be benefited by the parks to a large extent are persons who have no other means of getting recreation from the labors of the week. I have had from different persons who are connected with the city government of Orange a request to appoint Mr. Kelsey. I have, in addition to that, letters and recommendations from a great many persons in the city of Orange who are interested in this project, and who are large taxpayers, who desire his appointment. I have no means of saying what proportion of the taxation of the city of Orange is paid by these gentlemen who presented the petition. I only know that it represents a body of the taxation in the city of Orange that is quite considerable. I have said with regard to the city of Newark that considerations of this kind have controlled my mind. I must apply the same principle to Orange in leaving off the two gentlemen who have served on the present commission with so much credit. I regret it very much, but personal considerations are not of the slightest weight in the decision of this public question, and it is not for any personal reason that I have made the changes that I have already indicated.

"The two commissioners selected from the body of the county will be Frederick W. Kelsey and Frederick M. Shepard.

"Now I come to Newark, and here I strike another cause of perplexity in making the selection.

"I have said that in selecting these commissioners I desire very much to obtain for the benefit of the public the experience and knowledge that they have, and I ought, as far as practicable, to give that consideration in the selection of the commissioners.

"Cyrus Peck and Stephen J. Meeker are on the present commission. They were both my personal selections, having regard to their fitness. They are men in whom everybody has, or ought to have, confidence. I propose to retain these two gentlemen. I can see no reason why I should make any changes.

"Mr. Peck lives in Roseville, at the northeastern limit of this city; Mr. Meeker resides in the Eighth Ward, at the north end of the city.

NEW REPRESENTATIVE FOR NEWARK.

"The southerly part of this city is without any representative, and while ordinarily that might not be a consideration of much importance, yet when it comes to the question of parks within the city, I believe that west of High street there is no park, and east of the railroad there is one park. I want to give the southerly part of the city representation, in carrying out the principle that I have already announced. When I undertake to make a selection in that part of the city I have a superabundance of material, but I desire to put on this commission, as an additional member, a man who is

well known; a man of public spirit; a man of intelligence,
one who knows the deficiencies of the city of Newark as
compared with the improvements in other cities; and, having regard to his judgment and to the interest he has taken
in this public park project, and the interest he uniformly
exhibits in all public affairs, I have selected for that place
Franklin Murphy.

"Giving the subject the most anxious consideration—
more than I have given to any duty of this kind since I
have been called upon to perform public duties—I think the
commission that I have constituted will be as good as any
commission that I could possibly select."

I have never doubted Judge Depue's sincerity in dealing
as he did with the taxation-representation phase of the
question, or that it was made to appear to him as desirable
that the sectional or local representation principle should
then be injected into the enterprise—although this very
principle of sectionalism, as I have already indicated, occasioned the wreckage of the park enterprise for Newark in
1867-72; was largely responsible for the failure to materialize of the commendable efforts of the committee of the
Newark Board of trade in the same direction in 1892; has
occasioned the failure of many public park enterprises all
over the country; and was the very thing that the first commission had made every effort to prevent, and which, having been prevented, was in reality one of the essential elements in the immediate indorsement of its plan by the public and the Legislature.

REASONS FOR COURT'S ACTION.

Nor do I doubt that it had been forcibly represented to
the judge that the better plan would be to reverse the divi-
sional lines of representation from three from the county at
large, as he had endeavored to establish in selecting the first
commission, and give the majority in the board to Newark,
as the portion of the county paying the larger proportion of
the county tax. Nor do I believe there is the slightest reason

to doubt that he had, from representations made to him, become apprehensive that in reality one of the most cautious and conservative members of the first commission might, from his deep interest "in the inauguration and pushing through of the scheme," drift away into the realms of extravagance and possibly shape the affairs of the commission in that direction.

Then again, from the viewpoint of the court at the time and under the swirl of varying influences brought to bear upon the judge in selecting that board, may he not have been sincere in thinking that merely the qualifications of a successful manufacturer or man of business, and those of an energetic chairman of a State partisan committee of his own political predilections, might constitute the very elements of fitness for the responsible position of park making? As one having a mind with judicial tendencies and attainments, and who had evidently never given the subject of creating an extensive park system theretofore special attention, a generous thought may, I believe, be accorded this action as to its intention, whatever may have been its practical results.

But some of the "interviews on the part of the people of the county" were not directed to the question of geographical representation of the new commission, nor of taxation, nor of the conservative, or extravagant tendencies of any of the candidates who were then under consideration; but to other and decidedly different phases of the subject. There were $2,500,000 of county funds to expend. "Who was to have charge of the handling of this great sum of money?" "Who was to control the patronage in this new and important Department of Parks?"

Subsequent events indicated, clearly enough, what these and other arguments and influences were which became potent factors in the final selection of a majority of the commission.

The change in appointing Messrs. Shepard and Murphy in place of Bramhall and Jackson was apparently something of a surprise to the public, and was variously commented upon by the press. The unexpected had happened. The plan of laying out "the best park system that could be devised" for the whole county irrespective of local and sectional lines, which had been the keynote and the foundation structure of the work of the first commission, and the reason for its popular approval, had been by this act of the court—where the appointing power had been placed for the express purpose of minimizing the chances of failure in the execution of the plan—completely reversed. And, in that enterprise, a new principle and prerogative was then and there established, with two-fifths of the board of new material, one new member an active and ambitious politician, both representing large corporation interests—men who had had nothing whatever to do with the formulative plans or the work of the first commission, and who were not conversant with the causes that had led to the popular success of the undertaking up to that time.

FORMER POLICY REVERSED.

Whatever may have been the intentions of the court, this reversal of policy was the practical effect, as was conclusively shown at almost the first meeting of the new commission and has been more fully demonstrated since. The Daily Advertiser referred briefly, though kindly, to the new commission. The News was editorially non-committal, as were many of the other papers, both in and out of the county. The Call, while having a good word for the new board, in an editorial note, referring to the appointments, expressed this sentiment:

"The omission of Mr. Bramhall from the park commission is incomprehensible. It was hoped and expected that his valuable services would be retained in the interest of the public throughout the county."

In an interview about the same time Senator Ketcham said:

"In appointing the permanent commission I am sorry Judge Depue could not continue in office the original commission."

Though "oft expectation" had, with many, in this instance failed, the appointments were made, the provision of the law in this respect had been complied with; the past was a finality beyond recall, and the question now became: What was forward, and would the current of park affairs flow onward as smoothly and rapidly as before?

On April 20, 1895, the newly-appointed commissioners, Messrs. Peck, Meeker, Shepard, Kelsey and Murphy, took the prescribed oath of office and the same afternoon met in the rooms of the former commission for organization. When the question of selecting officers was taken up, Commissioner Murphy, whose appointment was for the full term of five years, made the surprising statement that Judge Depue had expressed the wish that Mr. Peck should be president, Mr. Shepard vice-president, and himself (Mr. Murphy) the treasurer.

Two of these three commissioners, now placed in control of the board, who had just received their appointment and who then, for the first time, came into the park enterprise, all made and created, with the $2,500,000 to expend, were lifelong "always to be depended upon" Republicans, and were directly installed as officers at the request of the court.

Discussion, however, as to the judge's right to thus determine the organization followed. Why should he assume to encroach upon this prerogative of the board in deciding for itself who the officers should be? No satisfactory answer was given. Mr. Murphy was disposed to press the point, and promptly offered a motion that Mr. Peck be made president. Mr. Meeker said he thought the board competent to select its own officers. Mr. Shepard said he thought the vice-presidency should remain the same as in the previous commission. Mr. Peck was, as usual in discussion, silent.

"Mr. Meeker," I remarked, "has been an active member of the first commission and a satisfactory treasurer. Why this desire for change?"

As the prospect for differences in the board at the very outset was not an agreeable one to contemplate, and as no one then seemed to care who the officers were sufficiently to make a contest over the principle involved, the matter was allowed to stand, as the judge had requested. The three officials were chosen and the two officers of the previous board were changed accordingly.

In this record of the park undertaking—the truth of which will stand long after all of us engaged in its work and development thus far shall have passed to the beyond—not wishing to do the memory of Judge Depue or any living person any injustice, I will here state, that, while the judge might not have intended by this action to usurp powers that did not rightfully or legally belong to him, or to the office he was then administering, I am just as firmly convinced that such was the fact. The very first section of the law under which he was acting, "Chapter XCI., Laws of 1895," already referred to, distinctly provides that "every such board shall annually choose from among its members a president, vice-president and treasurer, and appoint a clerk or secretary, and such other officers and employés as it may deem necessary to carry out the purposes of this act."

If that clause does not clearly enough leave the selection of officers solely as a prerogative of the board to determine, and with equal clearness leave only the selection of the commissioners with the court, what language could be employed to express such meaning? If the judge, under this law, could assume to determine and direct by an expressed "wish" or otherwise, who the officers should be, why could he not with equal right or authority decide who the secretary, counsel, or any other officer or employe should be?

I do not think that at the moment when the expression as to the judge's wishes was made, or during the brief discussion that followed, any of the commissioners thought of the clause in the charter above quoted. And I have also the generous disposition toward Judge Depue's memory to believe that, in the extraordinary pressure brought to bear upon him regarding the appointments he had overlooked it or possibly may have never read it. There was, however, at least one of the commissioners present at that meeting who

knew, without a shadòw of doubt, that it certainly never had
been the intention in framing that law or the preceding
park act, to lodge with the presiding justice of the Essex
Circuit of the Supreme Court any power whatever beyond
naming the commissioners who were to be entrusted with
the park undertaking. With that appointive power securely
placed in the court by legislative edict, an officially expressed "wish" in such a matter as the selection also of officers, may, in the absence of counteracting influences or ad-
vices, be construed, as it was intended to be and was in this
instance construed, to have almost the force of a mandate.
The effect of that action has had a great influence in shaping the affairs of the Park Commission down to the present
time, and was one of the causes that a little later brought a
sharp turn in the rapid-flowing current of Essex County
park affairs.

The question as to who should be secretary of the new
board was soon determined by the appointment of the
former secretary, Alonzo Church. Then came the settlement
of two questions, the solution of which practically constructed a dam across the heretofore straight and smooth
course of the park movement, and effectually turned to one
side, and almost back upon itself, the current, in an entirely
reverse direction from that taken all through the work and
life of the first commission.

These questions, in the order disposed of, were: First,
the selection of counsel to the board; and, second, the policy
to be pursued relative to the location and acquirement of the
parks in establishing the county park system.

CHAPTER V.

QUESTIONS OF POLICY.

THE selection of counsel to the Park Board was, at the outset, recognized by all the commissioners as a matter of much importance. It was a new proposition, at least in Essex County, for an appointive board to have the right by law to make requisitions for large amounts on an elective board of the same constituency and area of jurisdiction. Such attempts, theretofore, in other places, had created jealousies and litigation. These conditions it was, by all of the members, deemed imperative, if possible, to avoid. There were also many questions, it was known, which would arise as the scheme developed, and which would require the advice and service of an able attorney. To this extent we were all agreed.

Soon after the organization of the board this subject was taken up. Commissioners Murphy and Shepard were both ardent and decided in their advocacy of Joseph L. Munn. Commissioner Meeker was as decidedly opposed, and favorably mentioned Henry Young. Mr. Peck said nothing. I was unprepared to make a decision and asked that the question go over. The matter was again brought up at the following meeting. Messrs. Murphy and Shepard were insistent for Mr. Munn's appointment. Mr. Meeker and myself objected. There was a prospective issue, for it was manifest that those favoring Mr. Munn's appointment were determined it should be made. The points as then stated in his favor were mainly that his knowledge of, and position as counsel with, the Board of Freeholders would be of assistance in establishing and continuing friendly and co-operative relations with that board. This all recognized as desirable—indeed, necessary, for the harmonious execution of the Park Board's plans.

"At the meeting May 7 it became evident that longer delay would retard the work of the commission. Previously I made inquiries as to Mr. Munn's character and qualifications. The replies from, and statements of, those I thought most competent to judge were conflicting. I was told that, while employed as town counsel of East Orange, and later by the freeholders, his attention was mainly given to political or party affairs and that he was extremely friendly, and most valuable, to the traction companies when they wanted new legislation or additional franchises.

In this dilemma of uncertainty I left the meeting referred to. The question was pressing for solution. Mr. Shepard and I came out together and boarded an Orange car. I then stated directly to him the result of my inquiries as to the two candidates, and my misgivings about Mr. Munn. That, as I seemed to hold the balance of power, I felt it "doubly incumbent that no mistake should be made in the decision." I said to him:

"Mr Munn has been your close neighbor for years. You must know him thoroughly well, his character and all about him. In this park enterprise you have now an equal responsibility with me. You are the older man and have far better opportunities of judging whether Mr. Munn will properly fill the requirements of that position than have I. I am suspicious of him and in doubt as to what is best to do."

The answer was in these words: "I have known Mr. Munn for years. He has been my counsel in other matters. If this expenditure of $2,500,000 was all of my own money I would not think of employing any one else but Mr. Munn." My reply to that statement was equally direct: "If you now say that to me as my colleague in this great undertaking I will withdraw my opposition at the next meeting and vote for Mr. Munn's appointment." He assured me that was his conviction. I then repeated my promise of giving Munn's candidacy my support—and did so.

At the meeting of May 9, Commissioner Murphy, knowing that Mr. Munn's appointment could then be secured, pressed for that result by moving that the salary for the counsel be fixed at $2,000 per year, and that J. L. Munn be the counsel. Mr. Shepard seconded the motion. Commissioner Meeker formerly proposed Henry Young. Mr. Murphy called for a vote. It resulted in 4 for and 1 against J. L. Munn; and he thus became the legal adviser of the Park Commission, with all the opportunities for good or evil which that name and position implied.

POSSIBLE STORM BLOWS OVER.

Immediately there were public mumblings of discontent. The previous December Mr. Munn had been "chosen" counsel to the Board of Freeholders at a like salary of $2,000 per year. The Republican politicians and "the boys" of that party had for a long time been berating the Democrats for having allowed, when that party was in control, one man to fill more than one remunerative office. Now that the same scheme, and for the same reasons, had become operative in their own party, the same principle was brought forward, and the question was raised as to why "the plums" falling from the Park Board's table should not be more evenly distributed. These advance monitions of a possible party storm, however, finally blew over, when it was found that "what's done" was not likely to be undone, and that the seal of fate had been set upon the hopes of many other lawyers who had been rated as of the faithful in party allegiance. Like the appointment of the commissioners, the thing was a thing of the past, and what was the use of continuing to mourn or agitate it, even though, to many aspiring attorneys' minds, the overturning of that overflowing milk pail had diverted the cream of some of the richest available county funds to one already gorged—considering the service he was performing—with the emoluments of public office.

The discussion, while it lasted, was entertaining. It was also instructive, in reflecting, as it did, the practical aims and ideals of many otherwise good citizens in dealing with questions of party control, and in showing how services, provided for at the taxpayers' expense, are, in party parlance, really looked upon as "the spoils of office."

The Newark News of May 29, 1895, gave an amusing account of this episode, quoting from some of the aggrieved publicists who thus had opportunity to vent their grievances.

"Why shouldn't the county pay the legitimate expenses of the man who goes to Trenton in its interests?" was the way one of the party statesmen expressed his sentiments. This observation might, by the cynically inclined, be deemed of much significance, in view of the appearance, a few months later, of Mr. Munn before the Assembly Municipal Corporations Committee in favoring the "Roll trolley bills." Then, with much earnestness, he contended that the control of all such county roads as Bloomfield avenue "rightfully belonged" to the freeholders, "the only logical body to control county roads"—a board then, as since, well under "trolley" influences. When objection was made to the "undue interest displayed by the Board of Freeholders in reference to the passage of those bills," Charles D. Thompson asked if Mr. Munn "represented the freeholders or the Park Commission, or appeared as the counsel of East Orange in this matter." Mr. Munn replied: "I do not; I represent myself;" but added that "he knew several freeholders who were in favor of the bills." As these measures sought to deprive municipalities and property owners of all control or voice in granting trolley road franchises, and vested that right exclusively in the Board of Freeholders—then, as afterward, to all appearances, under corporate and party boss dictation—the counsel's efforts to secure their passage was, indeed, significant.

POLICY IN SELECTING PARKS.

In public matters, as in other affairs of life, there are

certain general principles which with reasonable certainty foreshadow ultimate results, much as, under the application of the axiomatic rules of science, like causes produce like results. Anticipating that park making on a large scale might involve these principles, the first Park Commission had, as indicated in the preceding chapters, continuously dealt with the park system as an entity, hoping thereby to avoid the pitfalls of sectional differences, and, by treating the proposition as a whole, thus to be in a position to better determine the probable limits of cost for "a system of parks in its entirety."

QUESTION OF POLICY.

After the second commission had completed its organization, the question then before the board, briefly stated, was whether the pledge made by the first park commission in respect to the policy of establishing the park system should be carried out, or a new policy on other lines be inaugurated. The consideration and discussion of the subject went on for months.   At almost every meeting it received attention. Although free from personalities or acrimonious reflections, the arguments for and against the proposition stated were earnest and persistent.

Mr. Murphy was emphatic in his advocacy of a new policy in saying "I am here to lay out the parks and to expend the money appropriated for that purpose as in my own judgment I think best, without regard to what the former commission may have said or done."   When in answer, in espousing the cause of continuing the plan and policy of the first commission that had received such cordial public indorsement, I referred to the conviction forced upon me, "to consider the pledge of that board as a binding obligation upon its successors, for it was upon that pledge the court, the Legislature, and the electorate of the county had acted in passing the charter and in granting the large appropriation then available," we were reminded that the first commission was no longer in existence, and that it had no right to bind the present board in any way whatever.

There were certain parks, it was claimed, that should be selected first. When these were provided for, and the boundaries, etc., established, others could be taken up. Weequahic was one of these, although that lake, with a railroad on one side and mosquito marsh on the other, had been rejected by every one of the landscape architects employed by the former park board, and the commission had also passed it by as too costly to improve, and having too many other disadvantages to even give it consideration as a probable location for a future park.

Again, what appeared to be the defects and dangers of a change of policy were pointed out. If we were to start in by selecting piece by piece and park by park, without regard to other locations and requirements throughout the county, who could estimate where the board would finally come out on the plans, or what the ultimate cost would be? Would the cost not be more than double the amount the first commissioners had assured the people the expense of the entire system would not exceed? If the proposed policy should be adopted would we not be in the position of the man beginning to build a residence within a definitely estimated price for the house complete, and then starting the foundation without regard to the cost of the superstructure, only to find when foundations and frame were up that the money provided had disappeared with the building but half completed? If the Newark parks were first determined upon without any reference to the mountain parks or the parkways, or vice versa, would not the board be in similar situation long before any part of the proposed system was completed?

SITUATION UNCHANGED.

At the close of each meeting the situation remained substantially as at the beginning. Arguments were unavailing. The logic of events and experiences of the past were met by a statement of condition and of intention to go ahead on new—and to the park enterprise—untried lines. Whether right or wrong in my contentions, the more I thought of the confidence and generosity extended on all sides to the first commission, of the sincere and loyal support of the various elements in the county and State, of the direct pledge we had made in the reciprocation of that confidence, and of the possible—or what seemed to me almost certain—dangers involved from such a radical change of policy, the more I shrank from it. Not content in relying upon my own judgment, I sought the counsel and advice of those outside of the scene of action, away from any of the persons or influences directly involved, and in whose character and judgment I believed I could place implicit confidence in such matters. Among my acquaintances there was one for whose judgment I entertained the highest regard— Mr. D. Willis James. I had known of his philanthropic deeds, his kindly nature, his public spirit and withal exceptional judgment on large financial operations, and on matters pertaining to the carrying out of large undertakings. I met Mr. James at his summer place at Madison. Without mentioning the names of the commission or giving any intimation as to which side of the question any of them stood on, or the slightest inkling of my own views on the subject, I presented the matter to him precisely as it was then before the park board; stated the claims at issue, which had been put forward by each of the commissioners; explained to him the amount of the appropriation and that it was intended and was appropriated for a park system for the whole county; and set forth the plan that had up to that time been followed by those having the enterprise in charge. His reply was earnest, emphatic and directly to the point. It made a lasting impression upon my mind.

A PIECEMEAL POLICY.

"Do not make the mistake," he said, "of attempting to carry out any piecemeal policy in such an undertaking as that. It will cost you more than twice what you anticipate before you get through, and if you start that way you will never be through.

"In my judgment," he added, "there is but one way to

proceed in an undertaking of that magnitude, and that is to have the whole scheme laid out in advance before any commitments are made. In this way you can see the end from the beginning and at least approximately know at the start where you are coming out."

Those statements are now as clear in my mind as though Mr. James had made them but yesterday. At the next meeting I reported the conversation to the board. Mr. Murphy reiterated the answer:

"I am here to spend that two millions and a half of dollars as I think best. Newark pays about three-fourths of the county taxes, and, as one of the representatives of this city, I propose to be free to favor such parks here or in the county as I wish."

On May 20, 1895, a conference was held with Landscape Architects and Engineers Messrs. N. F. Barrett and John Bogart, who had made the most original and suggestive plans for the first commission. On the recommendation of the committee on landscape architects—Mr. Shepard and myself—these gentlemen received their appointment and went immediately at work on data for the preparation, later, of landscape plans. Mr. Bogart was chosen with the view of his having especially in charge the various engineering problems which it was soon recognized the commission, in carrying out the plans for such varied topography as existed in Essex County, would have to solve.

About the same time, Messrs. Murphy and Meeker acted as a committee in conferring with Mayor Lebkuecher to obtain his views in regard to the transfer of lands belonging to the city of Newark which might be desirable for use in the new park locations. Requisitions for funds were made on the freeholders—one for $5,000 on May 9—and promptly honored, and that board was advised that the commission "would probably require the current year $750,000." On June 17 a conference with the Finance Committee of the freeholders was held. This was followed a week later by another requisition for $50,000, which amount was promptly forthcoming.

NUCLEUS OF NEWARK PARK.

While the question as to the general policy of the board was yet undecided, there seemed to be no doubt that the Branch Brook reservoir property should become the nucleus of the central park for Newark. The location was central—although far north of the center of the large population in Newark. The tract belonging to the city, had in December, 1899, owing largely to the active efforts of the Roseville Improvement Association, Charles H. Pell and others, been transferred by the Aqueduct Board to the Common Council, and a few days later was dedicated to park purposes and came under the control of the Board of Works—the right being reserved to use such part of it as necessary for reservoir purposes. There had been more or less agitation in favor of having the transfer of this tract made to the Park Commission. The Mayor recommended it and the press favored it. It was "as good a place to begin with as any, and all should help hasten the development of the park system. Let there be some practical results shown as soon as possible." That was the way The Call put forth its claims for a park site to public favor. The tract as transferred contained about sixty acres. Adjoining on the easterly side, within the park site soon afterward chosen, were many residences, always very costly in acquirement for park uses. But the reservoir property was already in municipal control and held for park improvement, and in July, 1895, was transferred by the Newark Board of Street and Water Commissioners to the Park Commission.

At the board meeting of July 18 the landscape architect and engineers were requested to prepare a map indicating their best judgment as to the lines for a Branch Brook Park. The lines soon afterward recommended, did not then, as now, include either the central or northern divisions, and on the north extended only as far as Fifth avenue. This plan was approved July 30, 1895.

The subject of a county bond issue for the parks was also

under active consideration during the summer, and early in August it was decided to make a further requisition for $945,000. It had also been determined to locate a small park in the eastern district of Newark, where all agreed a park was needed, and where opportunity offered to obtain about thirteen acres of unimproved city lots in the midst of a built-up and populous district.

The acquirements of nearly all this land from the single owner, John O'Brien, of New York, enabled the commission to avoid the expense and delay incidental to condemnation proceedings, and made the improvement of that park the first work completed.

Early in July, I brought before the board the matter of encouraging gifts of park land, etc., from private owners, and the following statement was approved and appeared in most of the Essex County papers about that time:

"THE ESSEX COUNTY PARK COMMISSION,
"Newark, N. J., July 25, 1895.

"In order that Essex County may possess as elaborate a park system as possible, the Park Commission has thought it wise to invite the people to assist in increasing the area and attractions. This is the only commission in the United States where the park movement embraces an entire county, and the splendid possibilities which follow from such an almost unlimited choice of magnificent natural features make most desirable the hearty co-operation of the press and people in every portion of the county.

"The experience of other localities shows that park development has been materially assisted by liberal gifts of land and money, and in almost every community the park systems are a monument not only to the wise public policy but to private benefaction as well.

"Of the 425 acres in the Springfield (Mass.) park system, more than 300 acres have been by gift from individuals and but 116 acres—less than one-third—acquired by purchase.

"Within the past two years the city of Hartford (Conn.)

has received donations of 180 acres of park lands and several hundred thousand dollars by bequest from one of her late citizens.

"Cleveland, Detroit, Pittsburg and many other communities have received similar munificent gifts for like uses.

"In all cases the results are as gratifying to the donors as the public. Land forever dedicated to public park uses is an enduring monument to the giver.

"The Park Commission hopes that the experience of other localities may be repeated here, and gifts of land and and money will be gladly received. The plans under consideration admit of the selection of alternate sites for the county system, and it is important that notice of the intention to present land be given to the commission as soon as possible, in order that all lands accepted may be developed in harmony with the park plans.

GLAD TO RECEIVE PROPOSALS.

"The commission will also be glad to receive proposals for sale of lands suitable for park purposes from individuals or other owners desiring to co-operate in the acquirement of lands on advantageous terms to the county.

"The commission will make public acknowledgment and suitable recognition of all donations, whether land, money or bequests. Gifts of money will be used according to the directions of the donor in any way which tends to increase the beauty of the parks.

"Suggestions have already been made of gifts of certain tracts, and offers of others at nominal prices, and the Park Commission feels sure that the public spirited will respond liberally to the call and render it possible for Essex County to possess one of the finest park systems in the country.

"CYRUS PECK,
"FREDERICK M. SHEPARD,
"FRANKLIN MURPHY,
"FREDERICK W. KELSEY,
"STEPHEN J. MEEKER."

The commission afterward received from the Messrs. Ballantine a gift of thirty-two acres, and from Z. M. Keen and William A. Righter one of about twenty acres, all valuable land in northern Newark, and now included in the northern division of Branch Brook Park, north of Bloomfield avenue. In 1896, a number of public-spirited citizens in Orange and East Orange made a donation of $17,275 in cash toward the acquirement of the triangle tract there, now the Orange Park.

REAL ESTATE EXPERTS.

As the preliminary work of the board early in 1895 continued, it was found that one of the intricate, if not difficult, obstacles to overcome would be the acquirement of the land needed for the parks. It is unfortunate, but true, "and pity 'tis 'tis true," that whenever realty property is required of private owners for public uses there is, in most instances, an immediate increase in the owner's estimate of the value; and not infrequently the demands become so exorbitant as to price as to leave no other resource excepting either to abandon the purchase or resort to troublesome and frequently costly litigation. Although the commission had guarded its plans, as had the previous board, there was a general impression that soon appeared to pervade the district immediately contiguous to the reservoir site that a park would in all probability be located there at an early date. In order to accomplish, as far as possible, the acquirement of the land by purchase, it was decided to employ, as a part of the working organization of the commission, two real estate experts, who would undertake this important work of land purchase, and on July 18 Messrs. B. F. Crane and E. E. Bond received the appointment of land agents. Both of these gentlemen performed most valuable service, especially Mr. Crane, who was continuously active and earnest, and by kindly and tactful effort was very successful in acquiring a great number of the small lots and residence properties within the Branch Brook Park area. His loyalty to the interests of the commission won the confidence and esteem of all the members, and by his death, in February, 1896, the Park Board lost one of its most trusted and careful assistants.

In January, 1896, A. L. Cross was chosen as assistant land agent, in place of Mr. Bond. The purchasing agents were not always successful, even in instances where there had been no intimation to the owners that the lands inquired for or under negotiation were for public use. No one outside the board rooms knew of the decision of the commission regarding the East Side Park location, as mentioned, or, as far as I know, at the time negotiations were opened for the land, no one in that part of Newark had any thought or knowledge that the subject was under consideration.

Messrs. Bond and Crane reported that J. M. Lummis was the agent of John O'Brien, who owned the 134 unimproved lots, and constituting nearly all of the thirteen acres required for the park, bounded by Adams, Walnut, Oliver and Van Buren streets, in eastern Newark. They were authorized to negotiate with Mr. Lummis and to have a careful appraisement made, including their own valuation of the property. Later they advised that $148,000 was the price asked, and reported the appraisement, which they said had been carefully made, at $95,700. The board declined to pay any such price as that asked. After some further negotiations the selling price was reduced to $125,000, as "the very lowest price" that would be accepted. At the board meeting of December 31, 1895, a resolution was adopted authorizing condemnation proceedings toward securing the property. Not long afterward I received word at my place of business in New York that Andrew H. Green, whom I had pleasantly known and whose office was convenient to mine, desired to see me. In the interview following Mr. Green informed me that as a lifelong friend he had, as a personal favor to Mr. O'Brien, consented to look after his property interests in Newark; how both he and Mr. O'Brien disliked either to stand in the way of such public improvements or to go into litigation; and that he had sent for me because from our past acquaintance he felt that "we could amicably settle the question of the purchase of the lots, if any one could settle it."

COMMISSION'S METHODS EXPLAINED.

I explained the methods employed by the commission in arriving at a basis of fair valuation of the property—considered alike fair to Mr. O'Brien and the people of the county who were paying for it, and how we should be glad to reciprocate the spirit of civic improvement that had been so marked a characteristic in his administration of public affairs. I endeavored to make it clear to him that the Park Commission, in its position of trustee of public funds, in placing the limit of the purchase price at the appraised price and what we believed a fair and equitable price, was acting as he had so many times acted in similar positions of trust, when duty and loyalty to the obligation as trustee had been the paramount consideration.

Mr. Green then asked me when condemnation proceedings would be begun. I replied that authorization had been made for them to be instituted directly. He then wanted to know if we could not "divide the difference between Mr. O'Brien's last asking price, $125,000, and the appraised valuation as reported of $95,700." He declared that this seemed to him preferable to litigation for both sides, and that he had understood Mr. O'Brien had for some time considered the property worth $150,000.

"Were it a personal transaction or the commissioners were negotiating individually," I replied, "we might very likely get together on the principle of dividing the difference, as you suggest, but in this instance I think the commissioners are agreed that we should stand on the agreed valuations of our experts, in whom we have the fullest confidence. Unless this price is acceptable to you and Mr. O'Brien, we should prefer to have the court proceeding for acquiring the property to go on, rather than increase the limit of price." He said he should like to confer with Mr. O'Brien, and that I would hear from him soon.

The following day Mr. Green called upon me, and wrote

out the following authorized acceptance, at the valuation
the commission was willing to pay for the property:

"New York, February 7th, 1896.
"Mr. Fred'k W. Kelsey, Commissioner.

"Dear Sir—I am authorized by Mr. John O'Brien to sell
to your commission all the property belonging to him in
blocks Nos. 964, 965, 966, 967 and 968 on the revised map
of the O'Brien property (of Ward & Tichenor of September,
1885), situated in the city of Newark, at the price of
$95,700, payable on or before the fifteenth day of March,
1896, or sooner if satisfactory examination of title can be
made.

"Yours truly, for John O'Brien,
"And. H. Green."

At the next meeting of the board, February 10, the purchase agreement was formally closed at $95,700, as pro-
posed in Mr. Green's letter. From the later experiences
of the commission in acquiring park lands by condemnation
proceedings there can be little, if any, doubt that this action
of Mr. Green's was the means of a direct saving to the taxpayers of Essex County of at least $30,000, to say nothing
of the delay that would have resulted in the improvement
of the East Side Park through the acquirement of the land
by legal process.

A TRUST OBLIGATION.

The question as to the still unsettled general policy of
the commission in establishing the park system was yet
before us. The subject would be discussed, put over, and
come up again whenever definite locations or estimates of
cost of proposed park areas were under consideration. A
solution seemed no nearer than before. The sectional
piecemeal plan was, notwithstanding, gradually taking
shape. The landscape architects were, as requested, preparing plans and studying boundary lines for different

parks, not for a park system as a whole. There was nothing whatever in the way of carrying out the other policy while the different sites were under consideration or being informally acted upon. The situation at this time may be readily understood from the following letter to Commissioner Peck of October 2, 1895:

"Dear Mr. Peck—On my return home last evening I went carefully over the report of the first commission, with the view of ascertaining whether I was not in error in my impression that the present commission was under a trust obligation to carry out substantially the recommendation of that report. Even a casual reading would have made my impression as to such obligation a conviction.

"As the meetings of our first commision were held in executive session, that report and the bill accompanying it were the only direct and official statements to the public of our conclusions and intentions. The confidence of the public in the recommendations made was evidently strengthened by the reiterated statements in the press as to the high character and aims of the commission.

"About 6,000 copies of the report were distributed throughout the county and in the Legislature. From that report, and upon the recommendations and statements there made, the press, Legislature and public approved the report and adopted the charter recommended. Every one of our names was signed to that report (in duplicate), and to the statements of fact and intentions there stated.

"If, under these conditions, a trust obligation does not rest upon the present commission, how could one be created? If the careful preparation of that report, with our signatures attached, does not clearly specify such conditions, how would it be possible to present a subject that would involve trust obligations?

"If we were borrowing a large amount of money for our personal account, would not the stipulations and statements accompanying the loan become important factors in the use of the money? What distinction or difference can be made in this instance, where the interests of 300,000 people are directly affected, after the loan has been made, the confidence reposed and powers conferred, based upon these statements?

"Surely there was nothing in the report that indicated there was the remotest thought or intention of adopting a piecemeal, sectional policy. On the contrary, every statement and inference was that a 'system' of parks was to be created; that they were to be laid out on the general plans as outlined in the report, for the good of the whole county, free from local entrammelments.

"If this view be the correct one, it seems to me that it is incumbent upon our board to change its policy, and instruct our architects to at once proceed and lay out a comprehensive plan for the county before we decide upon any other large areas, besides the Branch Brook tract, as a starting point already agreed upon.

"You will recollect I suggested to you this plan soon after the organization of the present commission. It has been my conviction from the first that it was the proper way, and, indeed, the only way, that we could make effective progress and lay out a system that would meet the obligations entered into with the public on the acceptance of our statement and charter, or that would avert adverse criticism and keep the work of the commission on broad lines, acceptable to the people of the county and the State.

"I have not more strongly advocated this plan before because I have deferred to the feelings and judgment of the other members of the commission who, I felt, would, sooner or later, from their own convictions, arrive at the same conclusion. Very truly yours,

"FREDERICK W. KELSEY."

The reasons why it seemed desirable to carry out the policy of the first commission, as above indicated, and many others, had been repeatedly stated at the board meetings, where, as I have already mentioned, the discussions, although earnest, were always in good nature. Believing that there was a vital principle involved, I also wrote Com-

missioners Shepard and Murphy on similar lines. In a
letter to Mr. Shepard, October 11, 1895, I wrote:

"If the plans outlined by the first commission, and so
cordially approved, are to be changed to a piecemeal, sectional policy, without regard to where we are coming out in
the expenditure of the two and a half millions provided in
the charter, should we not so state, openly and publicly, in
the beginning?

"To my mind our duty is clear in the obligation we are
under to keep faith with the public in fulfilling the stipulations and in making the conditions conform to the statements upon which our charter was formed."

In his reply Mr. Shepard submitted an estimate of the
probable cost of the park sites then under discussion,
amounting to $1,900,000, and stated that he thought the
architects should make a connecting plan "with parkways
as suggested."

"This meets the obligation we have inherited," he wrote,
"and when our plan is settled and we have some developed
work to show, we can apply to the people through the Legislature for sufficient money to complete the work."

Referring to the estimates and his proposition, I replied:

"If we start on Lake Weequahic I think the least we can
safely estimate for getting out of it with anything like ad-
missible results would be over rather than under $500,000,
and it might largely exceed that sum. Even if a half
million were a limit, or if it were more in the center of the
county or of the population, the proportion would look to be
less formidable, but it is almost on the county line—in
reality almost as much for Elizabeth and Union as for
Newark and Essex. My feeling is that when that tract is
improved for park uses Union County should unite in the
undertaking and contribute at least one-third of the
expense."

I again wrote Mr. Shepard on November 22, 1895:

"Our park enterprise was laid out and the preliminary work carried out on broad lines; successful because sectionalism was avoided and the pledge made that the money was to be expended for the benefit of all the county, rather than with special reference to particular localities.

"The majority sentiment at the meeting yesterday focalized directly on the negative side of those principles. No matter what arguments or facts favor the successful original scheme, it must now be superseded by a local policy plan, as distinct in its aims and objects and as much at variance with its former methods and policy as can possibly be.

"Whether the cable tract is or is not taken is not more vital, it seems to me, than this breach of faith with the public—the change of policy with its natural sequence, and the question of one's duty and obligation under such circumstances.

"If the change be made, it will be extremely expensive. It will tend soon or later to disintegrate any commission or public body entrusted to carry out a great public improvement, as surely as local and personal jealousies separate individuals and communities. If our enterprise can be anything of a success under such a load it will be a mere matter of good fortune.

"Should not this matter of policy be outlined and agreed upon before we go any further?"

Again, December 1, I wrote: "If the majority plan is adopted, the trust obligation we are under to the public is ignored and the experience of other local commissioners unheeded. Feeling as I do that nothing that you or I or any individual can do will prevent the final outcome and result of these two fundamental policies, the thought still uppermost in my mind is as to our duty, and the best course under the circumstances."

But further argument was useless. The work of the commission in establishing the lines and acquiring the land for the different parks was going on apace. The relative bearings that one park should have to another, or that any of those determined upon should have to the park system as a whole, was lost sight of, or considered as "wholly secondary." Each park was treated as an entity, as though the plan for a unified system had never been under consideration. The location for one park as a distinct proposition as exemplified in the East Side Park in Newark, had accentuated the pressure brought to bear upon the commission to locate others.

The suggestions of the court as to local "representation," and the two new commissioners appointed to carry out that principle, had borne fruit, and, before the close of 1895, the sectional policy for the Essex County parks was well established and became the controlling principle, as it has, subject to minor modifications, since remained.

CHAPTER VI.

THE FIRST $1,000,000.

WITH the great mass of people, to whom the matter of income vs. expenses is a present and ever-recurring problem, there are, perhaps, few characters in fiction more interesting or that have attracted wider attention than Wilkins Micawber. His object lesson in correct finance, showing the happiness that may follow from an income of "twenty pounds a year" and expenses of "nineteen pounds nineteen shillings and sixpence," when compared with the misery resulting from a like income and the expenditure of "twenty pounds one," illustrates in a few words a principle of very general application.

Thus, in the park enterprise, each of the commissioners, favoring the policy of being pecuniarily forehanded in public matters as in private affairs, was of one mind as to the desirability of providing ample funds before incurring liability for land purchases or other financial obligations.

After the organization of the department was completed and the first requisition for $5,000 on the Board of Freeholders in May, 1895, had been made, the commission then took up the subject of a bond issue for a large amount. This was arranged through a joint meeting with the Finance Committee of the freeholders on June 17. At this conference it was agreed that, as the proceeds of the bonds were under the law to be turned over to the park board, the commission should take the initial and active steps in the negotiations for the bond issue.

TO CONSULT WITH BANKERS.

The meeting was entirely harmonious, and I was appointed a committee, with the counsel, to consult with some

of the leading New York bankers having resources for
handling such a loan and as to the kind of bond that could
to the best advantage be issued. Soon afterward several
conferences were held with the United States Mortgage
and Trust Company, Kuhn, Loeb & Co., and J. & W. Seligman. All recommended a "four per cent. gold bond" for as
long a time as practicable, and, if maturing at different
periods, that the average date of maturity should be not less
than thirty years. These recommendations were approved
by the commission, and a circular letter was prepared inviting proposals for the bonds. On June 28, 1895, the New
York Bond Buyer announced that it had been "reported
June 17 that the Board of Freeholders of Essex County,
New Jersey, had decided to issue bonds at not exceeding
four per cent. to the amount of $2,500,000;" and that "the
Finance Committee, after consultation with the Essex
County Park Commission, had decided to issue them in
three lots" of four per cent. semi-annual twenty-year gold
bonds, two issues of $750,000 each, and one of $1,000,000.
The bonded debt of the county was given as "$780,197; as-
sessed valuation, $154,071,200; tax rate, 6.22." With the
exception of the time stated for maturity of all the bonds,
this announcement was substantially in accord with the plan
as then agreed upon.

About this time I brought the subject of the proposed
bond issue to the attention of J. Pierpont Morgan. He had
just returned from Europe. I had known for a number
of years, as does every one having business relations with
him or his firm, that he was the master spirit, exercising
the deciding mind on all important matters there. For this
reason we had awaited his return, while conferring with
the other bankers mentioned. In calling upon Mr. Morgan,
I stated briefly the situation. He replied that he would look
into the matter, and that he thought it a favorable time to
bring out such a bond issue. He was then accredited with
having just closed in London some exceedingly large financial transactions, and spoke of the low rates of interest
prevailing both "there and here." A few days later, June

24,1895, I wrote Mr. Morgan, enclosing "copy of the act authorizing the issue of Essex County Park bonds referred to in our conversation," and adding: "As a committee of the commission to look up this matter, I should be pleased to again confer with you personally, and will try and call on you in the course of a few days."

Soon afterward I again wrote Mr. Morgan, as follows: "In looking into the Essex County (N. J.) Park loan, I believe you will find the bonds now to be issued of the very highest class; indeed the very best. Under the county system of New Jersey there are special safeguards thrown round the county organization which give county measures such as the issue of bonds almost the prestige and resource of a State. This, with the fact that county claims have preference over local and municipal payments on all taxes collected, makes such an issue as the Essex Park bonds doubly sure."

A PRIVATE BOND SALE CRITICIZED.

While the subject of the bond issue was under consideration, an incident occurred that settled one point, regarding the method of placing the bonds, most effectually. A transaction in Newark bonds by a committee of the freeholders with one of the local financial institutions had excited much adverse comment. Even the grand jury made a presentment on the subject of the bonds having been disposed of at private sale at a price below the prevailing market.

The amount was not large, but the transaction was held up also by the press as a warning against the further disposition of any city or county securities in like manner, or in any other way than by competitive bids. As these criticisms were aimed directly at the proposed issuance of the park bonds, the commission and Finance Committee of the freeholders were in entire accord in deciding that sealed proposals should be invited for the new bonds, and that they should not be otherwise disposed of. It was also deemed advisable in this way to extend the credit for such securities, and the advantages which might accrue to the community should foreign capital be employed in investment in the bonds were considered.

On the afternoon of July 9, 1895, I went over the bond matter quite fully with Mr. Morgan. He said that it was a good bond; that it would sell for a good premium; that he would take the whole two and one-half millions authorized issue and pay a good price for the bonds; and that he would arrange payment so that the commission could have the money as fast as needed or whenever wanted. I asked him if he thought the bonds with a rate of less than four per cent. "would go." He said: "Yes." "Three and a half per cent.?" I asked. "No," he replied. "Well, then, what rate would you suggest as being safe for insuring a sale of the bonds below four per cent.?" He thought a moment, and remarked: "Some people like the idea of a cent a day on a hundred dollars, or a 3.65 interest rate," and intimated he would take the bonds himself at that rate; also that he thought they could be sold at a small premium. I told him that we should be glad to take up the negotiations with him, but the decision had already been made that the only way the bonds could be sold was by competitive bids, under the usual specifications. He replied that he would not go into competition, but would probably pay as good a price for the whole issue as likely to be obtained from others. Events soon demonstrated the correctness of Mr. Morgan's observation.

Immediately after leaving his office I conferred with Commissioner Peck, who agreed with me that we should favor the change in interest from four per cent. to 3.65 per cent., notwithstanding that reports like those above quoted had gone out to the effect that the park bonds were to be "four per cents," and the form of advertisements and circulars inviting proposals at the four per cent. rate were then in proof ready for printing. The same afternoon I wrote Treasurer Murphy and Counsel Munn as follows:

"NEW YORK, July 9, 1895.

"My Dear Sir—From the bids on the Brooklyn and Philadelphia bonds, opened yesterday, and from information received here to-day, Mr. Peck and myself fully agree that the interest on our park bonds should be 3.65 per cent. instead of four per cent.

"We believe that the other members of the board will concur in this view in considering the matter further at the meeting on Thursday.

"While this may delay the printing a day or two, we deem it a matter of considerable importance, and as the addressing of the lists for proposals can be completed in the meantime, it need not necessarily delay the publication but a little to defer the advertisements and sending until after our Thursday's meeting. Very truly yours,

"FRED. W. KELSEY."

"Franklin Murphy, Treasurer."

At the next meeting referred to, the conversation with Mr. Morgan was reported, and a resolution, offered by myself, that the rate of interest be changed to 3.65 per cent., was adopted. The following printed letter, inviting proposals for the bonds, was soon afterward sent to the leading bankers and bond brokerage houses generally:

$2,500,000 ESSEX COUNTY, NEW JERSEY, PARK BONDS.

"The Board of Chosen Freeholders of the county of Essex, New Jersey, proposes to issue bonds to the aggregate amount of $2,500,000, pursuant to the provisions of Chapter XCI., of the act of 1895, which act has been approved by a vote of the people of said county, for the purpose of establishing a system of parks and parkways for said county.

"These bonds will be dated August 1, 1895, payable as follows: $500,000, August 1, 1915; $500,000, August 1, 1920; $500,000, August 1, 1925; $500,000, August 1, 1930; $500,000, August 1, 1935.

"They will be of the denomination of $1,000 each; will bear interest at three and sixty-five one-hundredths (3.65-100) per cent. per annum, payable semi-annually; will be coupon bonds with the option to the holder to have them registered or exchanged for registered bonds; will be executed by the county officers, and the whole issue duly countersigned, principal and interest payable in gold coin.

"The proceeds will be required for use by the Park Commission from time to time during a period of not less than two, nor more than three years. At least $750,000 will be required during the present year.

THE COUNTY'S INDEBTEDNESS.

"The county of Essex has a population of 300,000, and an assessed valuation of $178,165,000. Its present total indebtedness is $766,859, or less than one-half of one per cent. of the assessed valuation.

"The act under which the bonds are issued requires the annual levy of a county tax sufficient to meet interest and principal when due. A county tax for any purpose is entitled to priority in payment over local taxes for municipal purposes.

"Sealed proposals will be received by the Finance Committee of the Board of Chosen Freeholders, at a meeting, to be held by said committee, at the freeholders' room, in the courthouse, at Newark, N. J., on Tuesday, July 30, 1895, at 3 o'clock P. M., which meeting will remain open until 3:30 P. M. Proposals should be:

"1. For the whole of said bonds, to be issued at once.

"2. For $1,000,000, to be now issued.

"3. For the whole amount, to be issued in instalments of not less than $500,000 during a period not exceeding three years.

"4. For any part of said bonds.

"The purchaser to pay the interest accrued on said bonds to the time of delivery.

"Under the statute, no bids can be received at any other time or place.

"The Finance Committee reserves the right to reject any and all proposals, if in its judgment the interest of the county requires such action."

Of the responsible bids received, the United States Mortgage and Trust Company offered 101.25 for a million bonds at four per cent. interest; J. & W. Seligman, 100.34 for a million of the 3.65 bonds—$500,000 payable on delivery of the bonds and $500,000 six months later; New York Life Insurance Company, "par flat for a million," $300,000 on delivery and $100,000 per month thereafter; Vermilye & Co., 100.77 for a million, averaging thirty years' maturity; and the Howard Savings Institution, par for $50,000 of the bonds as advertised.

The award was made to Vermilye & Co. and the $1,008,400 proceeds were received by the freeholders in a certified check for that amount on August 26, 1895; $945,000 was paid over to the Park Commission five days later, $55,000 having been previously received. And thus was closed the first transaction whereby a 3.65 rate of interest bond issued by a county at par had, so far as could be ascertained up to that time, been sold.

In commenting upon this sale, The Call said editorially: "The sale of a million of county bonds bearing interest at $3.65 per $100 at a slight premium showed that the Park Commission and freeholders of the Finance Committee who worked together in this matter had gauged the bond market pretty accurately in fixing the interest."

While this observation was no doubt correct, it was the suggestion made by Mr. Morgan, in the interview as stated, which resulted in a direct saving to the people of Essex County in their taxes for the thirty years' average life of the bonds, of $3,500 per year in the interest charge alone; and the particulars are here narrated, as having an important bearing, as will be mentioned in a succeeding chapter, at that juncture of park affairs.

ACQUIRING PARK LANDS.

With an abundance of cash in bank—these funds having been promptly deposited in various county banks and trust companies of accredited standing, subject to call and with interest at two per cent.—the commission proceeded as rapidly as possible with the acquirement of park lands and other work of the board. The land agents were requested to expedite purchases. The counsel was authorized to begin condemnation proceedings, directly owners were found who would not sell at a fair price, or in cases where such action was found necessary to correct or complete title. The commission held frequent meetings, often twice a week, to pass upon those questions and to determine the boundary lines of each of the parks as soon as a location for a park was decided upon. In almost every instance these locations, after they were determined, brought up anew the question as to extensions.

As has already been stated, the first outlines of the Branch Brook Park, agreed upon July 30, 1895, extended only so far as Park avenue on the north and to Orange street on the south. Almost immediately afterward extensions in both directions were under consideration. No sooner had the official map for the East Side, or "Down Neck," Park been prepared, than petitions and delegations from that section asked that the park area there be enlarged. This result followed quite generally, and as the majority of the board had determined upon the plan of dealing with each of the park sites separately, rather than as a part of the system as a whole, the importance of each location was unduly magnified accordingly. In order to give the reader a correct view of the progress of this work, perhaps an account of the selection of each of the parks in something like the order of their location may here be of interest.

While a number of the park sites as afterward chosen were under consideration simultaneously, a final decision was more readily evolved with some than with others, and these decisions, in a few cases, were deferred for many months.

The same day (July 30, 1895) that the commission accepted formal control of the reservoir property, the landscape architects and engineers were requested to prepare a map indicating their best judgment as to the lines for a park with the sixty acres transferred by the city of Newark as a nucleus. At that time the estimated cost of the land and buildings, between Fifth avenue and Orange street, above mentioned, was $361,685. It soon became apparent that a creditable "Central Park" for Newark and for the county could not be established within those lines. By January, 1896, the Sussex avenue extension and the block east of Clifton avenue, the Garside street addition had been included. The questions as to these additions were not long pending.

BRANCH BROOK PARK EXTENDED.

The extension from Park avenue to Bloomfield avenue was a more serious matter. A large acreage of city lot property was involved and the estimated cost was nearly $300,000. Such an expenditure, together with the cost of improvement, would make a heavy drain on the available funds, before the needs of the other portions of the county could be considered. The proposition was finally carried, however, and on January 9 that liberal extension through to Bloomfield avenue was also included in the Branch Brook Park.

But the lines were not to stop there. Pressure had been brought upon the commission to carry the northern limits of the park still farther. North of Bloomfield avenue and east of the Morris Canal on the line of the park, the land was mostly low, swamp property, impossible of improvement without draining, and until thus improved, practically worthless. In the springtime, or during a rainy season, many acres there were practically as impassable to a person on foot as the jungles of Africa. In the spring of 1896 the commission made two or three tours of inspection there, but no one would take the risk of sinking in the swale by attempting to explore the inner recesses of the waterlogged tangle of grassy bumps and hummocks, then known as the old Blue Jay Swamp.

On December 4, 1896, this northern extension matter was the special order of business. Commissioner Murphy had offered a resolution the July previous that the northern boundary of the park be at the old Bloomfield road. At the meeting of December 2, this resolution was offered: that "all speeches be limited to five minutes, and only two speeches be permitted from the same person." An amendment to the main resolution that "the territory between Bloomfield avenue and Fredonia avenue be treated as a parkway," was lost—2 ayes, 3 nays; likewise by the same vote an amendment providing that the cost of land in the property extension should "not exceed $150,000." This 130-acre tract, estimated to cost $160,000, was thereupon added to what seemed then, and has since proven, an already heavily ballasted financial load; although the redeemed land and the present attractive features of the northern section of the Branch Brook Park of to-day afford some compensation alike to the public and those responsible for the accession.

The financial part of this undertaking kept full pace with, or quite outran, the acreage accumulations. The estimated cost of $361,685 of June, 1895, had, at the close of 1896, mounted to an actual cash expenditure for land alone of $850,687; and a year later to $1,129,086, or nearly one-half of the entire county park appropriation for this one park of 278 acres. There were very many buildings acquired with the land purchased, especially in the portions of the park south of Fifth avenue; but these, mostly inexpensive residences, realized but little. At an auction sale on April twenty-fifth, these houses were disposed of at from a few dollars to a few hundred dollars each, and the costly experience of making public parks from improved city lot property was again exemplified. Only about $16,000 was realized from the buildings in this park, that had cost more than $500,000.

HURRYING THE IMPROVEMENTS.

Concurrently with the consideration of park sites came the question of beginning park development. All the commissioners were anxious that the practical work of improvement should proceed. The public reflected this sentiment through the press in urging that "something be done." It was now April, 1896. The commission had been in office a year; a million of dollars had been available for months, and why should not the work go forward? On April 11 the landscape architects and engineers were "requested to formulate a plan for the improvement of Branch Brook Park and for employing 200 men." By May 25 sufficient progress had been made to invite proposals, to close June 3, for the work, and to pass a resolution "that this work be done through contractors, who will agree to employ upon it citizens of Essex County on a basis of cost, and at such compensation as can be agreed upon by such contractors and the commission."

The plan of giving preference to residents or business houses within the county, other conditions being equally favorable, had already become an established rule of the board. The work to be done was in what is now known as the southern division of the park, south of Fifth avenue. A number of proposals—more than twenty—were received. They were as varied in specifications and offerings as were the qualifications and facilities for doing the work of the various bidders. The bids ranged from the offerings of a few horses and carts to those proposing to do all the work complete. After a moderately successful effort to properly classify these complex propositions, the rejection of all bids was deemed the only solution that could be properly made.

The meeting when the bids were opened was, as usual, in executive session. There was, in this unofficial and unbusiness-like procedure, no discourtesy to any of the bidders; none was thought of or intended. Nor, so far as I can now recall, would any of the commissioners at that time have been likely to have objected to the presence of the public. The bids were called for in the regular course of business, and no occasion for secrecy could or did exist.

The fact was that, owing to the topography and peculiar situation of that property, it was a most difficult matter to draw any specifications for contract work, as a whole, that would give the commission, through the architects and

engineers, the necessary reservation for directing the work
—a matter so vitally important in park improvements of
that character.

In the second communication inviting bids, this right of
direction by the engineer in charge was noted in the specifications and "any work directed by the engineer should be
included." It was also provided that all "tools, machinery,
etc., must be satisfactory to the engineer," and that bids
should state "upon what percentage of payments actually
made to the employés and for materials" the contractor
would undertake the work.

Six bids from all those to whom this communication was
sent were received. These were also opened at an executive
session of the board. The contract was, on the same day,
June 9, 1896, awarded to the Messrs. Shanley, whose bid, all
things considered, appeared to be the most favorable. All
the commissioners, I believe, concurred in this view, which
was also in accord with the recommendations of the chief
engineer. As soon, however, as the action became known,
there was a "hue and cry" directly.

Whether right or wrong, the commission was taken severely to task, both by some of those whose bids had been
rejected and by the press. One of the bidders in a published
letter wanted to know: "Are not the books and records of
the Park Commission public documents and open to inspection at any reasonable hour? Are not any moneys expended
by the Park Commission under such contract expended contrary to law, in direct violation of chapter 181, laws of
1894?"

COULD NOT SEE BIDS.

The writer went on to say that he had "called at the office
of the Park Commission and asked to see the twenty-three
bids received June 3," and "was informed by the secretary,

Mr. Church, that they were not for the public and could not be seen."

One of the leading Newark papers, in commenting editorially upon the incident, said: "The Park Commission should be compelled to expose to public view the contracts made. To keep confidence with bidders is one thing, but to let the public know the facts regarding actual business completed is a duty which admits of no argument. Every detail of such an arrangement should be available. The commission are occupying themselves with expenditure for the public of money from the public, and owe official existence to the public; confidence reposed in the public would seem to be nothing more than a report of a servant to a master."

Another editorial criticism pointed out that "the bids relate to public business, and any citizen who asks for the privilege of making examinations of them at a reasonable time and in a proper manner should be accommodated. The park commissioners ought to understand that they are public officials and that the fact that they are men of standing in the community and have had reposed in them a great trust, does not mean that they should be permitted to transact public business as if it were a matter entirely personal and private to themselves."

And again: "The people of Essex County do not desire to have two standards set up for the conduct of public boards and officers. They do not want to have some so exclusive or so lofty in their own esteem that open records and open meetings are intolerable to them. As men active in public life, the members of the commission will make a grave error if they try to assume any such position as that."

These cogent and convincing reasons were so thoroughly in accord with my own convictions that I soon afterward gave notice that later in the year, when the park locations were more definitely determined and the needed purchases to establish value in each park were made, I should offer a resolution providing for all regular meetings of the board to be held in open session. Such a resolution was accordingly offered, and before the following April—at which

time my term of office as commissioner expired—it was two
or three times called up for action, but each time "went
over" by request.

SECRET SESSIONS DISFAVORED.

While the discussion on the bids during June and July,
1896, was going on, at least some of the commissioners appeared to be impressed by the circumstances occasioning the
adverse comments on secret sessions. This is shown by a
statement made by myself after the board meeting July 22,
1896, in response to an inquiry from the News as to the
attitude of the commission regarding these executive sessions, and published the day following. This statement was
in part as follows:

"We have about concluded all that part of our work
wherein we considered that the interests of the county
might suffer by premature publication, and I know of no
reason why our meetings should not be open to the public
hereafter. We are simply the agents of the taxpayers, who
have placed at our disposal the expenditure of $2,500,000.
While our selection may have been due to confidence reposed
in our judgment, it is natural that the public should express
anxiety as to the manner in which we are executing the
trust. By affording every facility in this direction, we will
remove all causes for criticism and make our relations with
the public more pleasant.

"It is admitted that much of our work was of a character
that would suffer by premature publicity.

"We considered that the interests of the county would be
best served by conducting our negotiations for property
quietly and without publicity, which might tend to cause exorbitant prices to be demanded in certain sections. Now
our labor in that direction is about complete. We have
nearly all the land necessary for the Branch Brook and the
East Side parks. The same may be said in reference to the
Eagle Rock, South Orange Mountain, and Waverly parks,
and options have already been tendered on land for a West
Side Park. The balance of our work, in my opinion, can be

more advantageously conducted in the same line as that followed by other city and county boards, and for that reason our meetings hereafter should be open."

The article continued: "The speaker's sentiment was echoed by other commissioners, and Mr. Munn says he is satisfied that in the near future all the business of the board will be transacted publicly."

In the first report of the "board of commissioners" for 1896, issued early in the year 1897, the following paragraph (pages 3 and 4) appears: "The sessions of the commission have always from the beginning been held twice each week and have hitherto been executive in character. The commissioners feel that, as custodians of a public fund, it was necessary for them to adopt such a course as long as the purchase of land formed the chief topic of discussion."

When I afterward presented the resolution to carry this sentiment for open meetings of the board into practical effect, it was objected to by two of the commissioners, Messrs. Murphy and Shepard, as was the case whenever the subject of passing on the resolution was brought up. This resolution was left with other commission papers in the drawer of the board-room table at the place I occupied when my term expired, the April following. Why there was objection or why this resolution, or one of similar purport, has never been favorably acted upon, I have never known. Perhaps some future historian of the parks may ascertain, and elucidate this question.

LABORERS' WAGES FIXED.

Another incident that attracted much attention at the time, and may here be of interest, was the action of the commission in June, 1896, in making it a condition in the contracts for work on the park that "laborers be paid $1.25 and foremen $2.50 per day respectively, and for cart, horse and driver $2.50 and for double team and driver $4.25 each per day," and in notices to contractors that "the rates to be paid for services be fixed and approved by the commission."

There was, at that time—the summer of 1896—a very

large contingent of laborers in Newark, as elsewhere, out of employment. The Presidential election was pending, and the great struggle between the McKinley and Hobart sound money forces and the persistent advocates of a silver currency, under the leadership of W. J. Bryan, was going on and had already resulted in an extended business depression. The labor situation was still farther depressed by the continuous arrival of hordes of emigrants, especially Italians, many of whom found their way immediately to Essex County. The commissioners understood that this class of labor was then being employed by contractors on railroads and other large works at prices as low as ninety cents to $1 per day. They wished to have the work done as cheaply as it could be done, and done well, and at the same time to insure the laborers receiving whatever rate was paid. This would prevent the large margin, which, without some such restriction, might be exacted; as in cases then occurring where the contractor would be paid the contract price (of perhaps $1.25 per day), but actually pay the laborer much less.

In establishing the prices noted, the commission intended that they should be the fair current rates for the service named. This view was not shared by some of the other public boards, and the action was severely criticized by some of the labor representatives.

The Board of Freeholders at the meeting June 11, 1896, voted down a drastic resolution offered by one of the members protesting in vigorous language against such a restriction "in fixing the pay of the laborers on county park work at $1.25 per day, as we do not believe good men should be compelled to work for so small a compensation." There was a lively discussion over the resolution. Freeholder Medcraft denied that he had offered the resolution "for election purposes" on his own behalf. Mr. Condit suggested that "if the Park Commission should pay any more than the market prices for labor, they would be doing wrong, and taking money wrongfully out of the pockets of the taxpayers; and the rate per diem of wages was evidently the market price for labor, or they would not be able to get men to work for the figure named." When it was farther brought out that the passage of such a resolution would be an open criticism of one county board upon the official action of another public body of the same county constituency, oil was poured on the troubled waters and the resolutions were defeated.

OIL ON TROUBLED WATERS.

When there came to be a better understanding on the part of the objecting officials, the labor leaders, and labor unions, the agitation ceased, and the work, under the contract, including the specifications that had occasioned the discussion, went smoothly on to completion.

In the initial work at Branch Brook Park, there was a question in which another public board was directly concerned, that did not work out so readily. This was the authoritative closing of the streets; and later, the matter of transferring to the commission other land under control of the Newark Board of Street and Water Commissioners, besides the reservoir property within the park limits, which soon became a part of the same negotiations. Still later, in 1897, the construction of the Millbrook sewer, directly through the southern portion of Branch Brook Park, was for many months a bone of friendly contention between the Newark board and the Park Commission.

Incidentally, too, the question arose as to the payment of assessments due the city on land acquired by the commission. On June 23, 1896, Mayor Seymour wrote the Park Board as follows:

"During the last week a number of bills for assessments for city improvements, levied against property, have been returned to the city comptroller with the statement that the property benefited has been purchased by the Park Board. An investigation shows that, while the improvements were made prior to the date of purchase by your honorable body, the assessments were not confirmed until after title had been taken by the commission.

COURTS AGAINST ASSESSMENTS.

"I am advised that under the decision of the courts these assessments cannot be collected. So far the losses discovered aggregate $1,000.

"This matter you will understand is a serious one to the city. Believing, however, that an adjustment can be made satisfactory to you and the county of Essex, I respectfully request that you attend a conference in my office Friday morning at 10 o'clock. An invitation has also been sent the counsel of your board.

"Pending the conference, the ordinance of the Board of Street and Water Commissioners vacating certain streets for park purposes will be held under consideration.

    "Very truly yours,
      "JAMES M. SEYMOUR, Mayor."

There was apparently no objection made to closing the streets, but, as this letter indicates, both boards were, so to speak, fencing for position. There were questions both of ethics and equity involved. The city officials were naturally desirous of recovering if possible on the assessments as they appeared on the official books, and to obtain as large a contribution as could be secured toward the costly sewer. The courts had ruled out the assessment claims as against the commission, but they were not omitted as a factor in the negotiations. After various conferences, $40,000 was the proportion or share the city officials asked the commission to contribute toward the Millbrook sewer expense.

The commissioners contended that the assessment matter was in no way under consideration; that the expenditures for park improvements were of great benefit to the city; and that to divert public funds from the purpose thus designated to pay for municipal necessities such as drainage, would be an unwarranted procedure, and, under the circumstances then existing, on the principle of "robbing Peter to pay Paul."

COMMISSION PAID CITY $20,000.

The city authorities, not wishing to delay work on the parks, had in the meantime, during the years 1896 and 1897, with reasonable promptness, taken proceedings to close the necessary streets leading to each of the parks—Branch Brook, East Side, and West Side—as located within the city limits. But the questions referred to were not fully disposed of until the offer of the commission, agreed upon at the meeting November 16, 1898, was accepted. Under that proposition and the final settlement, the commission paid the city of Newark, through the Board of Street and Water Commissioners, $20,000, together with the privilege of constructing the city sewer through the park; and, in consideration of this, the latter board ceded to the commission the two blocks of land—all the city then owned—in the Sussex avenue division of the park, between Duryee street, Orange street and the Morris Canal.

TURNING THE FIRST SOD.

The real work in grading, and for the surface embellishment of Branch Brook Park, was begun the morning of June 15, 1896. No special ceremony graced the occasion.

Three of the commissioners, Messrs. Peck, Meeker and myself, with the secretary and Engineer Bogart, were present. Promptly, at 8:30 o'clock, the president, with a new spade, turned the first sod. The contractors had a large force of men and teams ready, and, from that time, the work on this great pleasure ground went rapidly forward. Now that more than nine years have passed and more than $2,500,000 has been expended there, the work is hardly yet completed, and at the present rate of progress it may be another year before the bridge approaches and other improvements are finished.

When completed, this park of 278 acres will be one of the most attractive and interesting pleasure grounds of the size in the country. The topography is sufficiently varied to make practicable the different styles of landscape treatment em-

ployed. The lawn tennis courts and comparatively open
level surface of most of the northern division; the play
fields and open lawn features of the middle division, bordered with raised and closely planted banks on each side;
these are in pleasing contrast to the formal treatment—the
Italian gardens, arbors, pergolas, bordered walks and other
ornamental attractions of the southern division. The lake,
with the connecting waterways under Park avenue and
Bloomfield avenue, with the artistically beautiful bridges,
carrying both avenues over the park driveways and waterways, greatly enhance the other landscape features of this
park. In winter the merry faces and gay costumes of thousands of happy skaters enliven the scene, and turn the
somber effect of the winter season into a joyous moving
panorama for all.

That the people of Essex County may derive increasing
benefit and enjoyment from the very large expenditure for
this park, must be the earnest wish and hopeful expectation
of every one who is a sincere believer in parks, and whose
sympathies are touched by the needs for that uplifting influence to all classes, which only attractive public parks can
supply.

CHAPTER VII.

As noted in a preceding chapter, the decision to locate a small park in the eastern and densely populous portion of Newark was made soon after the organization of the commission in 1895. This determination was the outgrowth of a sentiment within, rather than from any particular pressure brought to bear from without, the board rooms.

In like manner, the ownership of nearly all the property to the extent of 134 city lots being vested with one person, and all that property unbuilt upon, was an important factor in deciding the location. Indeed, no other site in that portion of the city was, I think, at the time under consideration. All the commissioners were agreed that if there was a particular place in the county where a park was especially needed it was in that section, and by November the landscape architects and engineers were authorized to prepare a map for the park. The announcement of the location and the purchase of the O'Brien property soon afterward was well received.

The arrangement with the Newark Street and Water Board for closing the necessary streets was made at a conference with that board held at the commission's rooms, January 2, 1896. These city officials were also in favor of the park.

The press commended the action. One of the papers, on January 3, contended that "nothing the Essex County Park Commission had done will be received with more genuine satisfaction by a great population than the plan approved yesterday by the Park Board and Board of Works in joint session for a fourteen-acre park in the heart of the Iron-

bound District." A similar sentiment was reflected by other
editorial notes and published expressions of the opinions of
many persons entirely outside the district immediately
affected.

There was no adverse criticism that ever reached the commission until the board declined to extend the lines of the
park as originally established. These objections were, however, confined to those more directly interested, and evidently never got beyond the point of individual opinion.
The lines of the park were at first located at the limits that
it was desired should be placed in each direction. As soon
as the requisite property outside of the O'Brien purchase
could be acquired, the working plans were completed and
the contracts, in August, 1896, were let for practically all the
work for completing the park. This work, also undertaken
by the Messrs. Shanley, was pushed rapidly forward and
finally completed in 1897. It was the first of the county
parks to be turned over in a finished condition for public
use. The entire area was a level tract, and the landscape
treatment, with trees on the borders, walks, lawn, etc, similar to most city squares or parks of small acreage. The
park contains a little more than twelve acres, and has cost
upward of $160,000.

THE WEST SIDE PARK.

Although the decision to locate a park in the western portion of Newark was not in the order following that for the
East Side, the conditions controlling the selection were so
directly the reverse of those in the other case as to make the
comparison of them quite apropos here. With the West
Side situation, instead of the moving forces being from
within the commission, they were—at least during the early
stages of the discussion—wholly from without. The park
experts to the first commission had not made any special
recommendation for a park there, and none were included in
the plans of that board, as it was believed that a park of
creditable dimensions within the city limits there would involve in proportion to its size too great cost. While other

possible or probable park sites were receiving attention during 1895, no suggestion had come before the new commission favoring a "West Side" park, and not one of the commissioners had advocated such a location.

This was the status of affairs when, on January 30, 1896, a letter from Mayor Lubkuecher was received. It called attention to the need of the "Hill section" of the city for a park and bespoke favorable consideration of the claims of the people in that vicinity. Active agitation toward pressing those claims did not, however, begin until it became well known through the local associations in that district that the East Side park had become an established fact. Then the trouble began, and extended "all along the line."

If there was ever a public board literally bombarded with communications and delegations by which a strenuous constituency can bring pressure to bear toward favorable official action, it was the Essex County Park Commission, as the recipient object of that attack and siege during the year 1896.

First, on March 12, came a committee of citizens urging that a park was "a necessity in the West End." This visit was followed two weeks later by a resolution from the Newark City Council favoring the project for a park in the western part of the city. On the same day a committee representing the West End Improvement Association, including Mayor Lubkuecher, A. B. Twitchell, Commissioner Frederick Kuhn, of the Board of Works, E. G. Robertson, president of the association, and George H. Forman, made a forcible presentation of the subject before the commission. The speakers dwelt at length upon the imperative need of a park in proximity to the large public school there; they referred to the healthy location of the "Hill" district; contended that there were "close upon 70,000 people in that western portion of the city, or nearly a third of the population of Newark;" and added that it was their belief "that ninety per cent. of the people of Essex County were opposed to the Waverly Park site." They asked for a park "convenient to the population," such as the proposed site in

the vicinity of Eleventh street, Seventeenth street, and from
Sixteenth to Eighteenth avenue would provide.

DEMAND FOR PARK.

During April and May, 1896, four petitions, with aggregate lists of 1,717 names, were received; and during the
summer various delegations of citizens and associations
from that district attended the meetings of the commission,
urging favorable action. On October 29, a request from the
Newark Board of Works for a "conference" was received.
This was arranged for November 9, when Commissioners
Van Duyne, Stainsby, Burkhardt and Ulrich again urged
favorable action, recommending a location "somewhere between Springfield and South Orange avenues, west of South
Tenth street and including the Magnolia swamp."

At the meeting on October 2, President Robertson, of the
improvement association, and Messrs. Twitchell and Kuhn
appeared and reiterated the claims of the West End Association and the people of that district generally; and later,
during October and November, there were other delegations,
including one from Irvington, on November 19. All urged
that the locality favored should not be overlooked. How
could it be? There was the commission, with petitions to
the right of them and petitions to the left of them, while in
front of them delegations had "vollied and thundered."

The board had been reminded that, by its own official action, it had established a precedent favorable to the West
Side cause.

"You have located a park on the East Side," said the
West Side people; "why should you not now follow the same
precedent for the same reasons for our side? We, too, have
a large industrial population, and why not do something for
us also?"

WEST SIDE PARK.

Early in February, 1897, the commission having decided
to locate a West Side park, the requisite maps were ordered
and land options and purchases were authorized. At last it

was done, and the strenuous cohorts of the West End had won.

In December, 1896, the provisional estimate of cost for "a park on the West Side" was $75,000. One year later the cash disbursements for land and buildings there amounted to $172,234. This amount, however, covers about all that has been paid for land in that park. The improvements have now cost something over $100,000. The area is twenty-three acres. The varied topography has given opportunity for diversified landscape effects, with a small lake or pond feature, attractive stretches of turf, and effective tree and shrub plantations.

About $40,000 in value of the acquired land on the west side of the park, originally intended for a parkway, is still held in the name of the Fidelity Trust Company—the matter of the parkway extension having been suspended—and has thus remained in statu quo for years.

EAGLE ROCK RESERVATION.

Since "ye olden time" and the days of Carteret, and of "East and West Jersey," Eagle Rock has been famed for its commanding views and attractive natural surroundings. For generations residents and sojourners in Essex and neighboring counties have made it a place of pilgrimage to enjoy the views, and the numbers have increased with the growth of population and the added facilities for reaching "the rock." Situated as this point is, on the bold precipitous cliff of the Orange Mountain, 600 feet above tide water, yet but a short air line distance from it, with Montclair, Bloomfield and the beautiful Llewellyn Park on the side of the mountain in the immediate foreground, and the Oranges, Newark, New York, and the hills of Staten Island in view beyond—what more fitting place could be selected for the first choice of the outlying parks than this.

It was, therefore, quite within the natural order of things that the Park Commission should turn its attention to the location of a park at this place as soon as the selection of park sites was taken up. Immediately after the Branch

Brook location and that of the East Side Park were disposed of, this was done. Each of the commissioners favored the proposition. The only points for determination, therefore, were as to the lines of the park limits, and the acreage that should be included. The subject was under discussion during the summer and early part of the autumn of 1895, and on October 3 the architects and engineers were authorized to prepare a map of the outlines that they would recommend for a park, including Eagle Rock. A little later, H. D. Oliphant was appointed purchasing agent to look after land options and purchases within the established lines. These limits included a little more than 400 acres, extending along the mountain cliff something more than a mile north of Eagle Rock avenue, nearly to Upper Montclair, and about a mile westward; and besides Eagle Rock, containing many of the finest viewpoints in New Jersey. A road along the crest, since constructed, has opened up a great variety of beautiful views over the hills and valleys to the eastward, while from the western slopes the views of the surrounding section and of the Second Mountain beyond are unsurpassed.

MONTCLAIR DELEGATION HEARD.

While it was the intention of the commissioners to extend at the outset the limits of this park as far as it was deemed advisable to make them, a delegation of citizens from Montclair on January 20, 1896, urged that the northern limits might be still farther extended. The boundaries of the park remain to the present time substantially as finally agreed upon after a personal inspection by the members of the commission in 1896.

In November, 1895, the announcement that there was to be an Eagle Rock Park met with favorable response from the public. The press was cordial in its approval. All the county papers commended the selection. Some of the New York papers were equally outspoken in the indorsement of the project. An editorial in the Newark News of November 26, 1895, on "The New Park Sites," referred to it thus:

"Whatever other property the Essex County park commissioners may acquire, there is no question that they have acted wisely in securing Eagle Rock and the land about it. This is the show place of Essex County." On the same day The Daily Advertiser expressed this sentiment: "A county park system without Eagle Rock would be in the nature of an anomaly. That elevated point, overlooking an extensive and varied panorama of town, country and river, seems to have been destined by nature for a public breathing place." An editorial in the New York Press of November 27 stated that "the acquirement of the far-famed Eagle Rock the other day for park purposes was a great thing for the people. From this giant knoll the homes of tens of thousands of New Jersey's citizens can be plainly seen, and it is declared that it looks upon more homes and varied industries than any other natural elevation in the world."

And The Orange Chronicle of November 30 thus referred to the acquirement: "A more suitable or a more beautiful site for a park could not possibly be found. There is double reason for rejoicing at the announcement just made."

With the exception of opening roads through this reservation, some thinning of the natural growths and clearing in places the east brow of the cliff so as to open unobstructed views, little has been done in the way of improvement of this beautifully situated and densely wooded reservation, and it yet remains largely in the primitive state as of years gone by—a place to delight an Emerson, a Thoreau, or a Ruskin,, and to charm any lover of nature who revels in her rugged and unintruded haunts.

The estimated cost of this park in January, 1896, was for land acquirement, $202,775. The actual disbursements by January, 1901, were for land and buildings, $243,563. Up to the present time the total cost of the park, including the 413 acres of land, and the improvements, has been about $300,000.

A FINE PARK SITE NOT CHOSEN.

During the tours of inspection of the Orange Mountain by the first commission, in 1894, perhaps no one observation had more favorably impressed the members than had the plans and the forethought of Llewellyn Haskel in his scheme for the county boulevards extending from Newark to the mountain crest; these avenues in turn to be connected by a crest boulevard along the top of the First Mountain. In the study as to how this idea could be utilized in the park scheme then under consideration, it was practically agreed that the plans for the park system should embody this feature of a mountain boulevard, at least from the proposed Eagle Rock Reservation, south as far as the Walker road or South Orange avenue, a distance of two or three miles.

It was intended that this crest boulevard should be one of the great features of the park and parkway system, with its beautiful vistas and commanding views opening from the crest along the edge of the cliffs; then diverging back where extensive improvements existed, giving the western slopes and view of the mountain beyond; and then emerging again to the great view stretching out from the cliff itself—and by these changes enhancing the beauty of the whole. Also that Central avenue should be continued up the mountain after the Swiss Mountain road plan, winding or "zigzaging" up the mountain side at an easy grade, up which horses or vehicles might proceed at a fair rate of speed.

The object in extending the line, at least as far as the points indicated, was to make this intended mountain parkway at the apex of the park system topography accessible and convenient to the mass of people of the county. With the location and construction of this parkway there would be, from the base of the mountain below, an almost unbroken area of the compactly built up portion of the county from that line direct to the Passaic River. For like reason it was deemed in every way desirable that a park location of suitable size should be selected on and back of the crest, somewhere between the Northfield road and some point south of the terminus of the mountain cable road. In this way not only would the crest boulevard become a most attractive and convenient central feature of the park system, but a park at this point would, like Eagle Rock Park as a terminus at the north, greatly accentuate the attractions, not only of that crest parkway and the approaching parkways, as proposed from the east, but of each of the parks as well.

Moreover, this site would make a direct and convenient park and parkway entrance to the Great South Mountain Reservation, which the members of the first commission had from their earlier investigations also favored.

In August, 1895, this subject was brought regularly before the board for consideration in a resolution offered by me, "that it is now deemed expedient to acquire for park purposes:

"First, suitable areas of park lands and parkways on and adjacent to the crest of the Orange Mountains.

"Second, that such locations be selected with regard to convenient approaches; that the crest of the mountain be followed as far as practicable, and with reference to obtaining the best east and west views.

"Third, that the total area be not less than 2,000 acres, and that the architects and engineers proceed to locate the above parks and parkways connecting with Branch Brook Park and prepare the necessary maps and plans."

PARKWAYS TREATED SEPARATELY.

These resolutions were afterward modified, in accordance with the "piecemeal" or sectional policy already referred to, and the park locations were treated separately from the parkways.

As the subject of the parkways was such an important one to the whole enterprise, and for years occupied so much public attention as well as the attention of the commission, the progress of those events will be consecutively stated in succeeding chapters.

In November, 1895, the question of locating a park in what had then become known in the boardroom of the second commission as the "cable road tract," and as "a counterpart of the Eagle Rock Park" in so far as its being an objective mountain park, came up for formal action. F. W. Child had already been authorized to obtain options on the tract, and on my motion the matter was made a "special order" for the meeting of November 11. At that time a written report from Mr. Child was presented. It gave a list of the land options he had secured from George Spottiswoode and others and stated that he could then acquire the property—the 121 acres, upon which options had been requested—for $67,000, or possibly $65,000—"a very low figure."

On November 23, I wrote Commissioner Shepard, who also favored the purchase, that I was "very much impressed that a reservation for the future, south of South Orange avenue, is entirely a secondary consideration to the cable tract, in that central location; and that I believed no further action should be taken toward acquiring those outside reservation lands until the more important in location, convenience, value and other respects are first considered."

And the same day I wrote Commissioner Franklin Murphy: "Unless I am greatly misinformed, it will be a long time before the trolley will overcome in practical use the long steep grade of South Orange avenue, and when it does that section will still remain entirely at one side and out of the reach of the mass of population. Surely, for the present, we ought not to have a reservation at the expense of a park accessible at once to all the county.

"As to any commitment regarding the reservation track, with the exception of the statements upon which our charter was obtained, it is my conviction that we are committed to nothing, save the interests of the people, the county and the parks."

ORANGE MOUNTAIN PROPERTY.

At the board meeting November 29, I offered a resolution "that the property on Orange Mountain at the head of the cable road between Northfield avenue and Walker road, be acquired, and that F. W. Child be authorized to purchase at a cost not exceeding $65,000 the 121 acres in that tract." There was considerable discussion. Two of the commissioners expressed the view that, with the needs of the Newark and other parks then practically agreed upon, the purchase could not be afforded. This was answered by a reference to the fact that that park would be "at the very door" of, and directly convenient to, most of the people of the whole county, and would be in reality a corner-stone of the chain of parks, and, like Eagle Rock, the mountain key to the western portion of the park system.

It was also pointed out that the whole 121 acres, extending for such a long distance on the mountain crest back to the proposed South Mountain reservation, would cost far less than the single city block of the Branch Brook Garside street extension east of Clifton avenue. In view of all this it was asked how could we afford not to acquire it.

As Commissioner Peck had all along been one of the most earnest supporters of the mountain park and parkway projects, it was thought by at least some of the commissioners that he would without a question of doubt favor the resolution. Mr. Shepard and myself were known to be in favor of the plan. Mr. Shepard called for a vote. It was lost. Two ayes, Messrs. Shepard and Kelsey; three nays, Messrs. Peck, Murphy and Meeker. The options were allowed to expire, and as the subject had been gone over very fully, it has never, so far as I know, been brought up for consideration since. The following day, in sending to the park board's office the return of the papers, I wrote Commissioner Peck as follows:

"Nothing that has occurred since the inception of the enterprise has been such a surprise to me as your action and statements on this subject yesterday."

In March, 1896, the commissioners paid Mr. Child $250 for his services and expenses in obtaining the options, and the proposition to acquire this most accessible of all the mountain locations was then most regretfully closed. The opportunity of obtaining this magnificent park site, the most direct in communication with Newark and the nearest to the centres of population of the county, was thus lost to the public; and the value and loss to the park system is, I believe, difficult to estimate.

SOUTH MOUNTAIN RESERVATION.

Large reservations of natural scenery have become one of the attractive features of a modern park system. Nor is the movement confined to localities especially acquired or reserved for park uses. The general government, and many of the States, have of late years included in their forestry reservations large areas of timbered lands, with the object at the same time of conserving also the feature for recreation and attractive natural environments. The movements toward the preservation of the big trees (Sequoia Washingtonian) of California; for a natural park and forest reserve along the Appalachian Mountains; and the White Mountain forest reservations in New Hampshire, are some of the better known efforts in this direction. In the Massachusetts Metropolitan Park's system the great Blue Hills reservation, with its more than 4,000 acres of beautifully wooded slopes and valleys; and the Middlesex Fells on the other side of Boston, with its 1,800 acres of timber lands, lakes, open fields, etc., are recognized as special attractions there, as have become Van Cortland and Pelham Bay Parks in New York, Epping Forest, outside of London, and the many other outlying natural reservations lying wholly without the large cities.

The Essex Park Commission of 1895, like the preceding commission, was in favor of a liberal acquirement of these lands in such a reservation for the park system here. There was but one location which in size, relative convenience, varied topography and attractive natural and wooded features, seemed to meet the requirements. That was the extensive tract between the apex of the First and Second Mountains, and principally south of the Northfield road. Former Commissioner G. W. Bramhall had always advocated this proposed reservation. In September, 1895, he was requested to assist the commission. Up to that time it had not been the intention of the commission to extend the lines of the reservation south of South Orange avenue. This was the view of the first commission, although the subject of the southern limit of the proposed park had been left in abeyance. At the board meeting of September 6, 1895, Mr. Bramhall was present. The result of the conference was that he was authorized to make purchases on behalf of the commission of such lands between the mountains or including the crest of the First Mountain south of South Orange avenue, as he could acquire and would recommend within an expenditure of $20,000. This action was the beginning of an acquirement of one of the finest reservations of natural scenery in the country, and in comparison with the population of Essex County is proportionately one of the largest to be found in any of the park systems. In February, 1896, the lines of the reservation were still farther extended in Millburn, and the closing of several of the land options secured through Mr. Bramhall was authorized. Later, in August, the lines were extended and purchases were authorized for practically the whole length of the valley and of the First Mountain to the south, and from the crest of the First Mountain to the sky line of the Second Mountain. The lines of this reservation as agreed upon in the official map then, as now, contain about 2,500 acres, and the cost has been approximately, within the estimates of December, 1896—about $250,000.

When in August of that year, the announcement was made that there was to be "a 2,000-acre mountain park," the project was referred to in some of the papers as "an ideal site for a public park," and Frederick L. Olmsted's remark that "he thought it one of the best locations for a park that he had ever seen," was freely quoted. The reservation is about three and three-quarter miles in length north and south and has an average width of about one to one and one-quarter miles. Its natural beauties are greatly accentuated by the water effects of the two reservoirs of the city of Orange water supply. These reservoirs cover a maximum area of about seventy acres, and, being located in the valley, along the West Branch of the Rahway river, make an added attraction from many viewpoints within the reservation.

WEEQUAHIC, OR WAVERLY PARK.

The first that was heard of a Weequahic Park was the suggestion from Commissioner Murphy, soon after the organization of the Park Board in 1895, which was in effect that that was "one of the best locations for a park in the county." The first commission had, as indicated in a preceding chapter, treated the possibility of a park there, and without any pre-formed prejudice, with scant courtesy. If for no other reason, the mosquito pre-emption and unrestricted occupancy of the tract was thought a sufficiently serious matter to negative any favorable consideration of locating one of the county parks there. Moreover, the uncertainty as to the large cost and as to the future of the springs that fed the lake and water supply; the direct proximity to Elizabeth and Union County—neither of which would, under a county park plan for Essex, contribute to the large cost of acquiring or expenses of maintaining a park there—were all factors in the decision that, for many reasons, other park sites more within the county were deemed preferable. That Mr. Murphy entertained a decidedly different view, was apparent almost from the first meeting of the second commission.

On July 18, 1895—only the three Newark commissioners present—he offered a resolution that "the landscape architects and engineers be requested to prepare a map, indicating their best judgment as to the lines for a park at Waverly." Later, as the subject was discussed, the proposition was not enthusiastically received. Messrs. Barrett and Bogart had not thought well of the Weequahic district in their earlier investigations and reports as experts to the first commission. The situation, however, had now changed, there being in the board an aggressive element in favor of the scheme to locate a park there. With the exception of Commissioner Murphy's ardent advocacy of the project

there appeared to be little interest in the subject, either
within or without the commission. During the autumn
(1895) it continued to be a frequent topic for discussion at
the board meetings. The land agents were requested to ascertain at what prices land that might be needed could be
secured. Their reports indicated that the cost would be
large, and that, if a park was established there, it "would
come high." Finally, on October 28, the report from the
architects and engineers was received. It was very moderate in tone and conservative in character. Of Weequahic
Lake they wrote:

"We feel that it is our duty to say that this lake and its
surroundings can, in our opinion, be made an attractive and
valuable adjunct to the park system, at a moderate cost, and
that it will, when so improved, provide what is desirable
in this section of the county."

This was, I believe, the first expert opinion making any
favorable reference to that park site which had been received. It seemed to modify the convictions of some of the
board who had entertained adverse views on the question.
I am free to admit that the report brought up in my mind
the question as to whether I had not been mistaken in the
conclusions I had before formed from the examinations of
the tract and of the surroundings. The project still made
slow progress in the commission, notwithstanding this report and the urgent advocacy of Mr. Murphy.

In November, 1895, it was decided to acquire some of the
property—the Cooper tract, the Ougheltree farm and land
belonging to Daniel Price—in the Waverly district, but not
including Weequahic lake, upon which the land agents had
obtained options. The estimated total cost of the land
within the lines of the architect's map that had been tentatively agreed upon was, at this time, $180,000.

FAIR ASSOCIATION'S STOCK.

One of the stumbling blocks in the way of making progress in either direction toward any definite result was the

property of the New Jersey Agricultural Society, better known as the Waverly Fair Association. This property consisted of a number of acres, a racetrack and the usual paraphernalia of country fair grounds, and was the focal point of the district. The association owning the property had had financially a varied and varying career since its incorporation in 1858. In good seasons the receipts might result in a dividend on the $90,000 of capital stock of perhaps five per cent. With bad weather and poor attendance, an assessment on the stockholders for the deficiency growing out of the light receipts was not an uncommon occurrence. As a result of these conditions, the price of the stock had for years, up to 1895, oscillated between 30 and 60, or, in extreme cases, 80. Transactions were few and far between, and if a holder must sell he was usually at the mercy of the buyer, somewhat after the order of the unsuspecting merchant of old who once met that world-renowned individual who demanded "the pound of flesh."

There were 3,600 shares of the stock, of a par value of $25 per share. It was "well distributed." Nine stockholders, however, with their combined holdings, controlled the association. They held the majority of the stock. These stockholders of record at that time were: P. Ballantine & Sons, 60 shares; Franklin Murphy, 186 shares; E. A. Dodd, 70 shares; E. B. Gaddis, 122 shares; H. H. Isham, 721 shares; L. H. Jones, 230 shares; G. B. Jenkinson, 109 shares; Jacob Skinkle, 125 shares, and E. A. Wilkinson, 139 shares.

This was the situation when it was reported in the papers that in all probability there would be a park at Weequahic. As the indications and reports grew more favorable, the price of the Waverly Fair Association stock increased proportionately in value. What would have been considered a good sale, at 60 or 65, at the time the reports were first emitted, was no longer a fair price. The stock was soon reported "worth par and none of the large stockholders would sell for a penny less." The history of this enterprise was not known in the Park Board rooms—certainly not to all of the members—when a proposition to make some of the land purchases in that locality was agreed to.

Some of the commissioners firmly declined the proposition of paying par for the stock. It was agreed that an effort should be made to acquire it at a price nearer the current value. Negotiations were in consequence suspended. Those anxious to sell the stock, after three years of "great expectations," got tired of waiting, and the Fair Association directors finally gave an option, No. 415, for the Park Board to consider. The association delegated E. B. Gaddis and H. H. Isham to close the sale, and on March 13, 1899, they had a conference with the commission on that subject.

The question then before the board was: Would it be better to pay something like the asking price for the fair association stock, or go through an expensive and tedious litigation in an effort to acquire it. The former plan, on the recommendation of those in the board who were understood to be well informed on the subject, was agreed upon, and, in March, 1899, $75,000 of the available park funds were thus disposed of.

The proposition to locate a park at Waverly had, in the meantime dragged along, and apparently evoked but little public interest in any direction. A small delegation from Clinton Township appeared before the commission at the meeting November 19, 1896, and spoke in moderation in favor of "park improvement of the district about Weequahic." This was the only delegation or petition favoring the park there that I can now recall or find record of. The adverse comments were not so limited. Reference has already been made to the statement of the West End Improvement Association's delegation at the hearing March 12, in opposition to the "Waverly park site." The press was also non-responsive; or, if any comments were made when the announcement was given out that a Weequahic Park was no longer a matter of doubt, they were either distinctly conservative or positively chilling. One of the leading papers asked editorially if "mosquito bars were included in the purchase." One of the old established New York papers referred to "the State fair grounds and Lake Weequahic, with its eighty-five acres of watery expanse," and said: "As this park will be nearer Elizabeth than Newark, Union County citizens are rejoicing at the philanthropy of the Essex commissioners."

My own convictions were quite fully stated in a letter to Commissioner Murphy, dated Saturday evening, May 23, 1896, which was as follows:

"Dear Mr. Murphy: Mr. Peck and I have spent the afternoon looking over "West Newark," Weequahic and the southern parkway question. The situation troubles me. A double track on Elizabeth avenue at once disposes of any prospect of making a park in that vicinity a part of a creditable connective park system. It is the only avenue available or worth considering for parkway purposes. The width is only fifty or sixty feet between the curb lines. Another track there will make it merely a tramway thoroughfare, like Frelinghuysen avenue—both dangerous and unsightly —and preclude any thought of ever making it a parkway approach.

"If the Board of Works will grant the franchise regardless of facts or conditions, we have then to meet the situation of a site for an important park of the county system, isolated from suitable driveway approach from the great center of population of the county, bounded on both longitudinal sides by railroads; a swamp tract with most unattractive features at one end, and a cemetery and Union County line at the other—with a large area of swamp in the center, the expense of dredging which opens up a perfect kaleidoscope of possibilities as to cost which no man can now determine.

COMPLICATIONS IN THE SITUATION.

"I cannot be frank with you as my colleague and associate in this enterprise without expressing to you these impressions as I looked over these conditions to-day. I was forcibly reminded whether the adverse report of four of the architects of the first commission, and the unfavorable criticism we have thus far received since the location has been under consideration, may not be correct and well founded. If the selection be not judicious, the public will soon find it out as they study these very conditions, and the whole enterprise thus imperiled.

"The situation is complicated, too, by the action of the traction people, the Fair Association, and the speculators in the adjoining property.

"As I read the signs of the times, the people are becoming very suspicious of corporate control of boards transacting public business, and this of itself makes the situation a delicate one, both as to the avenue and the association property.

"The natural park lands, such as the Nye property to the north and west, also north of Clinton avenue toward the West Newark sites recommended, appear more desirable as to location and parkable features, and come nearer meeting the requirements of the petition we have received; also of the park system. In those locations, too, the ratables would be largely increased in every direction by park acquirement.

"These conditions have never impressed me so forcibly as they did to-day. Mr. Peck will tell you of his own impressions, and I believe they were on similar lines.

"I wish to act most heartily with whatever is determined upon as best by the majority of our board, but I feel that this is a subject of great importance and should have very careful consideration under the conditions as we now find them.

"I enclose clipping giving some data showing reasons why our traction friends do not feel that they 'can afford' to give up these valuable and available thoroughfares.

"Sincerely yours,
"Fred. W. Kelsey."

A SERIOUS QUESTION.

When the practical work of improving the Weequahic reservation was taken up by the Park Board, in 1899-1900, a serious question arose as to the treatment of the lake. In

1896 the engineers of the department had advised that the raising of the lake for the purpose of improving the appearance of the surface and retarding the growth of rushes, etc., from the bottom, was of doubtful utility. On May 14, 1900, Engineer M. R. Sherrerd, in a special report to the commission, recommended the raising of the lake level five feet by obstruction to be placed in the outlet. The landscape architects, in their report at the same time, emphatically disapproved of this plan of treatment, stating at length the legal, engineering and esthetic objections. It would be experimental, they contended. Percolation of the water through the raised banks might make the result uncertain. It would "inevitably destroy the handsomest and most valuable part of the beautiful fringe of fine forest trees now existing most of the way around the lake." The resulting loss of water flowing from the lake, under the binding contract between the Park Commission and the Lehigh Valley Company of June 4, 1897, and with the Pennsylvania Company, that the commission would "not directly or indirectly do, or cause to be done, anything which would in any manner interfere with the natural flow of the waters of said Bound Creek," should the raising the lake seriously diminish or stop the overflow, would make the Park Commission "liable to prosecution."

As the loss of water from raising the lake five feet was by the engineer estimated at 550,000 gallons per day of a normal minimum flow of only 1,500,000 gallons daily, the point thus raised may at any time become a most serious one, and result in heavy claims for damages against the county.

COST OF PARK.

The estimated cost of dredging and properly treating the banks of the lake at its natural level was $250,000; and for raising the lake five feet, cleaning out the bogs, etc., with the destruction of the best part of the wooded banks and the prospective litigation with the railroad companies involved in this plan of treatment, was $50,000.

It was, therefore, largely a matter of Hobson's choice with the commission as to which horn of the dilêmma should be taken. The matter was held in abeyance and left undecided for years. Commissioner Bramhall, who had previously taken an active interest in the question, afterward wrote a formal letter to the board protesting against the lake raising level plan. That plan was, however, adopted, and, at the Park Board meeting August 9, 1904, bids were received for removing the bogs and other growth from the lake. These bids were for amounts from $32,000 up to $97,500. The contract was awarded to P. Sanford Ross at his bid of $32,000, and the work began in October, 1904. The lake water is now at the raised level and the bog cleaning contract is practically finished. This lake and the surrounding bog marsh comprise about eighty acres. When dredged and portions of the borders filled in, the lake area proper will be between fifty and sixty acres.

The old race track of the fair association is used under a nominal lease by the Road Horse Association. The "play stead" is used, as was intended (mosquitoes permitting), for athletic sports.

The cash expenditures for land for the Weequahic reservation, including the $75,000 to the fair association, grew from the estimated cost in 1895 of $180,900, to the cash expenditure up to December 31, 1901, of $243,563. The improvements up to that time had cost $67,258. Large expenditures have since been made, and must continue to be made, before this park of 265 acres can well or effectively answer, to any marked advantage, the purpose for which it was acquired.

CHAPTER VIII.

SELECTION OF ORANGE PARK.

THE Orange or Triangle Park, the last of the county parks not already referred to, has a unique history, quite unlike the other seven locations described. The selection of the Orange Park involved a continuous contending of differences between the commissioners themselves on the one side, and the almost unanimous sentiment of the public on the other side. That those favoring the project finally won, after two years of persistent effort, was the outcome of an incident which may be of interest here.

As a prelude, however, it may be well to give a very brief history of the events leading up to this conclusion. Nearly forty years ago, after the triangle bounded by Central avenue, Harrison street, East Orange, and Center street, Orange had been formed by the opening of these streets, it was a favorite topic for discussion among those in the Oranges who had a spirit of civic pride and forethought for the future, to refer to this tract as a place for a public park, which would be much needed in the time to come, and which, from its topography, would be one of the most attractive of parks, at a comparatively small cost. Although the central portion of the tract was low, swampy, marsh land, this was surrounded on each of the larger sides of the triangle with gentle slopes to higher ground the entire distance. Among the pioneers of civic betterment at that time who continued to refer to the desirable improvement were Llewellyn Haskel, Mr. and Mrs. Ross Browning, of Llewellyn Park, and Edward Gardner, then proprietor of the Orange Journal. Some of the articles published in The Journal many years ago on this subject, show how clearly and correctly these early advocates of the Triangle Park saw the possibilities which have, by latter events, become actualities.

While this discussion was going on, nothing toward practical results then came of it. These advanced thinkers were, like so many of their class, a little ahead of their time in the agitation, and it was, therefore, left for the first Park Commission of 1894 to take up the question where their predecessors in advocating the project had left it. With the first commission there was no difference in conviction, either in the minds of the commissioners or of the landscape experts as to the desirability of establishing a park there; indeed, the reasons, as they then appeared, in favor, were so many and so ample as to have left no question of doubt, that I had ever heard expressed, upon that question.

OPPOSITION TO PARK LOCATION.

When the second commission of 1895 was appointed, an entirely different situation was presented. For some reason which I have never been able to fully account for, the two new members of the board, Messrs. F. M. Shepard and Franklin Murphy, were radically and persistently opposed to the project. When, during the summer of 1895, the subject was referred to as one that in all probability would require the attention of the commission at a later time, the triangle was slightingly referred to in the commission as "a back door park." When later the petitions began to come in, urging favorable action, the opposition gradually increased, instead of the reverse.

In September a long petition was earnestly presented by a citizens' committee from East Orange and Orange. This document recited the reasons for the park—the natural advantages, the proximity to dense populations, the attitude of public opinion in favor of it, the reasonable cost, etc. The communication bore the signatures of Frank H. Scott, chairman; William Pierson, L. D. Gallison, W. S. Macy, I. Bayard Dodd, E. V. Z. Lane and R. W. Hawkesworth. It was followed in December by one from the city officials of Orange, as follows:

"Orange, N. J., Dec. 20, 1895.
"Honorable Park Commissioners of Essex County, Newark, N. J.:

"The undersigned members of the city government of Orange, N. J., would respectfully recommend to your honorable body the favorable consideration of the proposed plan for a park to be located in the triangle between Central avenue, Harrison street and Center street. The natural advantages of the situation, with its unfailing springs of clear water, must be evident to you, and its location as a link between two of our county roads, namely, Central avenue and South Orange avenue, will readily appear as a feasible part of your system of parkways belonging to the county. Hoping you will find it possible to carry out this recommendation, we remain,

"John Gill, Mayor of Orange; Louis D. Gallison, President of Common Council; Hugh J. Brady, Henry G. Miller, Irving M. Genung, Edward S. Perry, W. H. Henderson, Daniel McCarthy, Joseph D. Holmes, Charles A. Meigs; Members of Common Council, Orange, N. J."

PETITION FROM EAST ORANGE.

"On December 16, 1895, a committee represented by Messrs. George W. Bramhall, Frank H. Scott and William S. Macy also urged favorable consideration, as did the same committee again on February 10 following. On March 2 a petition signed by every member of the East Orange Township Committee and by 160 representative citizens of East Orange was received. This communication referred to the proposed park as "particularly desirable," and as "not opposing in the slightest degree the proposed plan of a speedway north and south in East Orange," adding that, "although the larger part of this land lies in Orange, it is nevertheless as convenient to East Orange residents as to those in Orange."

"We also advocate," said this petition, "the control by the Park Commission of Central avenue as a parkway, it being one of the most important avenues in the county and the most direct route from the center of Newark to the Orange Mountains."

At this time the citizens' committee had offered to make liberal donations in cash or land, or both if necessary, to secure the park which all desired. I moved that the proposition as proposed by Frank H. Scott, chairman of the local committee, be accepted; that the architects and engineers prepare an official map, and that "a separate map of a connecting parkway along, or adjacent to, Mosswood avenue, from Warwick avenue via Tremont avenue to the triangle tract," be included. The resolution was objected to, and the following substitute, as drawn by Commissioner Murphy, finally agreed upon:

"Resolved, That if the parties interested in the Triangle Park in Orange present a proposition to the commission satisfactory to it as to quantity of land, and involving an expenditure for land by the commission not to exceed $100,000, the commission would act upon it favorably."

Just where the adoption of this resolution left the proposition for assistance which had been made by the citizens' committee, I was puzzled at the time to know how they, or we, were going to find out. It was at this time considered very doubtful if the land could be acquired for that amount, in which event the resolution would defeat the project. The real crux of this situation lay in the fact that J. Everett Reynolds owned about sixteen acres of the land which it would be necessary to acquire for the park, and at what price he would be willing to sell this land, no one in, or out, of the commission had thus far been able to ascertain.

The city of Orange had built a large and costly stormwater sewer as far south as Central avenue. Mr. Reynolds, as a heavy taxpayer, and others, had been most urgent in petitioning the city to extend that line through his property, situated just south of the avenue. This extension would drain his and other acreage property there, and im-

mediately place all the land within the proposed site, on the
"city lot" basis. The extension had been deferred, pending
the decision of the Park Commission. If a park, then no
sewer extension. If no park, the extension would be
promptly built. With this see-saw of possibilities, the uncertainty continued for months. Mr. Reynolds would not
fix a price. The commission decided, owing to the opposition referred to, that it would not undertake to acquire his
property unless it could be secured by purchase. The local
committee did not know what proposition might, or might
not, be "to the commission satisfactory"—and thus the increasing doubt continued, to the advantage of the opposition, though not to the discouragement of those favoring
the park.

At last the uncertainty culminated. The Orange Common Council arrived at an understanding with the triangle
property owners that, if on December 7, there should have
been no decision by the Park Commission regarding the
park, proceedings to extend the storm-water sewer would
then be taken. The public agitation continued, more generally and more earnestly than before. All the newspapers
favored the proposition. There was not a dissenting voice—
outside the Park Commission. The citizens' committee and
the local authorities were becoming impatient at the delay.
Finally, on December 7, 1896, Mr. Reynolds was invited to
attend the Park Board meeting on that day. He was present. For nearly an hour we endeavored to ascertain his
price. These efforts were without success. It was then
after 6 o'clock. The Common Council was to meet that
evening. With the passage of a resolution to extend the
storm-sewer, there would be no triangle park.

OUTLOOK BRIGHTENS.

By one of those peculiar decrees of fate, when, at the last
moment, the tide seems irrevocably set in an adverse direction and is as abruptly changed, so in this instance a single
incident completely altered the drift of events.

"Mr. Shepard," I asked, "what, in your judgment, would

be a fair price for Mr. Reynolds' holdings there in the triangle—one which the commission would be justified in paying him by purchase?" After a moment's reflection, he
replied, "Twenty thousand dollars."

"Gentlemen,' I said, "will you entrust me to negotiate
with Mr. Reynolds before the council meeting to-night, and
close with him for his land at the limit which Mr. Shepard
has stated he thinks a fair price?"

We were all tired and anxious to get away. I think no
one believed, and I was myself in grave doubt, as to whether
any practical result would materialize from the proposition
which I had made for the purchase. I have always understood that a like impression was in the minds of the other
commissioners. But this resolution went through: "Moved,
that the counsel and Mr. Kelsey be authorized to offer Mr.
Reynolds not to exceed $20,000 for such of his property
as the commission desires, and if he (Reynolds) signs an
option to that effect they are authorized to state to the
Common Council of Orange that the park commission ex-
pects to locate a park in the triangle bounded by Central
avenue, Center and Harrison streets, Orange."

It was then nearly 7 o'clock. The council was to meet
at 8 o'clock. Mr. Shepard conveyed the word to Mr. Reynolds to meet me at the council chamber at 7:45 o'clock.
Before that hour I was in a coupé by the entrance there.
Mr. Reynolds soon came along and stepped into the carriage
as requested. I cannot now recall all of the conversation.
It is not important here.

PURCHASE OF LAND.

We were in the carriage together perhaps a half hour.
We then entered the council chamber together. The meeting was in session. F. H. Scott and others of the friends
of the parks were anxiously waiting.

"Mr. Scott," I said, "I have just closed the purchase on
behalf of the Park Commission of all Mr. Reynolds' land
in the triangle for $17,500 and you may announce to the
council that there is to be a triangle park."

Mr. Scott soon got the floor and made the announcement, which was loudly applauded by those present, even by some of the aldermen.

Early the next morning Mr. Shepard came to my office. Mr. Reynolds had already advised him of the result of our negotiations the evening previous. For eighteen months or more, both officially and personally, he had opposed the proposition for a triangle park with apparently all the resource he could command, and with a persistence against an emphatic public sentiment and the expressed wish of his own immediate constituency which challenged my admiration.

On the morning in question, however, in a gracious and agreeable manner he said: "Well, now that we are to have a park in Orange, let's go right ahead with it." The sentiment was accepted in the same spirit in which it was tendered, and from that time the acquirement and development of the park went smoothly forward. Mr. Reynolds soon received the $17,500—the agreed price—instead of the authorized price, $20,000. A direct saving of $2,500 was thus effected. The citizens' committee proceeded to collect their subscriptions for the park and turned over to the commission for that purpose in cash, as before stated, $17,275.

Commissioner Murphy's attitude, after the purchase was closed with Mr. Reynolds, was quite in contrast to that of Mr. Shepard. At the meeting of December 14, Mr. Murphy sent an official letter to the board "formally protesting against the purchase of property for the said triangle park until the sum promised by neighborhood owners shall have been received." On my motion Mr. Shepard was appointed "a committee of one to reply."

When, later, the official map of the park had been prepared and was signed by the other four commissioners, Mr. Murphy declined to attach his signature, and it thus remained for a long time unsigned by him.

Commissioners Peck and Meeker were all along favorably disposed toward the park, but when the decided opposition referred to developed in the early part of 1895, they were inclined to let Mr. Shepard and myself, as more directly familiar with the local situation, "get together" first. This, after months of earnest effort, it was found impossible to do; Commissioner Shepard repeatedly declining to accompany me in looking over the proposed site.

The announcement of the final decision favorable to the triangle park was everywhere most cordially received. All the Newark newspapers, and others in the county, contained commendatory references to the action. The Call of December 13, 1896, referred to the decision as one that will be hailed with delight, and added: "It is within the scope of the commission to make this park one of the garden spots of the county." A prediction that has been amply verified by results since.

In 1898, largely through the interest of Commissioner Bramhall, who had succeeded me as a member of the Park Board in April, 1897, the lines of the park were extended on the Central avenue side about 700 feet, and resulted in making the park, together with the finishing improvements inaugurated at that time, what it has since frequently been called, "The gem of the Essex County park system." The transition from the former swail and swamp conditions there, to those of a completed park of unexcelled attractiveness, was as rapid as the effects, to the public were gratifying. The low swamp portion of the tract is now a beautiful English park-like meadow. The attractions are greatly accentuated by the small lake of about one and a half acres, and the beautiful specimens and groups of well developed trees. The effective shrubbery borders, and rising slopes on each side of the park, make an appropriate frame to one of the most attractive and restful landscape pictures that have resulted from modern park-making. The total cost for the forty-eight acres of land and buildings, with the expensive additions of 1898 included, has been $185,213, and for all improvements about $115,000.

CHAPTER IX.

MORE BONDS AND "HIGH FINANCE."

With the many and extended land acquirements by the Park Commission during the latter part of 1896, and with some of the single purchases running into the thousands, money went fast. In February, 1896 a requisition was made on the Board of Freeholders for the remaining $1,500,000 of the authorized $2,500,-000 appropriation. By June 1, 1906, the commitments and assumed obligations were nearly a million of dollars. Bids were advertised for and received for the new additional bond issue under the same plan and method as employed in the disposition of the first million of bonds the year previous. Of the bids opened June 16, there were four for the full amount, $1,500,000. The new York Life Insurance Company offered 104.08 and D. A. Moran & Co. 101.68 for four per cent. bonds; Franklin Savings Institution, of Newark, in series of bonds at four per cent., 101.40 to 102, and J. & W. Seligman "10028" for a 3.65 interest issue—the same as the $1,000,000 of bonds awarded Vermilye & Co. in August, 1895. In comparing the bids, a controversy between the representatives arose over the omission of a period in the Seligman bid. This led to a series of triangular protests and an attempted withdrawal of some of the proposals; which, however, was not permitted. It was admitted by members of the Finance Committee of the freeholders, in charge of the bond-letting, that the bid in question, and all the bids, had been made in good faith, and that the meaning and intent of the "10028," minus the period, was "perfectly clear." It was there stated that the Seligman bid was "upward of $20,000 better than that of the New York Life," and that "the four per cent.

bonds, on a 3.65 basis, are worth 106¼,"—a statement the correctness of which was not challenged or denied. A lively discussion ensued.

The Finance Committee later retired and went into executive session. The bonds were there in secret awarded to the New York Life Insurance Company. The reasons for this action, as then given out for publication by Counsel Munn, were that, as the Park Commission might not want all the money "for five or six months," the interest account would be quite an item, which would not result from the acceptance of the Seligman offer; and that the bid accepted would, out of the $1,572,900 proceeds, allow the $72,900 premium to go to the sinking fund, for the subsequent redemption of these same bonds. This disposition of the premium received was soon afterward made.

An interesting incident in sequence of the action of the Finance Committee occurred in the payment for the bonds. Although the award was formally made to the life insurance company, the certified check received a few days later in payment for the bonds, bore the signature of J. & W. Seligman.

After the requisition referred to had been made, the Park Commission took no farther formal or official action regarding this issue. Treasurer Murphy had a few weeks before been appointed one of the sinking fund commissioners of the Board of Freeholders, and as both he and Counsel Munn were at that time "close to" that board, the individual members of the Park Board did not deem it consistent to take up the subject farther than to express their convictions in an informal way as opportunity presented. This I did, both at the Park Board rooms and in conversations with the president, treasurer and counsel.

BOND SALE RECOMMENDED.

On May 1, 1896, I wrote Counsel Munn as follows:

"Personally, I have for some time had the feeling that if handled rightly the remaining issue of bonds can be placed during the coming 'dull season'—say June to August—at the same rate, 3.65, as before; and private sale, in my judgment, is the best way to accomplish the most favorable results.

"You recollect Mr. Morgan told me he would take the whole two and a half millions at private sale, but he would not go into competition for an issue of that size.

"There has been no perceptible change in the underlying conditions as to rates of interest in the moneyed centres. English consols touched the highest price last week they have ever sold for. The demand for high-class bonds was shown the other day, when Brooklyn's million and a quarter loan, 3.50 bonds, were bid for two or three times over above par.

"All there is in making a good sale of bonds now is, first, a good bond; second, the right method of handling it."

I was free to confess then, as since, my inability to grâsp even the possibility of advantage to the taxpayers of Essex County from the proposition for them to pay in $5,250 extra every year for thirty years (the average life of the bonds) in interest, for the privilege of having a sinking fund of $72,900 in the hands and under the control of the sinking fund commissioners of the Board of Freeholders, instead of the $5,250 each year being saved and retained in their (the taxpayers) own pockets. That the bonds of a 3.65 interest rate were then saleable "at not less than par," as provided in the park charter, was manifestly shown by the Messrs. Seligmans' bid of 100.28 for the whole $1,500,000 issue.

"MODERN HIGH FINANCE."

What the actual loss to the people of Essex County by the issuance of those bonds at four per cent. and the additional $2,500,000 of bonds since issued for the parks at that rate instead of at the 3.65 rate, as with the first million issued, may, I think, be properly left to the future and for the public to determine. From present indications, it will not be long before the question of detriment to the public at large, from the methods of modern high finance, and the concentration of large sums of other people's money in the hands of a few men to control, will be readily understood and the false principle upon which the operations are based generally appreciated and measured at their true worth.

At the close of 1896, within fifteen months after the receipt of $2,450,000, the commission found that its financial limit had been practically reached. The results of the policy of individual selection of the parks, rather than that of a careful prior study of the requirements for the park system as a whole had, in this comparatively brief time, fully materialized. Although the balance sheet of December 31, 1896, showed a cash balance on hand or $1,209,559, the outstanding obligations for land and other liabilities and contracts were then sufficient to absorb all but a relatively small portion of this unexpended sum. At the board meeting of December 2 the landscape architects and engineers submitted, under a resolution of September 17, 1896, a "general plan of the system of county parks and parkways," including a formal estimate of the cost of the parks already determined upon. These estimates were made after consultation with the land agents and other employes of the department, who were then in charge of the various phases of the work. This estimate was as follows:

Estimated cost for land at various parks:

Branch Brook	$1,076,000
Lake Weequahic	180,000
Eastern (East Side)	125,000
Eagle Rock	227,000
Millburn (South Mountain)	250,000
Orange Triangle	100,000
*South Orange Park.............	25,000

*This item of $25,000 was for park or parkway lands out in South Orange, on or near Grove road; formal action regarding which had not then, and has not since, been taken.

West Newark (West Side)......... 75,000

Total ....,....... $2,058,000

Approximate estimates of park improvements suggested for early construction:

Branch Brook improvements from Sussex avenue to Old Bloomfield road $350,000
East Side Park...................... 40,000
Weequahic Park 25,000
Eagle Rock Reservation............. 25,000
Triangle Park, Orange.............. 25,000
West Newark Parks................ 25,000

Total $490,000

As will be seen from these figures, they represented a total actual and estimated expenditure of $2,548,000, from an appropriation made but the year previous "for a system of parks in its entirety" of $2,500,000. This, notwithstanding the conservative estimates for the cost of the remaining land yet unacquired in the different parks, and the extremely limited amounts noted for improvements in those parks, other than in Branch Brook, where contracts were made and improvement work was already well under way.

THE FINANCIAL SITUATION.

Although the subject of the impending dificiency was not referred to in the first official report of the commission for 1896, issued early in 1897, it became well understood in the park board room that there would be no object in longer "executive sessioning" the fact from the public. As Commissioner Franklin Murphy had been the most active and outspoken exponent of the sectional policy adopted in acquiring the various parks, he was delegated by his colleagues to convey in his own way the financial situation in the board's affairs to the public. This was done, and I think the first intimation the people had of that matter was ob-

tained through a published interview given out by Mr.
Murphy January 5, 1897. It was there stated that "unless
additional appropriations be made for park purposes in the
future, the system of public pleasure grounds and county
boulevards outlined in a general way by the Essex County
Park Commission will not be completed," and "that the
commissioners do not expect to turn all the property purchased into finished parks with the $2,500,000 that was
placed at their disposal for the purpose." Mr. Murphy
further said: "The board has no right to suppose that additional money will be furnished. On the other hand, it has
no reason to think that additional appropriations won't be
made. * * * The commission feels bound to give the
county certain completed parks for the money it has been
given, to satisfy the people, and this no doubt will be done."

"The conditions as to the Orange Park," he said, "are in
the air. Yes, we did agree to purchase the land, but there
were certain conditions that—oh, well, I can't tell you now.
* * * We cannot arrange for maintenance before we
have something to maintain. That question has not been
considered yet."

As a part of the same interview, Counsel Munn, the same
morning, was reported as having said: "The plans of the
commission have not been laid out on the theory that there
will be additional legislation."

APPOINTIVE OR ELECTIVE PARK COMMISSIONS.

These announcements were evidently something of a surprise to the public. The time had run by so quickly since
the appointment of the commission, only about twenty
months before, that many, even among the friends of the
park movement, hardly realized that the work of the commission was by that time well begun. The public utterances, for the most part, were not favorable. Mayor Seymour made a severe arraignment of the commission, and of
the appointive system of legislation under which it was
created. This law, providing for an appointive board, he declared, in a written statement a few days prior to the an-

nouncement of the Park Commission shortage, "should be amended." This method of appointment, he said, "is wrong and opposed to the popular notions of self-government."

"Under certain contingencies," he wrote, "it might remove the power of selection entirely from an officer of Essex County and place it with an official residing in some distant part of the State. This might occur in the event of the selection of a Park Commission being made during a vacancy in the Supreme Court in this county. Officers of such importance should be chosen by the people. A public board making such large demands upon the taxable property of the community should be in closer touch with the people of the community. According to the highest conceptions of popular government, that closer touch is to be had only through the medium of the ballot-box. The law should be changed and the Park Commissioners be compelled to take their chances before the community."

These forcibly-expressed sentiments, published both in the leading New Jersey and New York papers almost concurrently with the park deficiency statements quoted, apparently touched a responsive chord with many people throughout Essex County. While the Mayor's presentment was merely an elaboration of the anti-appointive commission plank of the Democratic city platform, as before mentioned, its reception by the public was no doubt accentuated by the disappointment which the call for more funds to complete the parks occasioned. The claim was at once made by the partisan advocates of the appointive plan, that the attack of the Mayor and those favoring his side of the question was in reality naught but an incident in the play of politics, and an attempted flank movement by which the Democratic minority hoped to secure a "vantage" point with the people over their Republican opponents, who counted upon then having a safe working majority locally as well as in the Legislature.

Senator Ketcham came at once to the rescue, and in a published interview told of his surprise at the Mayor's statements. He explained the features of the park law he had

so earnestly favored, and defended his support of that
measure in the Legislature on the ground of expediency—
as he considered the appointive Park Board under the existing conditions far preferable to an elective commission.

MONSIGNOR DOANE'S VIEWS.

Monsignor G. H. Doane was also a zealous supporter of
the Park Commission's cause. He, too, responded vigorously. While not touching in any way upon the political
features of the controversy, his optimistic thought in favor
of some of the things then accomplished toward the improvement of Branch Brook Park was clearly expressed in a
published letter January 9, 1897. In this letter, after referring to the skating he had just witnessed in the park as
being "Holland over again" and wishing he were "a boy
once more," he added: "The promise of the beauty of the
park is great, and the commissioners and engineers are
showing great judgment, skill, knowledge and good taste."

Others joined in the effort to repel the attack, and the
conflict of words soon had the appearance of a drawn battle,
yet actually leaving the appointive commission in possession
and victor of the field. The discussion, however, bore fruit
in largely extending in the public mind the objection to an
appointive commission. This was manifestly the result, as
shown by the resolutions of disapproval of that system in
the different political conventions since. Published individual opinions then and since have reflected a similar sentiment as existing in the minds of officials and publicists,
both in Essex and in Hudson counties and elsewhere, in
conformity with the generally accepted objection to specially
appointed public boards.

One of the persistent advocates of the elective plan contended that the only answer to the claim that the appointive system is in every way contrary to the fundamental
structure upon which our entire political and representative system of government is based, has been that "the law
so provides," and that such legislative results are "accomplished by log rolling, scheming and jollying of ignorant,

inexperienced and ambitious legislators." "The park commission law" is thus pronounced "radically wrong in its conception and construction."

Answer was made that such views belonged to the "Rip Van Winkle order of observation," ignored the teachings of experience with elective boards in inaugurating large schemes of public improvements, and disregard the fact that park making is in itself a special undertaking quite unlike the ordinary administration of public affairs.

The converts to the elective plan side of the question have apparently continued to rapidly grow in numbers. Since the discussion over the last million-dollar appropriation, and the question of mandatory maintenance in 1902, and the war for eight years waged over the parkways, it is extremely doubtful whether the number averse to an appointive park board has not been materially augmented: And equally doubtful whether if the proposition to continue the present appointive system were now submitted to the voters of Essex County it would not be by a liberal majority defeated.

PUBLIC NOT ENTHUSIASTIC.

In 1897, however, the agitation soon ceased. As there was no immediate prospects of the law's being changed, the discussion in January of that year soon turned upon the financial aspects of the enterprise. The attitude of the public, as voiced by the press, was not enthusiastic. It was, indeed, largely apathetic or distinctly unfavorable. Aside from the generous view, taken by Monsignor Doane and a few ardent supporters of the commission, the comments not infrequently conveyed a tone of severe criticism. The public was reminded of the promise of the first commission as to the completion of the parks and parkways for the $2,500,000 appropriation.

While many readily accepted the theory that all such appropriations were subject to additional or later demands, others were outspoken in their objection to the way the affairs of the Park Board had been managed. No charges of bad faith, which I can recall or find in the various records

I have examined, were made; but rather a subdued feeling of disappointment and of disapproval permeated more or less the mental atmosphere throughout the county. This sentiment was forcefully expressed in the editorials of the Newark News, January 6 and February 13, 1897, the former referring directly to Commissioner Murphy's statement above quoted.

As these articles then embodied a clear and evidently correct expression on this 'subject, the salient portions may here be of interest. Under the caption "The Cost of the Parks and the People's Power Over the Outlay" it was stated: "The letter, the spirit and the intent of the law under which the Park Board is acting require that, with the expenditure of $2,500,000, all the parks and parkways which they have the right to establish, shall be completed and turned over to the county of Essex. The commissioners, presumably acting with forethought and good intention, have chosen to set up a law for themselves by purchasing large tracts of land, to be held for future development, with increased cost to the people. * * * The park commissioners are going to spend $2,500,000 in the development of a few parks in Newark, and the purchase of certain lands outside. To improve these lands very large additional expenditures will be necessary. The present board, or its successors, will probably make an appeal to the Legislature for authority to issue more bonds. If the practice sought to be established by the present board be allowed to stand, and be imitated in the future, the legislative restrictions regarding public expenditures for parks will have no meaning. If the parks of Essex County are going to cost more than $2,500,000, who may say what they are going to cost? Will the total run up to $5,000,000 or $10,000,000 or $20,000,000?"

In commenting upon the report of the commission for 1896, issued early in February, 1897, the News, February 13, said: "The scheme of parkways is not discussed in the report. The commissioners have not yet determined as to the character and the scope of those great avenues which are to connect the various parks, and which are to add new charm to the beauties of the county. It is reasonable to expect that the improvements of these broad avenues will involve a large expenditure, and that this work, taken in connection with the improvement of the great areas already secured in the Orange Mountain district, will necessitate an expenditure of at least $2,500,000 more, and perhaps a sum in excess of that amount."

The correctness of this prophetic statement as regards the application for additional funds for the parks, was vindicated within a year by the issuance of the commission's report for that year (1897), in January, 1898. In the closing paragraphs of that report appears (page 18) the following statement:

MORE MONEY NEEDED.

"The Park Commission can expend the balance still on hand in completing as far as is possible the land purchases within the areas already selected, and in bringing the city parks to such condition as will make them useful, in a measure, to the public. But for more perfect development of the parks, for the acquirement of some further lands to improve the outlines of these parks, and especially for the expense of parkways, the need of which becomes more obvious as the system is developed and appreciated, the commission estimates that the further sum of $1,500,000 is needed. And this sum is, in the estimation of the commissioners, all that ought to be expended for acquirement and development of the system as laid out and designated."

This official intimation of the needs and the intention of the commission was put into practical shape by the preparation of a bill, which, at about the same time, early in 1898, made its appearance in the Legislature. This bill, containing a referendum clause providing for its submission to the electorate of the county in April, was soon passed by both houses of the Legislature, and was approved February 21, 1898. At the election of April 12, following, the vote stood for the law, 14,737; against, 9,954; or a majority in favor of only 4,783, although the Newark Board of Trade, the

New England Society, the Roseville Improvement Association and other organizations had, just prior to the election, passed resolutions favoring the adoption of the law, and the approval of the act by the voters.

Another factor which might have been favorable in deciding the vote was the impression and promise given out by the commission that the additional $1,500,000 asked for would be sufficient to complete the park system plans. The News of January 21, 1898, gave a detailed account of a conference upon the new appropriation bill "held at the home of Franklin Murphy, treasurer of the Park Commission," the night previous, at which meeting Senator Ketcham, a number of the Essex County assemblymen, and all of the 'park commissioners, excepting Mr. Bramhall, were present. It was there stated, according to this report of the conference, that while the amount ($1,500,000) "would not do all that might be done, for the commission could expend $5,000,000 if all the suggestions advanced were followed, yet it would, he said, be sufficient to leave the county in possession of a park system, properly connected by parkways, second to none in the country, and all secured for a total outlay of only $4,000,000."

SIGNIFICANCE OF SMALL VOTE.

The comparatively small total vote of 24,691—only a little more than half in the county—and the reduced majority of only 4,783, as against a majority of 8,321 for the first appropriation, April 15, 1895, clearly reflected the reduced interest in and lack of popular support of the commission and of the county park undertaking, as it was then before the public. On January 11, 1898, the commission made a requisition on the Board of Freeholders for the $1,500,000, as provided in the bill, "on approval of the bill by the people," and in April, directly after the vote on the bill, an unconditional requisition was made for $500,000 of the appropriation as then available.

The issuance of these bonds was delayed for several months. A technical question had arisen as to the legality of the referendum feature of the new law. Able lawyers differed upon the question. The freeholders declined to issue the bonds "until directed to do so by a court of competent jurisdiction." The question was taken into the courts by the friendly suit method. On July 8 the new act and the proposed bond issue was, by the Court of Errors and Appeals, declared valid. An instalment of $500,000 of the bonds was then, in August, 1898, sold. They were four per cent. gold bonds, similar as to form and time of maturity to those last issued. The sale was made under the sealed proposal method, as before.

There were seventeen bids. The award was made to the Illinois Trust and Savings Bank, Chicago, and Mason Lewis & Co., Boston, on their joint bid of 112.199. The remaining $1,000,000 bonds of that authorized issue also brought a good premium. They were disposed of in like manner, $500,000 in 1899 and $500,000 in 1900.

In the meantime methods had been devised for turning over to the Park Commission the premium realized on all these bonds, instead of retaining it in the sinking fund as theretofore. On August 3, 1900, the last $500,000 of this appropriation, together with $80,000 premium on the bonds, was turned over to the commission.

Thus, within five years, the people of Essex County had raised and contributed in cash for the park system promised them for $2,500,000, more than $4,000,000.

CHAPTER X.

EXPERIENCES WITH COUNSEL.

SOME of the causes indicating the increased cost of the parks over the previous estimates have been stated in preceding chapters. Another reason for the enlarged expenditure was the persistent inattention of the counsel to the duties of his office. This continued neglect by Counsel Munn of the interests entrusted to him began almost simultaneously with his appointment in May, 1895.

Any one having had practical experience in great enterprises where large financial operations, and intricate or varied legal questions are involved, recognizes the necessity of having in charge of the legal department not only a man of ability, but one alert in the grasp and direction of legal affairs. While this is directly applicable to all large undertakings, the principle applies with special force to a public enterprise, where there is such a temptation and tendency with people generally to take any and every advantage possible in securing from the public treasury the maximum amount of cash, for the minimum amount of land, goods or service, or whatever is to be given in exchange.

In the organization of the park department these conditions were supposed to be well understood, hence the importance of the care to be exercised in the selection of counsel. Relying largely upon Commissioner Shepard's strong advocacy of Mr. Munn's appointment, based upon his experience with Mr. Munn as his own counsel and neighbor, I had, as previously stated, reluctantly supported him for the position. This tentative confidence that he might prove the right man for the place was somewhat strengthened by the receipt of a letter soon after the appointment was made. In this letter Mr. Munn stated:

PARK POSSIBILITIES IN ESSEX COUNTY.

"My imagination was fascinated years ago by a statement from Llewellyn S. Haskell as to the possibilities of
converting Essex County into a world-famous park. The
present county avenues—radiating from Newark—were a
part of his plan, and we are indebted to his heroic advocacy
for the limited success achieved. If he had lived he would
be the enthusiastic supporter of the present park commission. I count it a great honor to be identified with a project
so noble, and the prospect of its success, in the hands of
commissioners so high in character and ability, constitutes
an incentive to all who are identified with the work to give
to it their best endeavor. To be able, also, to feel that
cordial relations subsist with the members of the commission, makes the work a pleasure, apart from its intrinsic
interest."

What more could one ask as to implied intention, or an
ideal sentiment in undertaking the work of a new enterprise, than was apparently by this letter expressed? But
the reality, and what soon afterward followed, was a very
different matter. At first, and during the early part of the
summer of 1895, Counsel Munn evinced a disposition to
fulfil the obligations of his office and thus to vindicate the
ideal sentiments above quoted. In looking up matters pertaining to the bond issue, he was reasonably attentive and
helpful. In the ordinary legal routine also, there were, at
first, no noticeable lapses. When, however, the work of the
legal department began to increase, his care and attention
to it commenced to decrease in a corresponding and ever
increasing ratio.

On the determination of the lines of Branch Brook Park
in July, 1895, the requirements in condemnation proceedings and other legal questions were rapidly augmented.
Aside from the reservoir property in that park, the entire
area was in city lots. With the desire of the commission to
obtain possession of all the property at the earliest practicable date, all the small holdings that could not be pur-

chased required prompt and vigorous attention. Later in the summer the work of the counsel began to get badly in arrears. In the autumn and early winter, when the East Side, Eagle Rock and South Mountain Park locations had been decided upon, matters went from bad to worse. In almost every direction there was evidence of negligence. The counsel, instead of attending the board meetings, where, with all the important matters then in his charge, it was considered his place to be, was frequently conspicuous by his absence.

LACK OF INTEREST SHOWN.

The suggestions and requests for better service and attention to duty met with no appreciable response. Through the spring and summer of 1896 matters went on in this way. The neglect was not only costing the county dearly in money, but was preventing progress in the development of the parks. This was having a demoralizing influence on the entire department. When the active work of the commission was taken up early in the autumn, I determined that I would not acquiesce in the prevailing conditions longer. First one commissioner, Mr. Meeker, then another, Mr. Peck, declared the same view. This was a majority of the board. Something must, therefore, be done, and that speedily. It was done—and this is the way it was done:

At the board meeting of October 6, 1896, immediately after roll call, the commission went into the most executive of executive sessions. Even the secretary, always present at our meetings, was excused. Only the commissioners were present. Counsel Munn's case was at once taken up. When he was appointed the "votes were there" to elect him. Now the votes were there to dismiss him. The question was well gone over. All concurred, or admitted, that his conduct was inexcusable; its continuance intolerable. The remedy suggested was immediate dismissal. One or both of the commissioners just mentioned concurred in that view.

At this juncture Commissioner Franklin Murphy began

to interpose palliatives and to plead for Munn. Commissioner Shepard joined in the pleadings. It would be very trying, they said, for Mr. Munn, as it would be for any attorney, to have a peremptory dismissal from such a board. We should not act hastily, they contended, in so important a case as this. The official relations with the freeholders were friendly.· Might not differences arise, should the proposed dismissal be made effective? Give Mr. Munn a trial —another opportunity, provided he would promise to do better, they urged. His salary was not large for a counsel in so responsible a position. Perhaps this may, in part, account for his lack of attention to his duties, they continued.

It was decided to call Mr. Munn in, explain the situation to him, and, unless he would promise to do better forthwith, that he should go. He entered. His manner was serious; his bearing courteous but grave. He took a seat at the end of the commissioners' table, where he could be closely observed. The status of matters was explained to him. He listened attentively, scarcely uttering a word. He was told how the business of the commission in his charge was suffering from his neglect; how serious the result was becoming; that it must be stopped, or a change made. His manner indicated more clearly than words that he realized the truth and the force of the charges made. I then looked him directly in the face and said: "Mr. Munn, if we retain you, can we rely upon your properly· attending to your duties here?" In a subdued but clear voice he replied: "Yes, you can!" He was excused.

The pleadings of Messrs. Shepard and Murphy for his retention then continued. He had made a pledge in the presence of us all; why not at least give him an opportunity to redeem that pledge. Who else could be selected, of all the attorneys in Essex County, who could then come into the department and have the grasp of the legal situation that Mr. Munn already possessed? These arguments prevailed.

It then seemed logical and consistent to give him a further trial before exercising our right of peremptory dismissal. Those of us favoring this latter course hoped for better results, and agreed to the time-and-trial extension proposition. Munn's answer to my question, as quoted, together with the arguments on his behalf, inspired that hope.

THE COUNSEI ETAINED.

As it was now agreed to give Counsel Munn the opportunity of redeeming his promise for proper service, Commissioner Murphy promptly offered the following resolution: "That the counsel's salary, from October 15, be $3,000, it being understood that, in view of the increased compensation, the counsel shall give additional time to the work which has now become necessary,." After further discussion, in effect, that if he did not thereafter adequately attend to his duties he should be dismissed, the motion was agreed to, and Mr. Munn was thus retained in that responsible and, at that time, most important position. Did he fulfil his new obligation? Never, to my knowledge, with the exception of a slight temporary improvement for a few weeks immediately after the described incident, and temporary, spasmodic efforts on exceptional occasions since. Nor was he dismissed until more than seven years afterward, when he had drawn from the taxpayers more than $20,000 in salary, and his negligence had caused losses to the commission difficult to estimate.

The incident in then retaining Counsel Munn, as detailed above, cannot in a few words be more forcibly or accurately expressed than in the humorous comment of one thoroughly conversant with the circumstances then and since, who has repeatedly said to me in referring to that incident: "You agreed to discharge Munn for cause, then turned immediately around and hired him over again at an increased salary."

INATTENTION TO DUTIES.

But the efforts to secure another counsel who would properly attend to the duties of the office did not rest here. When in April, 1897, George W. Bramhall succeeded me as commissioner, the affairs in the legal department were found to be in the utmost confusion. As a man of experience in model business methods, Mr. Bramhall's attention was at once attracted to this situation. It was not long before reports were in circulation of the conditions being so bad that some of the leading attorneys were considering the advisability of sending a protest to the Park Board against Munn's retention. Some remedy must be found. Two of the commissioners determined to get rid of him. They made an earnest effort with that end in view.

Upon further investigation, it was found there was ample cause. The neglect to advance the very many cases in condemnation proceedings was resulting in higher awards. These awards for increasing liabilities against the commission could have been secured for less amounts, earlier in the proceedings, when lower values on contiguous property had, by purchase and otherwise, been established. The failure to have deeds and other legal papers of the land acquirements promptly and properly recorded, as required under the Martin act, was making the commission liable for taxes and other charges. Valuable papers of the law department could not be found when wanted. Much inconvenience, delay and loss was being occasioned by the absence of the counsel when important meetings of the commissioners were held to take testimony in condemnation proceedings. The failure to attend meetings of the commission when matters of great importance and urgency were to be considered, continued.

With these conditions before them, the minority members endeavored to secure the necessary third member to constitute a majority for action. Commissioner Peck's attitude was felt to be too uncertain. Commissioner Shepard's position, in persistent advocacy of Counsel Munn, was well known. Commissioner Murphy went to the Park Board rooms, looked over the situation there with one of the other members, and admitted that the case was serious. The impression received was that he would unite in the vote for dismissal.

At the next board meeting the subject was brought up.

The secretary was again excused. It was warm weather, and the temperature was soon increased inside the Park Board rooms. The minority members, when they came into the meeting, thought there would be no doubt as to the result. They were mistaken. Commissioner Murphy at once joined Commissioner Shepard in a repetition of the pleadings of a few months before. The time had "not come for the dismissal of Counsel Munn." They would not vote for it. Commissioner Peck reversed his previous position and holding, as he then did, the deciding vote, gave the necessary majority to that side. The counsel was, therefore, retained. The incident was closed.

When legal work of importance must be done, special counsel was employed. On February 11, 1898, W. B. Southard was thus employed at an expense of $125 per month "to expedite condemnation proceedings." At the Park Board meeting, March 11, following, a bill of $300, of Riker & Riker, attorneys, "for services in the S. Howell Jones condemnation case," was ordered paid. On July 7 a bill of Robert H. McCarter for $500 in attending to "the park law mandamus case before the Court of Errors and Appeals," was presented. October 1, 1901, Cortland Parker's bill of $184.45 in the Watkins insurance case—the property on Orange Mountain then in process of condemnation—was paid. April 8, 1902, a bill of Corbin & Corbin of $200 for an "opinion on the constitutionality of the park law" was approved. August 19 of the same year Robert H. McCarter was retained as associate counsel in the matter of the certiorari proceeding of the Forest Hill Association against the Park Commission," and was paid $500 for that service. January 20, 1903, Henry Young was "retained in the litigation to test the constitutionality of the park act" and paid $250, with $250 more the following April. On the same day, April 7, 1903, Corbin & Corbin were paid $500 in the same case for services before the Court of Errors and Appeals.

On November 10, 1903, Secretary Church was paid an extra $600 "for services rendered and to be rendered for

1903." He had previously become an attorney of record, and the partnership of Munn & Church, consisting of Joseph L. Munn and Alonzo Church, had been formed, with offices, then as since, with the same entrance and adjoining the Park Board rooms at 800 Broad street, Newark.

Other and similar payments to the above from 1897, or early 1898 down to time Counsel Munn's "services" were dispensed with, January 1, 1904, were made. As to the propriety of these payments, or, under the circumstances, the partnership referred to, I prefer to make no comment. I merely state the facts as a part of this record.

That conditions regarding the services—or lack of service—of Counsel Munn had not improved for more than two years after Commissioner Bramhall's retirement from the Park Board in April, 1900, may be conclusively inferred from the action of the commissioners taken at the meeting August 13, 1902. The East Orange parkway was to have been the special order of business for that day, "but, owing to the failure of the counsel to report," the following resolution was adopted: "Whereas, the counsel has failed to report to the commission, which held a meeting at considerable personal inconvenience to the commissioners, for the express purpose of receiving his report; therefore, be it resolved, that the secretary notify the counsel that his negligence in failing to report as to the property between Main street and Central avenue has greatly inconvenienced the commissioners. Resolved, further, that the counsel be directed to report immediately to the chairman of the Committee on Parkways as to whether he intends to see the property-owners between Main street and Central avenue as requested by the commissioners, and as agreed by him.

"Resolved, further, that a copy of this resolution be sent to Mr. Shepard."

Since 1896 the question has been frequently asked: Why was this neglectful and faithless counsel retained by the Park Board for so many years?

CHAPTER XI.

A CHANGE OF COMMISSIONERS.

In the early afternoon of April 20, 1897, my former colleague on the first commission, George W. Bramhall, called me by telephone and asked for an appointment at my house that evening. It was accordingly made. From the time of our appointment on the first Park Board in June, 1894, our personal relations had been cordial, and, in park matters, intimate. After April, 1895, when I was reappointed on the permanent commission and he was not, we had conferred on many of the more important park subjects.

When his appointment on the first commission was recommended it was recognized that he was a man of cultivation and taste in park matters; that he entertained broad views on that subject, and that, as commissioner, he would have "no ax to grind" in bringing to bear on the problems involved his experience and ability shown in other directions. This estimate of his qualifications was, I think, vindicated during the two terms of his service as commissioner.

UNDERLYING CONDITIONS.

It may be well to here state the underlying conditions at the time of the conference mentioned. My two years' term as park commissioner expired that day. For some months, even prior to the Munn dismissal incident, there were powerful corporate and political interests, which for reasons that may be readily inferred from the reading of the facts contained in this history, were averse to my reappointment. This condition was materially accelerated by the contest over the parkways begun the November previous, and by my attitude in insisting that the counsel attend to his duties or leave the service of the commission. The traction companies up to that time had had quite smooth sailing in their successful efforts to secure coveted franchises, and the more valuable the public franchises were, the more successful the managers of the companies appeared to be in their efforts to secure them. Any individual aggressively opposing this "gift enterprise" business was soon made to feel that his future, politically or otherwise, would be far more agreeable, or, perchance, successful, if he should not "stand in the way" of what the "organization"—or in other words, what the corporations, then, as afterward, so closely allied with the party bosses—wanted. A park commissioner who would insist that the people should have what had been promised them, provided the execution of the promise interfered with the corporation plans for a valuable public franchise—notwithstanding the promise may have been for a park system that was being paid for from the tax budget—was not the kind of man the corporations wanted. The pressure brought to bear upon Judge Depue as the appointing power to leave me off of the commission, was, now that the die for the parkways had been cast and my outspoken position well understood, materially increased.

Commissioner Franklin Murphy's political craft had also up to that time had smooth sailing, and if he could unify the various elements in both the corporate and political fields, there was a fair prospect of his reaching his ambition in the climb for the Gubernatorial chair. Counsel Joseph L. Munn was regarded as one of his active political workers for furthering that object.

Commissioner Frederick M. Shepard, as the principal owner of a valuable water plant, which, with the assistance of "Counsel" Munn, it might be during the next few years desirable to sell at a good price to the municipalities of East Orange and Bloomfield—(as was accomplished in 1903)—was in full sympathy with, and extremely friendly to, these corporation influences and interests.

There were, perhaps, not many men in Essex County who then had a keener appreciation of these underlying condi-

tions than had I. The situation as to the efforts made with
the court to make a change in the appointment of commissioners in 1895, had been fully reported to me by my
friends, some of whom were then consulted by Judge Depue
before he made that change.

The final decision then made in my favor was the result
of the action taken by my friends, unknown to me until
after the commission was appointed.

My experience during the two years in the second commission had made the situation, as it existed at this time,
as clear as the noonday sun. It was perfectly evident from
Mr. Murphy's bearing and conversation with me that he
would do what he could to prevent my reappointment. Although our personal relations had remained courteous, and,
in a measure, to all appearances, friendly, our views as to
policy and method in the management of the park department were, from the outset, radically at variance. We differed on almost every vital principle, from the plan of procedure in laying out the parks and the impending contest
with the trolley companies over the parkways, to the retention of Counsel Munn. The official records and correspondence make this situation for that two years, from first to
last, perfectly clear. Every one knew, who knew anything of
the conditions as they existed in April, 1897, that both
Commissioner Murphy and Counsel Munn were in close
touch, directly or indirectly, with Judge Depue.

Weeks before the expiration of my term as commissioner,
my friends expressed to me their fears that the influences
so inimical to my reappointment might prevail. My answer was: That while I fully appreciated the circumstances,
I would not seek the appointment. The original suggestion
that the appointing power be placed with the court had been
made by me, and the full responsibility had, in accordance
with that suggestion, been by law conferred upon the judge;
that if appointed I would, at least for the present, accept
the office, but would not vary from the conviction and principle I had always believed in and adhered to—that the
office should seek the man, not the man the office.

Several friends told me they had written strong letters to the judge urging my appointment, and I learned afterward that many letters were sent of similar tenor.

A FRIENDLY CONFERENCE.

From the above, the reader may readily infer that Mr. Bramhall and myself were both prepared for a heart-to-heart talk on that evening of April 20, 1897, in question. We went over the subject quite fully. He explained to me how Judge Depue had sent for him—much as he had sent for me just before the appointment of the first commission, in 1894, as noted in Chapter II; how he (Mr. Bramhall), had frankly stated that he was not a candidate, could not accept an appointment, and his aversion to even appearing to countenance any action unfavorable to my reappointment. After further conversation with the judge, Mr. Bramhall stated, he said to him, "Mr. Kelsey is as well equipped as any man in the county to fill the position; his appointment is favored by me and I have so stated."

The judge then made answer: "I cannot consider his appointment. Pressure has been brought to bear against it." Mr. Bramhall said that he then asked the judge the direct question why my reappointment could not be considered. The answer was not forthcoming. Later in the conversation the question was repeated, but the information, he said, "could not be wrung" from the judge. Mr. Bramhall said he then indicated that, even though he should accept the appointment, he could not serve the full term. The judge was urgent. Mr. Bramhall finally assented to the appointment; but before doing so it was agreed between them that before the appointment was announced Mr. Bramhall should see me and that we should talk the matter over together. This we did without reserve.

A PROPHECY FULFILLED.

After he had related to me what had occurred during his conversation the evening before with Judge Depue, I stated that I was glad to be relieved of the duties, which for two years had been most exacting; that I was pleased that he had consented to accept the appointment in my place; that I was perfectly well aware of the influences brought to bear, and the reasons why my reappointment was not considered by the judge; and that those reasons would not be given to the public when his appointment was announced in court any more than they had been given him, on his urgent request, during their conversation in the privacy of the judge's home.

I hardly expected at that time, however, that the correctness of this prophetic remark would be so soon and so fully vindicated as it apparently was, when the appointment was made. The next morning I wrote Judge Depue as follows:

"Orange, April 21, 1897.

"Dear Sir—Mr. Bramhall called upon me last evening, stating that he had done so in accordance with an understanding with you that you were not to announce the appointment of my successor in the Park Commission until he had seen me.

"I was astonished at his statements. My relations to the enterprise, its inception and development since, and my work as commissioner have been such that my constituency and the public, so far as I understand, have been satisfied, and I am told have asked for my reappointment.

"If, in any way, my work has been unsatisfactory or not what it should have been to you, or to the public, I am open to criticism, and will gratefully receive it. Until then I feel, in view of the facts, that it is just and due to me to know why my services are discredited and my appointment not under consideration.

"It seems to me that this statement is due you. And that it is equally due me in consideration of the work I have done in the enterprise, and the time I have given it, that you advise me why my name 'cannot be considered,' as Mr. Bramhall states.   "Very truly yours,

"FRED. W. KELSEY,

"Hon. David A. Depue."

No acknowledgment or reply to this letter was ever received, and I never saw or heard from Judge Depue again. In the afternoon of the same day, and the day following my conversation with Mr. Bramhall, April 21, 1897, the appointment was announced in open court. The announcement was noticeable for its brevity. It also occasioned comment for not giving the public the slightest suggestion or intimation, any more than had been given privately to Mr. Bramhall, as to the reasons the judge had for making the change. This was in marked contrast to his extended remarks in making the change in the appointment of two commissioners two years before, as quoted from at length in Chapter IV of this history. Moreover, this change involved the displacement of a commissioner who had served continuously from the time of the appointment of the first commission in June, 1894. The judge said:

"I have the appointment to make of a park commissioner, to take the place of Mr. Kelsey. I appoint George W. Bramhall, whom I regard as capable and efficient. He has served as a temporary commissioner and is much interested in the work. As regards the situation now I consider the appointment a judicious one."

APPRECIATION FROM THE PUBLIC.

The Newark Sunday Call, in editorially commenting upon the appointment, referred to it as appearing to do "some injustice to Commissioner Kelsey, whose place is taken and who was chosen originally in preference to Mr. Bramhall. Mr. Kelsey's services have been satisfactory to the public, but it is gratifying that his successor is known as a man of taste, experience in business affairs and of special knowledge in this work." This sentiment was quite generally expressed throughout the county. The commendations of various county papers, and the letters and other personal expressions of appreciation and approval of my course as commissioner were gratifying. In The Daily Advertiser, the same day of Mr. Bramhall's appointment, the following statements appeared in an interview with Commissioners Shepard and Peck at the Park Board rooms that afternoon of April 21: "Mr. Shepard said that Mr. Kelsey had been a faithful member of the commission; that he had attended almost every meeting, and that he was an enthusiastic worker."

"Mr. Peck here added a few words in praise of Mr. Kelsey, saying that the retiring member had been keenly alive to his duties."

My non-appointment was, however, to myself a great relief. For nearly three years I had given a large part of my time and interest to the inception and formulative plans of the enterprise. The first year with the preliminary or original Park Commission, as may be inferred from the first three chapters of this volume, the work, though arduous, and at times confining, was treated as recreation, and was for the most part a pleasure. The two years' service in the second commission were indeed strenuous years, filled with forebodings, doubts and uncertainties, and, as one who reads these records of the events as they occurred at the time, can readily appreciate, were years of conflict in my earnest endeavor to hold on the lines of its original conception, to the best of my ability, this great enterprise, founded as it was upon an ideal of what a park enterprise should be, and for which I was willing to devote every effort and time to have carried out to the best practical result. If this were possible, I believed that the development of this ideal would be a constant pleasure, benefit and growing delight to the people of Essex County; and to myself an unfailing source of satisfaction in the results obtained. It was only after my retirement from the active work of the commission in 1897 that I better appreciated these conditions and what the effort had been.

But almost immediately, and continuing as it were from the very day of the expiration of my term of office, and growing out of the conditions then existing, arose another

or a part of the same question, viz: Whether the plan of
parkways for connecting the larger parks as then established, into a park system, and as repeatedly promised the
people, should or should not be carried out.

CHAPTER XII.

A full record of all that has occurred in connection with the parkways for the Essex County parks would fill volumes. The correspondence, the official communications, the public conferences, the private confabs, the petitions and the litigation for the parkways, the protests against destroying them, the resolutions of various civic associations, the public hearings, the massmeetings, the action of special committees—would each, if given complete, require a chapter or a volume. A chapter, too, might well be devoted to the different phases of the situation during the various changes in this interesting question.

How, on the announcement of the parkway plans by the Park Commission in November, 1896, the traction company began at once to scheme after the manner of public utility corporations for the defeat of those plans, and to be the first to obtain possession of one or both of the principal avenues that were designated for parkways. How, as this contest went on, with the people and, at the outset, the Park Commission on the one side, and the allied powerful corporate and political forces working through the "organization" machine as dictated by the party boss, on the other side, the proceedings in the county and local governing boards, in dealing with the question, were for years a continuous performance of the play of battledore and shuttlecock.

How shrewd attorneys and the interested politicians, working for the corporations, continued the policy of creating realistic phantoms and legal hobgoblins for the purpose of befogging the public mind and confusing honest officials, in order that the result of preventing the parkways and

172

securing the franchises might obtain. How the effort was made to use both the press, and even forged postal card ballots to accomplish these ends. How such representative organizations as the New England Society, the Woman's Club, the Road Horse Association, and other civic and good government associations joined the parkway forces and entered into the fray, where they remained to the finish.

A volume might also be written on the action of certain officials and the majority members in the Board of Freeholders, and of the municipal authorities in East Orange and Orange, who for years were seemingly so anxious to serve "the organization" (alias, in this instance, the corporations), that their official acts resembled those of toy officials and toy boards, where each, in time of emergency, sprang to rescue the situation for their superiors, and against the parkways and their constituents, as moves a jumping-jack when the strings are pulled by the man in power behind the scenes.

A chapter might also be of interest accurately describing the shifting of position of some of these officials; first upon the one side, and then upon the other of the same identical question, when their opinions and services were needed to comply with the needs and exigencies of the corporations as from time to time these requirements developed.

TOPICS OF GENERAL INTEREST.

Much might also be written of the changed attitude of the Park Commission, clothed as it was, and is, by its charter, with all authority and full power, from its original position of active interest toward securing the two principal parkways for a time after their announcement in November, 1896, to a somnambulistic condition of non-activity and seeming impotence, and an apparent indifference as to what became of its own plans, and as to whether the board should secure the parkways as it had planned, and had repeatedly promised the public, or should give them over, through the assistance later of the commission's own counsel, to the corporations for private uses.

Then, too, an extended account of the evolution of the parkway question into the agitation for limited franchises, which has since become such a live State issue, would fill much space: How the persistent determination of the traction companies' managers to defeat the parkway plans, and, regardless of consequences, secure the long-sought franchises, led to an investigation as to the reasons why the men responsible, who were accredited with having some public spirit in other matters, were on this subject deaf and blind to all appeals; how, when the indisputable facts were ascertained and recognized by the public as to "the millions" literally "in" such franchises, there was at once a response and popular uprising that has already found expression in the platforms of both the leading political parties—an uprising followed, as since, by the widespread popular demand for improved utility franchise conditions by the people: And how the majority of the Legislature of 1905, under the direction of the "corporation leader" of the House, juggled with this franchise legislation.

These might all be topics worthy of full description, and perhaps of interest, to the readers of this history of the parks. Space, however, does not permit. Nor is it intended that this history of the Essex County parks will do more than give a consistent, continuous, and truthful account of the more important facts, which record shall mirror the events of the past as they have occurred, and possibly throw some light on the situation of park affairs that may be helpful in the solution of this great problem for the present or for the future.

The general plan for the parkways, as agreed upon by the first Park Commission in 1894-5, was outlined with three distinct and objective points in view:

First—Convenience and accessibility to the great majority of the people of the county.

Second—Economy in the use of Park and Central avenues, inasmuch as these were the two parallel and broad

avenues, between the proposed larger parks, well adapted
for parkway purposes, and already laid out and constructed
at county expense; and

Third—Availability. As these parkways, with Park avenue on the north and Central avenue on the south of the
populous portions of the county between the Passaic River
and the Orange Mountain would, with the Branch Brook
Park on the east and the mountain parkway and parks on
the crest of the first mountain, constitute a compact, and,
to that extent, complete "park system" in the heart of the
county, readily and directly reached from any of the four
sides of the elongated square of parks and parkways that
would be thus formed.

AN IMPORTANT PARKWAY.

In order to utilize the more accessible and important
of these parkways, Central Avenue—important as being
by far the most convenient to the people of both Newark
and the Oranges—and to avoid the expense of new and
costly construction, or the removal of the railway tracks
then on the avenue in Newark, as far as the East Orange
line, the plan from the southern division of the Branch
Brook Park included the use of Sussex and Ninth avenues and Grove street, or Sixteenth street, for the direct
connection with the park as the eastern terminus, and a
direct extension by a zig-zag, easy-grade Swiss road up
the mountain to the mountain parkway, for the western
park connection of the system.

The advisability and practicability of this method of
establishing a convenient and economical county park system—one that could be promptly and at comparatively
small cost carried out, and at the same time constitute the
basic framework for the future park and parkway development within the county—strongly appealed to the members of the first commission. I am not aware that any
doubt ever existed as to the practical execution of the plan
on the lines indicated. For years the steep grades and "old-
fashioned" straight up and down roads of the Orange

Mountain had acted as a barrier to the growing population of the whole county below the easterly slope. The construction of the parkway of sufficient width to permit of the easiest grades, to practically overcome this barrier, would, it was believed, be much appreciated by the people, make the mountain section of the Central parkway a novel and attractive feature, and tend to open up the whole mountain section from the object lesson such a piece of parkway construction would furnish. Then, too, the crest boulevard or parkway, it was intended, should extend from Bloomfield avenue on the north, to possibly South Orange avenue or the end of the Mountain at Millburn on the south, and would, it was thought, provide a never-ending source of beautiful views and appreciable enjoyment to the people indefinitely, and constitute one of the most attractive and unique features of mountain parkway development in the country.

The first commission also contemplated, as a part of the general plan of the parkways, the connecting links in any future chain of parks. As the growth of population and financial resource of the county developed, the park experts recommended, and the commission then favorably considered, the future enlargement of their plan, so as to include, if possible, a parkway from a connection with the Newark park along the Passaic River road or via Fredonia avenue, north of Branch Brook, directly connecting with the Second River, thence by the most available route or routes, through Belleville, Bloomfield and Montclair, thus connecting again with the mountain crest parkway on the north.

Connecting lines were also favorably considered from the Second River near the Soho Railway station, to the Third River, a most beautiful section; and thence through Bloomfield, Montclair and the mountain, through territory still further north. In the southern part of the county it was thought in time a parkway should be laid out, extending from the southern or extreme southwestern portion of Newark, through Clinton, Irvington, near Vailsburgh,

South Orange to the foot of Bear lane at the Ridgewood road, and thence to the South Mountain reservation as a western terminus, and with the mountain crest parkway there.

While these designs for the future parkways were informally approved by the first commission, the whole subject was tentatively considered with the view that the future, and the future alone, could determine what portion of the extensive plans should be finally adopted, and indicate the opportune time for carrying them out.

FOR A PARK AND PARKWAY SYSTEM.

What the commission of 1894 did, however, intend should materialize, and be put into practical form at the earliest possible date, was the plan for the parks and the parkways, as outlined—"a system of parks in its entirety," as promised in the commission's formal report in 1895, already referred to. It was for this purpose that the liberal charter for the second commission was prepared; and had all the members of the first commission in 1895 been reappointed on that board, and the personnel and policy of the commission remained unchanged, I have now no more doubt that these plans would have been carried out and promises fulfilled, than I have of any future event which is considered a certainty, yet not having transpired.

What did occur regarding the policy of the first commission as to the parks has been indicated in the preceding chapters. What results, in turn, followed regarding the parkways, I shall endeavor in this and succeeding chapters to correctly but briefly state.

As the second commission, immediately after completing its organization, proceeded vigorously with the selection of park sites to the exclusion of any consideration of plans for a park system as a whole, the question of parkways was hardly broached for months. Indeed, under the local or piecemeal sectional policy of locating parks, why should it be?

In the discussions, however, favoring the reverse policy, the parkway subject was occasionally mentioned; but it was not until the summer of 1896, after the commission had been in existence more than a year, that the question came up officially and directly before the board. At the meeting, June 4, Commissioner Shepard brought up the East Orange boulevard, or parkway project. A delegation from East Orange had appeared on December 19 previous, and urged that a local park or "speedway" be laid out within the limits of that city. No action was then taken.

August 25, 1896, I wrote Commissioner Peck that, compared with the natural reservations of the (Massachusetts) Metropolitan Park system, "We have still greater opportunities in Essex. A crest boulevard or parkway, as originally suggested by Mr. Haskell, with the mountain acquirements already outlined, will give a feature of mountain park attractions not excelled, if equaled, in any other large parkway system so accessible to a great center of population."

On October 19 Commissioner Meeker introduced the resolution which the parkway-avenue controversy has since made historic. All the commissioners not being present, the resolution was entered upon the minutes for future action. On November 12 following, at a meeting held at Commissioner Murphy's residence, the resolution was seconded by Mr. Shepard, and was then, by unanimous vote, passed. It was as follows:

"Whereas, It appears to the Park Commission to be desirable that the avenues hereinafter named should be under the control of the commission as part of the system of parks and parkways,

"Resolved, That the counsel be directed to obtain, if possible, from the Board of Chosen Freeholders of the county of Essex a transfer of the care, custody and control of the avenues as hereinafter designated, to the Essex County Park Commission; as also from the other municipal corporations in the county a transfer of the same, so far as may be necessary, under the statute. The avenues now desired are as follows: Park avenue in Newark, East Orange, Orange and West Orange; Central avenue in East Orange, Orange and West Orange; South Orange avenue, from its intersection with Ridgewood avenue, westerly to Cherry lane."

It was also agreed that a copy of the resolution "should be transmitted to the Board of Chosen Freeholders, and to each of the municipal governing bodies directly interested, viz.: East Orange, Orange, West Orange and South Orange."

CORPORATION CONTROL.

At this time the parkway question, as applied to Park and Central avenues, had been well considered. The necessity of using both avenues for parkways, if any creditable park system should be established, was recognized and so stated by each of the commissioners. The action was taken after mature deliberation; and, as already indicated, was in entire accord with the recommendations of all the park experts and the recorded action of the first commission on that subject. Nor was there any reason to then doubt what the attitude of the traction company's managers would be. The matter had been under public discussion for some time. Petitions from Orange and East Orange to the Park Board, as already quoted, had favored early action to secure these parkways.

The trolley management had laid lines to counteract any such result. James B. Dill had been employed. The influences were actively at work. Within thirty days after the introduction in the Park Board of the parkway resolution as above, viz., November 9, 1896, application was made to the East Orange Township Committee by the Consolidated Traction Company for a railway franchise on Central avenue. This was the picket gun of a battle that was raged with unceasing vigor and aggressiveness for eight years. The firing became general and soon extended all along the line. Both sides were in a measure prepared.

The Park Commission had the law and public opinion in its favor. The traction company, grown greedy and arrogant from former franchise spoil, had the power of concentrated wealth, and the party machine, with the resource and influence of a domineering party boss to do its bidding. For years the corporate interest, then demanding the sacrifice of the parkway for the coveted franchise, had had full sway. The old Essex County Road Board, before it was abolished years previous by a reform Republican Legislature, was their willing tool. The succeeding Board of Freeholders, in control of the county roads, although riding into power on the popular wave which in 1893 and 1894 engulfed the race-track, coal-combine, corporation-ridden State-and-County-Democracy was equally subservient. From those unsavory legislative days of 1890, '92 and '93, the street railway companies had readily passed their own bills, both at Trenton and in Essex County, as they desired, and in their own way. The law permitting a traction company to practically pre-empt a street or avenue by merely filing a map and certificate of intention with the Secretary of State, and the payment of a small fee, had, prior to 1896, been availed of, and both Park and Central avenues were "on the map" of the traction company's routes as prescribed.

The Storrs bill of 1894 was intended to curb this hydra-headed giant of financial and political power by requiring the filing of consents of the owners of a majority of the street frontage before any road could be constructed under this "pre-emption law." As introduced, the bill exempted all non-taxable property from consideration in the matter of these consents. But, under this clause, the Cemetery of the Holy Sepulchre property, with its 966 feet of frontage in East Orange, would have prevented the company from procuring the necessary "consents" for appropriating Central avenue there, so the "reform" Legislature followed the example of its predecessors by amending the bill and striking out the objectionable clause as the corporations desired.

TRACTION COMPANY'S FRANCHISE.

The change in control of the county avenues from the
Essex Road Board to the Board of Freeholders was, as regards the manipulation by the corporations, a change in
name and party shadow only. The substance of corporate
dictation remained the same. In October, 1894, the Freeholders granted to the Consolidated Traction Company a
perpetual blanket franchise for Park avenue in Newark,
East Orange, and Orange, Bloomfield avenue, and Frelinghuysen avenue. The Call, in its next issue, characterized
this action as completing "the surrender of the Road Board
highways to the street railroads." The prodigal liberality
of that "surrender" to the traction company of that most
valuable grant of public property was, and is, amazing.
The scheme was defeated on a technicality in the courts the
same year, 1894.

In like manner, the East Orange Township Committee
had, on May 1, 1891, given the Rapid Transit Street
Railway Company an equally favorable perpetual franchise for Central avenue from the Newark terminus
to the Orange line. This was before the company's
lines were constructed in Newark; hence, prior to
the leasing of that short line to the Consolidated Traction
Company, as was afterward done, at a clear profit to the
promoters and owners of "a round million of dollars." The
Rapid Transit finances were not then—1891—in very flush
condition. It was largely a paper company, organized to
build and equip the road from the sale of bonds, and without the investment of much money in promotion or construction. The company was advised that the franchise
could be extended, or a new franchise had "at any time,"
in East Orange, and Thomas Nevins promised the same
result in Orange. The company for once failed to recognize the uncertainty of (franchise) human events, or to
appreciate "a good thing when they had it," and the franchise was, therefore, allowed to lapse, and the rails, which

had been distributed as far as Harrison street, were afterward removed from the avenue.

Locally the party organization in East Orange in 1896
was yet so overwhelmingly on the Republican side that
little doubt as to the authorities again lining up on the
franchise-granting corporation side was entertained by the
traction people or their attorney there. And they were
right. After exhaustive public hearings by the Township
Committee on November 30, and at three public meetings
in Commonwealth Hall in December, 1896, when the whole
situation as to the needed parkways had been fully outlined by many representative citizens, and in a way explained by the Park Commission, the new ordinance franchise for a railroad on Central avenue was passed on first
reading January 18, 1897. In the meantime, at the meeting of the previous week, January 11, the request of the
Park Commission for the transfer of the avenues had been,
by unanimous vote, declined. This declination was based,
as was then stated, upon "the reticence of the commissioners as to what they proposed doing with the avenues
if they secured them." Whatever the cause, when the railroad franchise was passed the town woke up.

The awakening had been accelerated by the methods employed by the traction company. The property owners'
consents filed with the authorities, were found to be those
obtained for the Rapid Transit Company several years before; and, owing to the favorable sentiment for the parkways, new consents were unobtainable—owners of two-
thirds of the feet frontage, and of three-fourths of the
property value on the avenue, having petitioned for the
parkway.

The morning after one of the public meetings, Counsel
J. B. Dill stated that "a resolution would be passed by
the Park Board granting the trolley people, whom he represented, a franchise for Central avenue, as soon as the
avenue came in possession of that board."

Not long afterward Rev. H. P. Fleming, of St. John's
parish, Orange, informed me that a well-known lawyer,

living in East Orange, had come to talk with him about the parkways, and had said, during the conversation, that, should the Park Commissioners be given control of Central and Park avenues, they would "have gates put up so as to keep the poor people out," when they thought it advisable or desired to do so.

These specious and misleading statements were quite in keeping with methods which were rapidly arousing an adverse public sentiment. New consents were finally secured and filed by the traction company, February 7, 1897.

MANY MEETINGS HELD.

The comments and rumors current did not tend to smooth the fighting ground of the traction contingent. There had been lively discussion and some warm words at the three well-attended meetings of the Township Committee, December 8, 14, and 21, held in Commonwealth Hall, as also at the citizens' meeting in the athletic club rooms, January 26. At these meetings the parkway claims were well presented. The friends of the parkways had not been idle. Committees having the subject in charge had sent out appeals. Meetings were held, and Commissioner's Shepard's co-operation invited. In January, 1897, after Orange had declined to make the transfer, he wrote, unofficially, "as a citizen," expressing "regret that the Town Committee should take abrupt and final action concerning the request of the Park Commission for the care of the avenues," adding:

"The commission made this request, believing it was for the benefit of every citizen of the county that it should be granted, and supported in this view by a written communication signed by a large number of the citizens of East Orange.

"If the Town Committee declines to co-operate, in all reasonable ways, with the Park Commission, it will prevent many things being done which will beautify the town and add greatly to the pleasure of living in it. That residence or business streets can be made attractive as parkways is proved in many cities, notably in Chicago, Detroit and Buffalo, where some of the finest streets are in the care of the park boards, and where there is no interruption at all of the necessities of daily life."

At the Township Committee meeting of December 14, 1896, I was present, and in response to an inquiry, stated the position of the commission as then agreed upon regarding the parkways. Counsel Munn also elucidated some of the points as to the intended treatment of the avenues, should the transfer be effected, "the status of the avenues to remain practically unchanged, but with parkway embellishments, footpaths, bicycle ways and bridle-paths added."

But, as the town was awakened, the franchise-acquiring forces were also active, and the trolley ordinance made steady progress. At the regular January meeting of the Township Committee in 1897, with David Young and Counsel Dill representing the traction company, various amendments to the ordinance were agreed to. As the popular tide for the parkways was rapidly rising, Mr. Dill stated to the committee that "the company was willing to agree that the avenue should be considered first as a parkway, and secondly as a trolley route, and, in the event of the avenue's being widened the traction company to be considered as a tenant, to pay one-third the cost, and one-third the cost of any other necessary improvements."

THE POWER OF PUBLIC OPINION.

The leverage which, in this country and under our form of government, will invariably call to an accounting and reverse the action of any legislative body—the power of public opinion—was now being actively focalized. At the very time the traction company's counsel and the members of the Township Committee were "fixing up" the trolley ordinance so as to make it satisfactory to all parties, a call was being sent out for a massmeeting in Commonwealth Hall for the evening of February 7. That call was signed by more than one hundred and twenty of the most representative citizens of East Orange, regardless of party or other local affiliations. The object of the meeting, the call stated, was to secure "intimate co-operation with the Essex County Park Commission, to the end that Park and Central avenues be placed in their charge as parkways, and the construction of the projected north and south boulevard be insured." Henry H. Hall acted as chairman, with a list of thirty or more vice-presidents.

The speeches by Messrs. H. H. Hall, A. P. Boller, H. G. Atwater, G. R. Howe, G. S. Hulbert, W. H. Baker, G. F. Seward and Hamilton Wallis were dignified, forceful and to the point. A letter from Mr. Shepard was read, in which he stated: "If Central and Park avenues cannot be included in the park system, then new east and west parkways could not be constructed through East Orange, because of the great cost of the land. This would compel their construction through cheaper vacant land at the north and south of East Orange."

The hall was filled. Enthusiasm prevailed. The effect of the meeting was instantaneous. The members of the Township Committee who had so readily declined the park commission's application but three or four weeks before, and were seemingly so willing to pass the traction company's ordinance for one of the avenues, soon saw new light. The proceedings of the meeting, with quotations from the Park Commission's reports, and the official map showing the avenue parkways for connecting the mountain and Newark parks, was printed in pamphlet form and generally distributed.

On February 15, 1897, the commission received a request from the Township Committee for "a conference as to the proposed parkways." This was held February 26.

In the meanwhile the reader may wish to know what had been going on in the Park Board rooms. There was nearly as much activity over the question there as in East Orange. When the traction company showed its hands—

or at least one hand—in November, 1896, differences at
once arose as to the attitude of the commission, and what
position should be indicated to the East Orange authorities and the public.

Commissioners Shepard and Murphy were disposed to
deal very lightly with the subject, and to appear non-committal as to any very clearly defined position on the real
issue, which all recognized was whether we should stand
independently and firmly for the parkways, or climb the
neutral fence, trusting the settlement to the localities where
the contest with the traction interests was actively in progress. Commissioner Meeker and myself favored a different policy. It was my conviction and contention that
we should clearly and explicitly define our position, as a
duty both to our charter and the people of the whole county,
which duty I believed transcended any and all local interests. Commissioner Peck was, so far as we could discover,
already on neutral ground. On November 12, before the
adoption of the resolution above quoted, requesting the
avenues' transfer, I proposed a substitute preamble and
resolution on the lines of my conviction just mentioned.
I believed a more explicit statement from the commission
to the freeholders and governing boards, alike due them
and desirable. May 15 previous (1896), in writing Commissioner Murphy regarding the general policy of the parkways, and regarding Elizabeth avenue, where the same
parkway-trolley question was involved, I said: "The matter of parkway approaches to our larger county parks is
so vitally important I believe we should now take the
initiative and clearly define our position to the local governing bodies and to the public. Having accepted the
trust to locate, acquire, and develop the parks, it appears
just as incumbent that we take the leadership in defining
the approaches. Without such approaches and connective
parkways from the centers of population, the county park
system will be most defective and always open to criticism."

After referring to the plans of the first commission, that
"new parkway construction in the built-up portions of the

county would be prohibitory, even were our appropriation double what it is," I added:

"The situation in the Newark Board of Works brings this question to the fore, whether we will or no. We have either to meet it, or evade it. A hesitating policy will, I believe, place our board in a secondary position, alike objectionable and disadvantageous. An uncertain position before the Newark local board, or elsewhere, will neither command respect for our opinions nor help public confidence in our official action.

"For these reasons I am in favor of prompt and decisive action on this question. I would make such action broad, comprehensive, yet definite and concise.

"Such a resolution as the form enclosed, will settle the question as to the attitude of our board on a very important matter, in which the people of the whole county are interested. The people have confidence in the commission; they are anticipating a creditable system of parks and parkways, and will stand by the commission if we show by our acts that we are competent to execute the trust in laying out the park system."

A PUBLIC DEMAND FOR INFORMATION.

When I ascertained the actual situation in East Orange, in December, 1896, I took up the matter again, both at the Park Board meetings and personally with my colleagues. January 2, 1897, I wrote each of the members as follows: "The matters referred to in the Stanley letter are so direct and important that our reply, it seems to me, should be equally explicit, if we are to retain the confidence of our friends and the public generally in dealing with the questions under consideration. The form of letter suggested by Mr. Munn will not, in my judgment, answer the inquiries or allay the agitation in the public mind on the matters referred to."

On January 16, 1897, I again wrote Mr. Murphy: "The governing bodies, press and public throughout the Oranges all appear to demand a clearer statement as to the atti-

tude of the Park Commission on the points raised in the
Stanley letter.

"It has been, as you know, my conviction from the first,
as stated at the meetings and as indicated in my letters
to you and to my colleagues, that we should meet these
important public questions promptly, fully and explicitly;
and it is still my firm conviction that this is our only
course if we are to avoid unjust suspicion and prejudice,
and retain the confidence of the public—so vital to the
present and future welfare of a great public undertaking."

On January 26 I wrote Commissioner Shepard: "It
seems to me that every day's delay in our defining clearly
to the public the relations between the Park Commission
and the local boards is resulting in serious detriment to
the commission." And on February 10, "I am impressed
that the action of the Township Committee last evening
throws upon us an additional burden of responsibility as
to our position toward that committee and the public on
the matters we have recently been considering.

"If our action in asking for the transfer of the avenues
for parkways was right, should we not openly so state to our
Township Committee friends our position on all the questions involved, as a matter of mutual interest affecting the
same constituency? It seems to me this cours is now incumbent; indeed, can we take any other?"

Again, March 6, 1897, I wrote Mr. Shepard: "I feel
very anxious about the affairs of the commission, both as
to our financial situation compared with the commitments
and needs of the department; and also as to the persistent
effort that is being made to use the commission by acqui-
escence in carrying out the schemes of the traction speculators and their allied politicians to the injury of the park
system. The articles in the Newark papers of to-day, while
no doubt inspired by the same influences that have all
along been creating distrust and injury to the commission,
yet assume a degree of assurance which makes it appear as
though the commission were favorable to the sacrifice of
one of the parkways at the behest of the trolley interests."

The Stanley letter, so-called, was received by the commission December 24, 1896. It was a long official letter from Edward O. Stanley, then chairman of the Committee on Parks of the East Orange Township Committee. The letter asked many questions, but bore the imprint of sincerity and desire on the part of the writer, to have brushed aside the cobwebs of misapprehension which then existed in the minds of the committee and throughout East Orange as the outgrowth of the seeds of prejudice poison that had been scattered by the traction company's representatives there against the parkways and the Park Commission, since the latter had openly favored the avenues for another purpose than their surrender for private uses.

The committee wished to know how the commission proposed to improve the avenues; whether, should the transfer be made, a trolley line should be run there; whether openings could be made by the township authorities for repairing gas mains, water pipes, etc., and made the request for a section plan of the avenues as they would appear when beautified and completed by the commission.

In the Park Board these questions precipitated the subject for a reply. It was evident that the platitudinous generalities in the previous communications from the commission were not sufficient to enable the parkway advocates to overcome the counter claims and assertions of the opposing corporation agents and representatives.

LANDSCAPE ARCHITECTS' AND ENGINEERS' REPORT.

On December 31, 1896, the landscape architects and engineers of the department made a report strongly reiterating their former "recommendations for extending Central avenue to connect with the larger mountain reservation," adding, "we have indicated upon the map an extension of this avenue from its present terminus at the Valley road to a point in Northfield avenue, and thence through Northfield avenue to the South Mountain Reservation. This extension makes use of a depression in the mountain slope which will enable a parkway to be constructed upon an easy grade and will give a desirable and useful approach to the mountain."

This report was in entire accord with the former reports of all the park-making specialists of both the first and second commissions. Frederick Law Olmsted who, prior to his retirement in 1897, and death in 1903, was accredited one of the greatest public park specialists known, had, in his firm's report of January, 1895, referred to Central and Park avenues as follows:

"Essex County is already provided with streets generally called avenues, that are essentially parkways of a formal character leading to the foot of Orange Mountain. To make them all that is desirable for your purpose it is only necessary that suitable building lines should be established on their borders; that roads should extend from them on easy grades up the mountain, and that certain improvements of detail should be made in them"—a concise and axiomatic statement, the correctness of which, as applied to the avenue-parkway situation in Essex County, no one has ever attempted to refute or even question.

At the Park Board meetings January 7 and 11, 1897, the reply to Chairman Stanley's letter was under consideration. Mr. Shepard presented and moved the adoption of a draft of letter in reply, which it was understood had been formulated or suggested by Counsel Munn. It contained these statements:

"As the larger parks must be outside of thickly settled districts, the commission favors every reasonable plan for reaching these, in parkways or otherwise, quickly and at the lowest cost, and without interference with the business or occupation of citizens.

"They recognize the fact that electricity is the coming power for the transportation of people in cities and suburban places. They would like to see methods in operation by which people could leave Newark and reach the Orange Mountain parks in fifteen minutes, and at a cost of three or not exceeding five cents. These same methods would, of course, enable people living in the country to reach their business or employment in Newark day by day in the same short time and at the same low cost."

As these were almost the identical "arguments" that were then being used to secure a franchise by the traction company's representatives in East Orange, and as used before the freeholders, two years before, for the same purpose, and as it seemed as though any person in reading such a statement might have—as of some of the utterances on the same subject by the commission later—some doubt as to whether the commission really wanted the parkways, in preference to having the trolley on the avenues, there was immediate objection. Even Commissioner Murphy thought the statement needed modification. As I was decided that such a reply would increase the feeling of indefinite uncertainty as to the attitude of the commission, rather than alleviate it, I there wrote out and presented the following:

"Resolved, That a full and explanatory statement of the position of this board relative to the care, custody, and control of Central and Park avenues be transmitted to the governing bodies directly interested."

Commissioners Murphy and Shepard at once objected to the resolution. Finally, after a lengthy informal discussion, the following reply, as a compromise answer to the Stanley committee's inquiries, was agreed upon, and it was promptly sent to Chairman Stanley.

REPLY TO STANLEY COMMITTEE.

"The object of the Park Commission in asking for the care, custody, and control of Central and Park avenues was to incorporate them in a system of public parks, and avoid the necessity of creating new and costly parkways to reach the mountain parks. They recognize the fact that these avenues are already great public thoroughfares, and they do not propose to interfere with the existing rights of property owners and municipal governments, but to put the avenues on a more decided parkway footing than can be done as long as they may be outside of the

control of the Park Commission. They would prefer that
rapid transit ways and parkways should be kept separate,
but they will not oppose the wish of the majority of the
property owners and municipal governments in this matter. If rapid transit tracks are to be put on Central avenue, the question should be decided at once; but it is not
the part of the Park Commission to make this decision
under existing conditions. It is, however, in our opinion,
inconsistent to attempt to operate a trolley road on a parkway only one hundred feet wide.

"In response to the request for section plan and detail,
it seems to be unnecessary for the Park Commission to
take up that question until the local governing body de-
cides the main proposition. If these avenues are not to
become parkways, further details will not be required."

The effect of this communication was distinctly unfavorable. The resulting action of the Township Committee
was, as already stated, a prompt declination of the commission's request. Some of the leading papers were outspoken in their criticism of the Park Board's position.
The day following, January 12, 1897, the Newark News,
under an editorial caption, "The Reticent Park Board,"
in referring to the Stanley letter and the commission's
reply, said:

"These were fair and reasonable questions. They were
not answered; they were even treated with scant courtesy
by the sending of a reply that the commissioners' proposed to construct parkways. The reasons for secrecy which
existed in regard to the purchase of lands and locations
of parks certainly do not apply to the extension or improvement of public highways." And again, February 4, "That
the application of the Park Commission was refused was
partly due, no doubt, to the manner in which that body
chose to preserve its air of dignified silence."

These and similar expressions were in marked contrast
to the almost unanimous sentiment of the press favorable
to the avenues' transfer, when the plan and resolution of
the commission were made public the previous November.

An aroused public sentiment in East Orange was, however, doing its work. When the conference between the commission and the Township Committee as arranged for February 26, 1897, already alluded to, was held, it was apparent that something of a change had come over each board. The commissioners had a meeting an hour before the appointed time. All the members then recognized that something more was demanded than the previous glittering platitudes as to the parkways.

Commissioner Shepard was delegated to speak for the board, and did so. A formal statement was agreed upon. It answered directly most of the questions that had been asked by the committee. Sketches were shown of the prospective treatment of the parkways. There was to be no obstacle to the construction or repair by the local authorities of gas or water pipes. Sprinkling would be considered a part of the maintenance. The transfer "could not in any way interfere with vested rights," either of the property owners or of the municipality. The question as to trolley roads on the avenues "should be decided by the property owners and the municipal authorities before the proposed transfer," for, with the present width of the avenues, "it would not be expedient for the Park Commission to accept the care of the remaining part, with the attending expense, as it is too narrow to admit of parkway treatment, and the expense attending the care would not be a proper use of park funds." Willingness on the part of the commission "to do everything in its power to add to the existing attractions in East Orange" was expressed, and a general spirit of co-operation on the part of the board was extended.

WHOLE SITUATION GONE OVER.

The Township Committee conferees were also to all appearances in a friendly and receptive mood. The whole situation was quite fully gone over. The question of widening the avenues was adversely considered, owing to the prohibitory cost. The policeing and lighting matters were satisfactorily disposed of; likewise the details as to surface embellishment. And the opinion was expressed by the commission, that after the transfer "the trolley people would find it necessary to have the consent of the Park Commission, in addition to that of the municipality, the Board of Freeholders and the property owners, as now." Then Committeeman Crippen put this poser of a question: "Now, I want to ask if the Park Commission proposes to bring the trolley if it gets possession of the avenues?"

The reply must have been a surprise to some of those who had relied upon the statements and insinuations of the traction company's agents and attorneys, for Commissioner Shepard promptly declared that "the trolley had never even been considered."

Finally the understanding was reached that the town's disposal works would, if transferred to the commission, be accepted for a park, and that if the avenues were transferred, the commission would promptly proceed with the work of improving them into parkways. The conference was then closed.

When the Township Committee members met the commission face to face, and ascertained that there was no intention of running away with the avenues, or of proceeding at once to place trolleys upon them, or of "keeping out the poor people" by the closed gates process; then there was, with the irresistible public sentiment of their East Orange constituents behind the transfer movement, no longer any delay or question as to the result. On March 15, 1897, the Township Committee, by a unanimous vote, passed the ordinance, as prepared by the Park Committee, transferring both Park and Central avenues in East Orange to the Park Commission for parkways, and, by the same vote at the same meeting, the "trolley ordinance" for Central avenue, then on second reading, was killed. At another conference soon afterward between the commission and the Township Committee all the details of transfer were finally agreed upon.

The popular verdict had won, and the curtain had been

rung down on the first act in this great play of the corporations against the people.

While the contest was being waged, one of the local committees, in order to test the sentiment of all the people of East Orange, obtained, through a return postal card vote, an expression on the question, which declared a preference, by a majority of more than three to one, in favor of the parkway for Central avenue to the exclusion of the trolley there, by a direct vote of more than one-half of the entire electorate of the township.

Soon after the transfer ordinance was passed the Park Commission, on April 20, 1897, on receipt of a certified copy of the ordinance, formally accepted the avenues as transferred. The matter was thus considered closed by the people, who had confidence in the commission, excepting, perhaps, all of those who knew of the determination and resource of the traction company, and recognized that the transfer proposition had still to run the gauntlet of both the Board of Freeholders and the city authorities of Orange, in both of which boards the corporation interests were, as was then currently understood, well entrenched.

Again the scene of activity had shifted—not now to the court, nor for the parks, but to destroy the contemplated parkways, and to secure, if possible, regardless of cost or effort, another almost priceless county road franchise.

CHAPTER XIII.

As an army, in taking every possible advantage of its opponent, uses pickets, scouts and spies in its preliminary operations; so a great and opulent corporation, bent upon securing from the public valuable franchises, not infrequently uses cunning attorneys and not over-scrupulous politicians, both in and out of office; and, by liberal contributions to both political parties, secures the service of the party boss; who, prior to the public awakening for better civic conditions in November, 1905, and through the apathy of good citizens generally, had become such a legislative factor in State, county and local affairs.

While this kind of self-interest, masquerading under the name of any party, constitutes a condition which is neither Republican, Democratic, Populistic nor Socialistic, but is essentially oligarchic—the poison germ, which soon forms the rotten core in any free government; yet this is, nevertheless, a situation that must continue to be recognized and appreciated by the people, if an adequate remedy is to be applied.

At the time the incidents related in the preceding chapter were formulating, in December, 1896, the traction company made application also for a Central avenue franchise in Orange. In the southern part of the city, as in East Orange, there was a contingent of the population which needed, and honestly favored, better east and west transit facilities to and from Newark. The large majority of the people earnestly and heartily favored the parkways and the locations of the lines of trolley extension in streets south of, and parallel with, Central avenue, where the facilities were needed. The corporate interests and influences referred to determined that the result should be otherwise.

The application to the Orange Common Council from the Park Commission for the transfer of the avenue was, on its receipt, promptly referred to the Street Committee. The chairman was Henry Stetson, who was one of the few men in Orange who had, with Mayor Seymour and others in Newark, strongly objected from the first to an appointive commission. "It's all wrong," Mr. Stetson said to me, when the plans for the first Park Commission were under way. He then assured me, as afterward, that he opposed that plan on principle. That he was emphatic in his objections no one who knew him, I think, had any reason to doubt. His views were not in the least modified when, in 1895, the second commission was appointed and the control of that board and its large appropriation was made politically Republican. Like the Massachusetts Democrat in that far-famed home of Republicanism during the exciting 1860-65 war times, he was thereafter, in parkway matters, unceasingly, and it seemed almost intuitively, "agin" the prevailing order of things.

The possession of the two ordinances, in January, 1897, apparently gave Mr. Stetson and his followers their opportunity. They were not slow in availing themselves of it. Theretofore the rule of procedure in the City Council had been that when the owners of a majority frontage on an avenue or street petitioned for an improvement, unless some legal or financial obstacle were in the way, the request would be granted. There had then just been presented to the Mayor and City Council petitions from the property owners on both avenues in favor of the parkways and "against the granting of any and all franchises on Central avenue for any purpose whatever, as such action on your part would embarrass the action of the Park Commission."

This petition for Central avenue bore the signature of

every resident on the avenue in Orange, and represented a frontage ownership of 8,106, out of a total of 9,213 feet. The Park avenue petition was still nearer unanimous of all the property owners there. All of the local civic organizations, without a dissenting vote, took the same position. The local papers were outspoken and emphatic on similar lines.

URGED TO TAKE ACTION.

The plans of the Park Commission, with the official maps showing the location of the two Avenue parkways, were before the public. During the first six months of 1897 constant appeals were made to the City Council and to the members there to pass the transfer ordinance. Some of the council members joined in the request that the transfer ordinance, without further delay, be favorably reported. But it was "in committee," and there it was held, until at the council meeting, July 12, 1897, it was reported— and then adversely. The report was a rambling presentment, criticizing the Park Commission; claiming the committee could not obtain from that board information it desired and had sought at a conference held at the commission's rooms a short time before; that "Orange had not been liberally treated" in the commission's plans; and was unfriendly in tone throughout. The principal excuse, as given in the report, was that the committee had in reality not been able to procure satisfactory replies from the commission. This view was apparently coincided in by some of the papers.

On June 20, 1897, when the conference with the commission alluded to was reported, the Newark Call made this editorial comment: "The Essex County Park Commission still maintains a discreet silence as to its intentions in regard to Central avenue, and all the attempts of the different municipalities to find out the treatment the avenue is to receive are met with glittering generalities."

Most of the county papers took the other view, and the Orange papers were up in arms directly the action of the

City Council was known. The Newark News editorial the day following on "The Inconsistency of the Orange Council" said: "It is difficult to understand, on any ground of public spirit or public policy, the refusal of the Orange City Council to assent to the transfer of Central and Park avenues to the care and control of the Park Commission," and, after answering at length the claims of the Street Committee, added: "It would be easy to show the clumsy inconsistency of the report and resolutions. It (the Street Committee) proclaims that it knows no good reason why those avenues should continue to be special wards of the county, and just below expresses its satisfaction with their maintenance at the general county expense by the freeholders."

The Orange Chronicle said that the opposition had been centered on Central avenue, "the latter being a possible plum for a trolley line"; adding, "Will some one who believes that the council did right please explain? The action was taken without a single word of open debate, and in the face of eloquent and able pleas by prominent citizens. In language, the report of the Street Committee is verbose, ambiguous, and involved in pessimistically impugning the Park Commission."

The Journal also commented at length upon the council's action, and said, among other things: "The Common Council has thus placed the city in a false and embarrassing position, which would be repudiated by its citizens if they had the opportunity to express themselves on the subject at the polls."

Counsel J. L. Munn, in a statement July 13, the day after the council's refusal to make the transfer, no doubt struck the keynote of the whole situation, from his standpoint, in saying, as reported in the News: "The root of the matter is that the trolley company desires a franchise on Central avenue, and there are many who favor it. Perhaps, under the circumstances, it would not be best to transfer Central avenue into a boulevard for pleasure vehicles or bicycles. But that is simply one phase of the question." Events, as they afterward transpired, duly emphasized this statement.

In December, 1897, through the active interest of leading citizens of Orange, in co-operation with some of the members of the Common Council who had become earnestly favorable to the passage of the transfer ordinance, the matter was again taken up. An effort was made to forestall and answer the objections that had been raised against the previous transfer ordinance. The opposition had become extremely solicitous (?) for fear the property owners in and adjacent to the avenues might be assessed for special benefits, although none of the property owners residing on or owning property there had made that objection. A clause was, therefore, inserted in the new ordinance, "that the Park Commission shall not institute proceedings that will result in the condemnation of rights of property owners in their land, or levy any assessment for any improvements made to the avenues." Thomas A. Davis was then the city counsel. He advised that the proviso was sufficiently clear and explicit. Thus it seemed to the average reader and those favorable to the parkways; and, at the Orange council meeting January 3, 1898, the new ordinance was passed by a unanimous vote of 16 to 0. But the anxiety of the opposition for the safety of the property owners from assessments was not appeased. A new flank movement was conceived. This is the way it was executed.

AN INTERESTING CONFERENCE.

At the Park Board meeting January 11, a communication was received from the Street Committee of the City Council advising that there was to be a meeting of the committee that same evening to consider the avenue transfer question. It was decided that Counsel Munn should attend. He was present. He was accompanied by Engineer Cole to meet the city conferees of the Street Committee, President Snyder of the council and Counsel Davis. The reader must draw his own inferences as to what occurred in that meeting, for the reports were then, as since, conflicting as to the facts. One of the city officials who was present at the conference stated for publication the next morning: "You can take this as inspired prophecy— that Central avenue will never be made a parkway, but the commissioners want it to turn over to the trolley companies for roads to the mountain parks; while Park avenue will be widened and the entire cost of making it a parkway will be borne by owners of abutting property, unless a decided and united stand is taken now by those interests, and the commissioners are compelled to take the public into their confidence and tell them what they intend doing."

This and similar public comments were looked upon unfavorably as regards the Park Commission. Intimations of bad faith were, by the doubting ones, freely expressed. The counsel and, by the statements accredited to him, the commission itself, were both placed on the defensive. Counsel Munn soon afterward made a lengthy report of the meeting to the commission.

The gist of it was that he had previously replied to the inquiries of Counsel T. A. Davis as to widening the avenues: First, that a transfer made under Section 18 of the park act did "not alter the status of such avenues as existing public highways"; second, did not confer upon the Essex County Park Commission the power to widen said avenues; or, third, the right to make assessments. That "no revolutionary subversion of these avenues has been thought possible by the Park Commission," but, "if at any future time it shall be deemed necessary or advisable to widen these avenues at any point or place, new and different proceedings will have to be instituted under the other powers of the park act, and the whole matter will then proceed as if this present contemplated action had not been taken."

The conference, the report stated, was of "a pleasant and agreeable character"; also stated that the ordinance pending before the Common Council "was unobjectionable in form, except for one clause therein"—the restrictive clause "not to institute proceedings at any time for the purpose of widening such avenues" or for "making any assessments," etc. This clause, the counsel reported he said to the committee, "was probably against public policy and void, and the Park Commission might decide not to accept the care, custody, and control of the avenues with such a provision inserted"; and further stated that he had advised that "there was no such reason for hasty action as to require a decision upon the question by the Orange Common Council at its next meeting."

The publication of this so-called report brought out a vigorous rejoinder of even greater length from Councilman Stetson, as published in the Call of January 30, 1898. In this reply, after reference to the erroneous "inference that the letter of Mr. Munn was perfectly lucid and clear in its replies to City Counsel Davis' letter of inquiries," Mr. Stetson contended that it "was not deemed so by a majority of the members of the Orange council"; that "it was not until the conference held on the eleventh instant that Mr. Munn gave information which might be deemed adequate"; that "Mr. Munn stated over and over again to the committee that the Park Commission had not the power to levy an assessment; but it did not follow from that that no assessment would be levied. The Park Commission can go to the courts and ask for the appointment of a commission to levy assessments. So you see the Park Commission really wouldn't levy assessments, but there is a way, all right, by which the assessments can, and doubtless would, be collected. Mr. Munn admitted this frankly, and he did not say that the Park Commission would not take that course."

The letter then reiterates the position of objection as from one "who voted to refuse the request" of the commission for the transfer of the avenue; adding, "I have not as yet seen any good reason for changing the opinion then held," and proceeds to again score a point unfavorable to an appointive commission.

Among the City Council members who at that time were

actively in favor of the avenue's transfer, was the president, Edward H. Snyder. On January 15, 1898, three days after the conference referred to, Mr. Snyder came to my office in New York and confirmed what Councilman Stetson afterward publicly stated, as above quoted. Mr. Snyder then made quite a full statement of what occurred on January 11, which was written out by my stenographer at the time. In that statement, now before me, is the following:

"Colonel Snyder says that Mr. Munn stated in the conference at the outset, that the ordinance would not be satisfactory to the Park Commission and that, if it was passed in its present form and thus accepted by the commission, he should advise going into court to have the restriction relative to levying assessments nullified. Stated further that assessments could not be levied unless the avenue was widened. Looking toward Mr. Stetson, he remarked that 'you want the trolley on Central avenue,' adding that if the avenues were transferred and not widened there ould be no trolley on Central avenue; but if they were widened, assessments could be levied and arrangements made for the trolley. Further stated that there was no hurry about the transfer; that the commission could not improve the avenues at present, and stated that the ordinance had better remain as it was for two or three months.

"Colonel Snyder says that he was greatly surprised at Munn's statements, and that after the conference Mr. Stetson said to him (Colonel Snyder) that he did not know what to make of what Munn had said.

"Colonel Snyder also said that he did not know how much I knew about what was going on, but that he was satisfied, and almost knew, that some scheme was going on with the Park Commission to get the trolley on Central avenue.

"He also stated that, at the close of the conference, Mr. Stetson asked him to repeat to Mayor Gill what took place at the conference, which he did, quoting the same statements as he has to me, and said that the Mayor thereupon appeared greatly surprised at Munn's position.

"Munn inquired how the question as to the avenues came to be brought up at this time—no one could answer."

STATEMENT CONFIRMED.

In attending the City Council meeting two days later, January 17, 1898, I asked Mr. Stetson regarding this conference, and told him the substance of Colonel Snyder's statement to me. He replied that the statement was correct; that Munn said "that, if the avenues were widened, the trolley could be arranged for, and we were given to understand that the commission favored a trolley on Central avenue," and that he (Stetson) thought "the commission wanted the avenue for the franchise." This conversation was brief, but Colonel Snyder had gone over the subject fully. His bearing was unassuming and earnest; his manner and conversation straightforward, and evidently sincere. The statements troubled me, and I knew meant trouble for the Park Commission; and the more from what had gone before.

After the contest over the parkways had begun in East Orange, in November, 1896, and during the early part of 1897, as described in the preceding chapter, a number of friends in East Orange, some of them neighbors of Counsel Munn, had come to me, or in conversation regarding the parkways had warned me to "look out for Munn," stating that they believed, regardless of whatever he might say or do before the Park Commission, that he secretly favored, and would work for, the trolley company "every chance he could get." My answer to these charges was in each instance in substance the same, viz.: "While thus far Munn's conduct as counsel had 'not been satisfactory,' I had not yet discovered any evidence that he was not carrying out the instructions of the commission regarding the parkways."

A CANCELLED CONSENT.

"Do you expect to catch a weasel asleep?" replied one who had spoken to me on the subject. "Do you think the counsel would go around with a brass band, and a traction placard on his back, if he were really doing this business?" said another. I admitted that no such expectations could be reasonably entertained; but these were not, under the circumstances, pleasant reflections. I was aware of Counsel Munn's action in revoking his former consent to the traction company, during the height of the excitement in East Orange, in January, 1897. His letter, canceling the consent for a railroad he had previously given for more than three hundred feet frontage on Central avenue, was an autograph letter as follows:

"To the Township Committee, Township of East Orange:
"If there is any attempt to use the consent given by me several years ago to the application on behalf of the Rapid Transit Company for a franchise for its street railway on Central avenue—as a consent to a new application or to any application for such purpose at this time by any organization, I hereby give notice of my protest against such use.

"And I hereby withdraw, revoke and annul any and all consents heretofore given by me, or by Mary P. Munn, whose sole heir at law I am, for the location or building of any street railway on Central avenue in East Orange.
"JOSEPH L. MUNN.
"January 9, 1897."

This revocation was, however, a year prior to the conference with the Street Committee in Orange, and to the "inspired prophecy" just quoted, and of the current rumors of Counsel Munn's real purpose in January, 1898. While my term as commissioner had expired in April, 1897, I had known much of what was going on in the Park Board rooms, and was forced to the conviction that the state-

ments and the constantly recurring reports and insinuations against the counsel demanded attention. That
the traction people were much encouraged by the
"Orange conference" was indicated by the formal application directly afterward, on January 19, 1898, of the
Consolidated Traction Company to the Board of Freeholders for a franchise and permission to locate tracks on Park
avenue and on Central avenue through Orange and East
Orange, and by a statement from Manager David Young
before the Ampere Improvement Association of Newark on
February 10 following.

A NEW APPLICATION.

After then explaining how "we came here, trying to get
Central avenue, but the people kicked us out, and wouldn't
have anything to do with us, but we are coming again some
of these days," Mr. Young made this prognosticating statement: "The way in which residents in this beautiful township are to reach their homes is to have the trolley on the
avenues, Park and Central, and then get off at the cross
streets and go to their homes. You cannot have a parkway on a one hundred-foot roadway. It is out of all
reason, never has been done, and never will be."

When it is remembered that it was on March 15, 1897,
less than eleven months previous, that the East Orange
authorities had, in response to the emphatic mandate of
public opinion, and without a dissenting vote, passed the
parkway ordinance and rejected the Consolidated Traction
Company's application, and that these statements were
made within thirty days after the parkways conference in
Orange, and the new application for the avenues above mentioned, the coincidence was indeed significant.

Whatever may have been the intention of the Park
Board's counsel and the opposition to the parkways, or,
perhaps, more correctly speaking, the forces working for the
trolley interests, the practical result of befuddling the whole
question, was, apparently to those favoring that course,
most gratifying. Some of the members of the Orange

Common Council at the time, stated that it had been the intention to pass the transfer ordinance on third and final reading at the meeting, February 7, 1898. Public sentiment and the press were as unitedly in favor of that action as had been the people in East Orange the year before. Excepting for the objection raised by the commission's own counsel and the local Orange objectors referred to, there was not a discordant note unfavorable to the parkways or to the action. Once the conference controversy became public, the conditions favorable to early and unanimous action by the City Council, as had obtained in January, were changed to those of uncertainty. The Newark papers elaborated on the points. "Abutting property to bear the cost of widening county roads;" "Orange residents up in arms against the scheme;" "Little probability that the Orange Common Council will agree to transfer Park and Central avenues," These were some of the heavy type captions of the articles giving an account of the Orange conference in the Newark papers of January 26, 1898.

PARK INTERESTS ENDANGERED.

Having an appreciation of these conditions, and not then being a member of the Park Board, I wrote the commission February 10, 1898: "The situation here is assuming such proportions in the undercurrents of public opinion that I feel it a duty I owe to the park enterprise, and to you as the present responsible representatives, to call your attention to the matter. The statements made by Counsel Munn to the Street Committee of the Common Council here at the conference on the eleventh ultimo, are likely to give rise to complications that may seriously endanger park interests;" and "the vital difficulty is the vantage ground given the opponents of the commission and of the park undertaking, from the alleged statements made by Mr. Munn at the conference. The presentment, coming as it did directly from him, as counsel to your board, is accepted by many as official and representing the majority of the commission.

"I believe the conviction is almost universally shared in by the public that it is not only the province, but quite within the limits of duty, for the counsel of a public board, to defend the charter creating it—not to attack or assail it, either as to what it contains or what it was clearly intended it should not contain.

"If the alleged statements are correct, the counsel of the commission came before the official representatives of the second city of the county, and gave those gentlemen,to understand confidentially—'not for the reporters'—that if the conditions (against widening the avenues and of assessment for benefits) are left in the ordinance in entire accord with the acknowledged limitations of the charter, and likewise in strict accord with what has repeatedly been announced as the definite plan and purpose of the commission, that such restriction might be deemed as 'against public policy and void,' and perhaps hereafter a court asked to nullify a condition which it was never intended should be other than restrictive, in so far as it applied to existing avenues or streets that might be transferred under the 18th section of the present park law;" that "this has placed the friends of the commission in all this portion of the county on the defensive, to explain, and, if not officially corrected, will be likely to unfavorably affect the additional park appropriation bill at the polls when the question is submitted to the electorate at the coming spring election."

Similar views were expressed personally and officially to the commissioners by others. On March 2, 1898, John D. Everett wrote Commissioner F. M. Shepard, and, after expressing the doubts in his own mind, referred to the parkway situation in these words: "There were, and are, no doubts in the minds of the good people of Orange since the conference of the Street Committee of the Orange Common Council with Mr. Munn and some one else representing the Park Commission on January 11 last.

"It is publicly reported and generally believed in Orange, by both Republicans and Democrats, that Mr. Munn stated to the Street Committee that the ordinance, which had passed one reading, was unsatisfactory to the Park Commission, and that if passed and accepted in its present form, he would advise the commission to go into court to have certain restrictions relative to assessment and widening nullified as contrary to public policy. That he turned to Mr. Stetson and said: 'You want a trolley on Central avenue, well, there can't be a trolley there without widening the avenue,. and we cannot widen the avenue without an Although under the resolution of the Park Commission of assessment.' "

November 12, 1896, requesting the transfer of the avenues, for parkways, it was specifically made the duty of "the counsel to obtain, if possible," such transfer from the freeholders and local governing bodies, no action on these and similar communications was taken by the commission. Inquiries and appeals were being continuously sent to ascertain just what the attitude of that board would be in view of the conflicting statements then current. Finally, at the Park Board meeting of March 4, 1898, a letter was received from Colonel E. H. Snyder, as president of the Orange City Council, asking the direct question as to the intention of the commission regarding the avenues. The following reply and authorized statement was the same day made public:

PARK COMMISSION'S REPLY.

"The Park Commission does not intend to widen Park or Central avenue in the city of Orange, and is advised that the transfer of the care, custody, and control of those avenues does not confer upon the commission the power to widen them. It follows, therefore, that the Park Commission cannot make assessment on abutting property."

To many of the active supporters of the park movement and those having confidence in the commissioners rather than in the confusing and contradictory statements to the contrary accredited their own counsel, this concise promise of intention was accepted as made in good faith and appeared to settle the question on the points indicated. To the opposition and all those under corporation influences favoring a railroad on one or both of the avenues, the statement had just the reverse effect. The experience in East Orange the year before was in many respects repeated. The method of Manager David Young and the tactics of Counsel James B. Dill there, in sowing the seed of doubt and suspicion as to the commission's intention, were again actively though quietly promulgated. The contention that Central avenue at least "would never be made a parkway" was continuously and with increasing aggressiveness repeated, notwithstanding the promises held out in the second annual report of the commission for 1897, issued early in 1898, and as quoted in Chapter IX. This report confirmed the official map made public early in 1897, indicating both avenues as parkways, by the statement that "a system of parkways has been determined upon which forms the final feature of park development." This was also acceptable to many as conclusive that the commission could be relied upon to defend its own plans, especially as in this same report, in asking for another appropriation of $1,500,-000, this statement (page 18 of the report) was made: "But for the more perfect development of the parks, for the acquirement of some further lands to improve the outlines of these parks, and especially for the expense of parkways, the need of which becomes more obvious as the system is developed and appreciated, the commission estimates that a further sum of $1,500,000 is needed. And this sum is, in the estimation of the commission, all that ought to be expended for acquirement and development of the system as laid out and designated."

NEW APPROPRIATION FAVORED.

These implied promises, following those theretofore made regarding the parkways, were considered a definite pledge of the commission, and the bill authorizing the additional appropriation having been passed by the Legislature and approved February 21, 1898, was favorably voted on by the

CONTEST FOR PARKWAYS CONTINUED 211

electorate of the county at the spring election, April 21 following.

The same report, of 1897, in referring to the parkways (page 15), also contained a clause which was at once construed by many as a sop to the traction interests. It was thus treated by the opposition as another evidence that the Park Commission was not, after all, averse to a "trolley on the avenue," when it officially there stated: "The location of the county parks will induce, no doubt, the rapid transit company to seek ways of approach thereto, and the commission will aid this endeavor so far as, in its judgment, is consistent with park treatment and use. Parks must be made accessible to the people, and any reasonable plan for rapid transit will be favored by the commission. In fact, almost all the parks are now accessible and by different routes."

This feature of the commission's report in inserting a "but," an "and" or an "if," became a marked characteristic of its later utterances on the parkway question; and, indeed, to an extent that was as bewildering to its most loyal friends and supporters as it was encouraging to the opposition, which was steadily and unceasingly making the most of every opportunity to take advantage, either of dissension or uncertainty, to advance the scheme of appropriation of the avenues for railroad uses. This was distinctly the effect in Orange. Councilman Stetson had, at the spring election in 1898, been chosen Mayor. It was currently reported, and not to my knowledge ever denied, that the traction company made an exceedingly liberal contribution then, as afterward, to his "campaign expenses." His prestige as Mayor in opposing the avenues' transfer was proportionately increased, for now he had the veto power, which, under the system of government in this country, whether with the President, the Governor of a State, or the Mayor of a city, is a powerful leverage.

The transfer ordinance continued to slumber in possession of the Street Committee. The pleadings by press and public urging further action by the Park Commission continued. On July 27, 1898, Mayor Stetson sent a special message to the City Council beginning: "At this time, when you have before you for consideration the ordinances in relation to the transfer of Park and Central avenues to the Essex County Park Commission, I would respectfully call your attention to the following:

"Now that the courts have decided legal the proposed issue of park bonds by the Park Commission, and the same are about to be sold, and the work suspended by the commission on account of the lack of funds will no doubt be pushed, it would seem to be an opportune time to direct the attention of the Park Commission to the desirability of the establishment of a park, centrally located, within the limits of the city of Orange. There are at the present time several desirable sites which could be purchased at moderate cost, upon which there are few, if any, buildings."

The appointment of a committee is then recommended "to confer with the Park Commission with this end in view," and the message closes with a commendation of the Street Committee "for the good work the street department is doing on the streets."

EFFECT OF THE MAYOR'S MESSAGE.

Excepting the opening paragraph quoted, not a word was mentioned regarding the real question then before the council—the disposition of the avenues transfer ordinance, which was then "put over." The Orange park was at that time well under improvement, and the Mayor knew, when he wrote that message, the difficulty and objection in the commission to locating even that favorable site for an Orange park. The practical effect of the message was to show the intention of the opposition to still further create discussion and issue over the main question. It had this effect on some of the members of the City Council. The document had, however, with the other influences referred to, the effect on the Park Commission of inducing that board to give out another statement. This was presented by Commissioner Bramhall at the meeting of the Orange Common Council July 8, 1898. There were also present Commissioners Shepard and Peck, and Counsel Munn of the park department. George Lethbridge, president of the council, presided.

The statement was conciliatory and explanatory, and began: "If there are any differences between the boards in conference here to-night, I am sure they are due to a misunderstanding and not to cross purposes. Both are public bodies seeking public good, and the action we desire the council to take is, we think, decidedly for the welfare of the city, as much as for the welfare of the county. Indeed, our request seems so little for you to grant that we are surprised that the necessity for it should arise.'

Assurances were then given that the commission "does not desire you to lessen one particle the municipal control you now exercise" or "to abridge in the slightest the rights of the property holders. ℐWe merely wish to be substituted for the Board of Chosen Freeholders, because the Park Commission is the only county board that has authority to beautify these thoroughfares and raise them above the level of ordinary streets. We ask you simply the privilege of adorning the streets of your city at county expense, and therefore I say it is surprising that any reluctance on your part should exist."

Then the commission's previous official statement, as to the non-intention to widen the avenues or attempt to assess benefits, was reiterated. Answer was also made to the claims of the traction company's representatives that the transfer would give the commission the right to at once permit trolleys on the avenues, in these words: "It has been asserted that we could turn over the parkways to the trolley. On the contrary, the consent of the council and of the property owners would be necessary as now, and our action is final only in matters relating entirely to decorative development."

An informal exchange of views followed. Commissioner Shepard said that "small parks were more in the nature of play-grounds than they were of parks, and that, as such, they came under the control of the municipalities and could not be included in a general scheme of the entire county."

PARK BOARD'S CHARTER.

After Counsel Munn had given a somewhat confusing reply to the widening and assessment question, the transfer ordinance was taken up. The commission then peremptor ily declined to accept the ordinance as it stood, particularly the section binding its successors never to apply "to any court or other power" for the right to levy assessments for the improvement of the avenues. This, notwithstanding the first section of the charter, in creating "such Board of Park Commissioners and their successors a body politic," then, as now, gives the commissioners ample authority to act for their successors, as, indeed, in most practical affairs, they had theretofore always done, and, from the necessities of the case, must continue to do, so long as the commission, under its present charter, exists. This right and prerogative has been, from the first transaction, unequivocally established, and is constantly exercised in the acquirement of land for parks and parkways; in the unquestioned right to make rules and regulations governing the parks, and in many other ways; and why the line should have been thus drawn on the advice of the board's counsel, on this particular occasion, I must leave to the reader to determine; for, unless it was for the purpose of continuing to confuse and befog the transfer question, I have never been able to account for it. The fair purport and clear logic of the statement of the commission's intention was, however, favorably received. To that extent it had an excellent effect.

Efforts to have the objectionable feature of the ordinance amended were then made. The pressure of public opinion to have some action taken by the City Council was continued, and accelerated by the passage of resolutions by a number of representative and public-spirited organizations. Among others, the Woman's Club, early in October, 1898, adopted a resolution, as follows:

"Resolved, That we women of the Oranges, represented by the Woman's Club, of Orange, earnestly favor the early transfer of Park and Central avenues to the Park Commission, to be improved and beautified for parkways, that the people may receive the benefit of such action.

"Resolved, That a copy of this resolution be sent to the Common Council of Orange, the Board of Chosen Free-holders, and the Essex County Park Commission, and the local press."

About this time, October 6, 1898, the City Council adopted a resolution, stipulating that the avenues, in the event of transfer, "should not be widened or any assessment for their improvement levied upon abutting property own-ers, this being in consonance with the views of the present commission." The resolution further suggested that "the clause referring to prospective park commissions be stricken out," as was done. A clause was then added "reserving police jurisdiction and control of franchises;" also a stipu-lation that "the ordinance must be accepted within sixty days," but should be "inoperative until the regulations em-braced in the ordinance are adopted and ratified by the council and the commission." This resolution was sent to the Park Commission.

The reply of October 17, 1898, stated that "your pream-ble and resolution, so far as they relate to this board, are in consonance with its views and purposes; so far as they relate to our successors, we are powerless to act. If your resolu-tion can be amended by the omission of the words 'now or at any time hereafter' and a simple resolution substituted in place of that clause in the ordinance, the transfer will be acceptable to the board."

The ordinance was, by the City Council, amended in ac-cordance with this request, the objectionable clause was stricken out, and on October 18, 1898, more than a year after its introduction, was finally and unanimously passed. This action met with general approval. But those who had hoped that the controversy was at last ended misjudged alike the reserve power of the traction company and the evident determination of the Mayor and his friends to de-feat the parkways' plan.

In an interview in the Newark News of October 22,

Counsel Munn came to the rescue by increasing the pending uncertainty in the accredited statement: "The question whether these avenues will ever become parkways is still open. No action has ever been taken by the Board of Freeholders, whose consent is necessary to establish the control of the Park Commission." He was then, as since, the counsel of that board.

MORE OBJECTIONS.

The activities of the corporation agents and attorneys continued. They were not in the least abashed or their efforts abated, and at the November meeting of the Orange Council, Mayor Stetson's veto of the transfer ordinance was presented. It was a remarkable document. He thought "it unwise for the city to part with its control of the avenues until it is definitely settled in what manner they are to be treated," and "unwise to strike out of the ordinance the words now or at any time thereafter," also "unwise to approve the ordinance until the regulations are agreed upon between the Common Council and the Park Commission, and until action on the proposed transfer is taken by the Board of Chosen Freeholders."

A long and rambling statement then follówed, but the gist of the alleged reasons for the veto is given in the quotations just noted. These "reasons" were promptly analyzed and their speciousness shown in both the editorial and news columns of the daily papers. Commissioner Bramhall had clearly defined to the councilmen themselves what the use of the avenues as parkways would be. It was "a waste of words," as The Chronicle expressed it, "to dwell upon the now or hereafter" clause objection. The very point the freeholders had ostensibly, all along contended for was that the municipalities directly affected should first express their preference in the matter of transfer.

The Jotrnal contended "that the Park Commission on one side and the Mayor and Common Council on the other" were both "to blame for the result."

PARK BOARD'S ATTITUDE.

Commissioner Franklin Murphy, in a published interview November 18, 1898, again sounded the keynote of uncertainty as to the future attitude of the Park Commission in the statement: "I feel as though we had gone as far as we should go in this matter. We have no desire to take the avenues if the municipality does not want us to have them. It is not likely that we shall take any action in the matter until the commission has progressed further with its work, and until the avenues become valuable as connecting links of the park system."

The reports regarding Counsel Munn's extreme friendliness to the trolley interests, and efforts in opposition to the parkways, notwithstanding the statements of the Park Commission, were becoming more and more frequent. The commissioners were fully aware of these reports current. In a statement in the Orange Chronicle of November 26, 1898, Commissioner Bramhall, among other things, said:

"Mr. Munn has been represented, or misrepresented, as saying much that is not so in relation to the transfer of Park and Central avenues. The truth is that the commission has spoken for itself directly and officially in this matter."

But the dissensions and differences were increased, instead of being allayed or diminished. The fact that the commission was saying one thing, and that the sayings of its duly authorized and retained counsel were being construed as meaning directly the opposite thing, gave the opposition and the franchise lobbyists just the opportunity desired. When, therefore, the Mayor's veto message of the avenue transfer ordinance came before the Orange City Council for action on November 21, 1898, it occasioned the knowing ones no surprise that the veto was sustained and the ordinance thus defeated by a tie vote of 7 to 7 in the council. And this directly in face of the evident fact, as stated in one of the leading papers at the time, "That the proposed improvement was favored by more than nine-tenths of the people;" 'that the action of the seven members who voted to sustain the Mayor's objections was "an affront to the people by whom they were elected to office;" and that, "by some mysterious influences," these men had "experienced a change of heart and literally stultified themselves by facing about without giving a single reason for so doing."

But the action had been taken. The parkways ordinance was dead. The curtain had been again rung down; now with the corrupting forces representing private gain and corporate greed, at the expense of the people and of the park system, for the second time triumphant.

CHAPTER XIV.

EAST Orange having completed the parkways' transfer, the Park Commission having formally accepted both avenues there, and the city of Orange having twice failed to complete the transfer ordinance, the parkway situation, early in 1899, might be compared to a well-equipped, safely ballasted, strong coach with a balking team. Every facility was at hand for the commission to mount the driver's seat of that coach, to quietly and firmly take the reins, and without resort to force, not even to the lash, to guide the load of obligations and pledges, which the board had already made to the public regarding the avenue parkways, to a safe and successful destination.

Not only did the Park Board possess ample power and full authority for accomplishing this result, but it had the press and the great majority of the people of the Oranges and of the county then in its favor, to approve and support any and every measure or action taken for the good and the protection of the parks and parkways which the commissioners were especially entrusted in their charter, by the people, to create and defend. One of the leading papers on January 7, 1899, voiced public sentiment in contending, editorially: "It is probable that nine-tenths of the voters of Orange are in favor of having Park and Central avenues receive parkway treatment."

PARK BOARD'S EVASIVE COURSE.

Similar sentiments were at that time so frequently expressed that there could be no reasonable doubt as to the attitude of the public generally upon this question. Instead

of the Park Commission taking any advantage of its opportunities at this critical juncture of its parkway affairs,
it was content to sit in secret session, month after month,
for several years, and give out statements or promulgate
manifestoes, restating its position that it had "not changed"
its attitude regarding the parkways; and at last, "declined
to take a partisan stand" on this matter, upon which the
board itself had taken the initial action in preparing and
publishing its plans, and had even secured appropriations
with the promise and understanding that the avenues were
to be made parkways.   And this question as to whether
these results should be secured, or the collusive corporate
interests should appropriate one or both of the proposed
parkways for private gain, was no more a "partisan" question than was the action of the Legislature in passing the
Park Commission's charter, or were the innumerable official
acts of the commission in locating the parks and parkways,
or in acquiring the requisite land, or in formulating rules
and regulations for the administration of the park
department.

But while the commission was for years resting upon its
declared intentions as to the two principal parkways, the
traction company, before the close of 1898, had its scheme
for securing at least one of the parkway avenues well in
hand.   And, at the time indicated, it was in possession of
both the reins and lash of the parkways' coach.   This condition had been, in the meantime, very materially strengthened by Counsel J. L. Munn, by his assistance in keeping
actively alive the controversy, not only in Orange, but also
with the Board of Freeholders.

In this board, some action was usually taken about the
time the Park Commission would issue another statement
of good intention, which would in effect nullify the commissioners' claim that they wanted the parkways, by creating still farther obstacles in the way of the avenues' transfer
being completed.

After the parkway-avenue resolution of the Park Board
of November, 1896, had been sent to the Board of Freehold-

ers, nothing was heard of it. While the contest between the
parkway forces and the trolley syndicate was being actively
waged in 1898, efforts were made by committees of various
civic associations to ascertain, if possible, why the freeholders were non-responsive and why such an important
request as that of the Park Board remained pigeonholed all
that time.

A PUBLIC HEARING.

Finally, on May 20, 1898, the Road Committee of the
freeholders gave a hearing on the commission's application.
The local committees were well represented. Mayor John
Gill, of Orange, and other well known officials and citizens,
were present. The reasons why the avenues should be used
as parkways were well presented. The petitions, signed by
nearly all the property owners on both of the avenues, favoring the transfer, were read, as also the resolutions of various
civic bodies. The former official and unanimous proceedings of the Orange and East Orange authorities, favorable
to action being taken, were noted.

The opposing corporation agents now offered a new line
of obstructive tactics. The Park Commission would, by
inaugurating new regulations after transfer at once "restrict ordinary traffic." The parkways were at best a local
question, they said: "The freeholders elected by, and the
direct representatives of, the people, should not surrender
control of these great highways and thus prevent the free
use of them as originally intended."

Although it was clearly shown that, under the transfer,
or eighteenth clause of the park law, the commission would
have no such right of restriction, and that the parkways, in
extending park treatment through the various municipalities by directly connecting the larger parks of the whole
county, could no more be considered a local question than
could the park system itself, yet the freeholders adopted the
opposition views and nothing was done. On October 25
following (1898) another "hearing" was given by the same

freeholders' committee. Frank H. Scott, F. W. Baldwin,
A. P. Boller, G. R. Howe and others made earnest and able
pleas, urging early action. But the listening freeholders appeared deaf to the appeals, and the conditions of persistent
inactivity were continued as before; although Chairman
J. B. Bray assured the petitioners "that a simple resolution
passed by the committee would not be sufficient to complete
the transfer"—a fact that was gradually beginning to dawn
on the minds of those who had heretofore believed that the
logic of the situation and merit of the transfer proposition
might be a potential factor in the proceedings before the
freeholders.

While the powerful hand of the Consolidated Traction
Company was clearly visible back of this inconsistent and
continuous inactivity, still it was a condition, not a theory
of official inactivity, which confronted the parkways movement. Attention was then again turned to the Park Commission. Here much the same uncertainty existed. Whatever may have been the cause, the wabbling attitude of that
board, aside from its executive session statements, was an
indisputable factor of large proportions in still farther extending the uncertainty of the conditions.

The commission was appealed to. The board was im-
plored to galvanize some life into its repeated claims of
intention. It was asked to show by its acts, as well as by its
words, what it meant; and was reminded that, "after the repeated reiteration of its plans and purposes as regards these
avenues, both the friends and most of the opponents of the
county park undertaking had formerly accepted that action as final," and that it was now being currently reported
"that the commission did not want the avenues, and that it
had never intended to make them parkways."

From the records it appears that the elements of uncertainty as to these parkways were also acutely active
within the Park Board rooms by or before the summer of
1899. At the meeting of August 1 of that year, Commissioner Shepard's motion was adopted requesting the landscape architects "to make a special report on the proper

location of an east and west parkway from Newark to the Orange Mountain, in the central part of the county."

The landscape architects of the department at this time were the Olmsted Brothers, who had succeeded landscape architects and engineers Barrett and Bogart, the September previous. In December, 1898, following their appointment, the Messrs. Olmsted had submitted two elaborate reports on the parkway subject—one December 24, the other December 31—of twenty-four pages of typewritten matter, and apparently covering most of the county. These reports were furnished in response to a resolution of the board of November 16, 1898, calling for "a report on parkways in general," and were, in outline, similar to the parkway features of the other tentative reports of the original five park specialists (their own report among the number) made to the first Park Commission in 1894 and early in 1895. These elaborate reports of 1898, however, although they treated of widely extended possible parkway locations, recommended special legislation for the acquirement of the requisite land; favored the establishment of building lines on future parkways. and desirable traffic restrictions, and the limiting of height of buildings. They also advocated "the extension of the East Orange parkway on to Weequahic," also to "the disposal works and to Eagle Rock," etc. Yet they made no reference whatever to the two great east and west avenue parkways already constructed, and which, as elaborated upon in that firm's own report of January 16, 1895, were then described as being "essentially parkways of a formal character," "on which, to make them all that is desirable for your purpose, it is only necessary" that "certain improvements of detail should be made."

OBJECTIONS BASED ON TRAFFIC.

No reference or suggestion was made in any of the earlier expert reports as to "the needs-of-ordinary-traffic" objection to the avenues being improved as parkways; but, after the traction company's franchise promoters had systematically exploited this claim, it soon entered into the parkway side of the discussion. In the Olmsted report of December 31, 1898, the heavy traffic "on Park avenue from the East Orange parkway to Branch Brook Park" is noted as an "objection" which it is "impracticable to exclude," though "the inconvenience might be less and less as time goes on." The report concludes "that the large proposition of parkways for Essex County is sure to lead to endless discussion."

Their special report of August 2, 1899, in response to the Park Board resolution, as above quoted, would, I think, have surprised the people of Essex County had it been made public at that time, or at any time during the five years following while the contest over the parkways was in progress. This report, according to instructions, was to have "regard for the various available routes, and to the financial limitations" of the commission. After noting that "no entirely new east and west parkway appears to be practicable, except at the north end of East Orange, through Clinton and South Orange," or possibly "from the northern end of Branch Brook Park westward to the mountain through the southern parts of Bloomfield and Montclair," etc., the report refers to Park and Central avenues as follows:

"As the board has not yet put this policy—of taking control of the avenues—into effect, there is still opportunity to reconsider the matter and to leave out of the parkway system either or both of these avenues. After a careful study of the existing conditions of the territory through which these two avenues run, it appears to us that the greater good to the greatest number of the citizens of the county directly interested, demands that Central avenue be left out of the parkway system, so as to be available for ordinary business traffic."

CORPORATION AGENTS SUPPORTED.

The reasons as then stated for this conclusion—surprising in comparison with that firm's prior report quoted, and in view of the fact that this statement was directly in line with the "points" which the trolley franchise agents and promoters had been for months actively circulating—were that "serious inconvenience and hardship to the business and personal interests of the people" would result. The commission's "financial limitations" would, according to this report, make "the expense of developing and maintaining both Park and Central avenues unwarrantable."

"It would be impracticable," continued the report, "to extend Central avenue with a width of 100 feet to the south end of Branch Brook Park, as would certainly be desirable, even necessary, if it is to be used as a parkway." It was also stated, that "the western part of Central avenue has four right-angled turns in it, which are so extremely ungraceful and inconvenient as to almost condemn it," and "it is already encumbered on both ends with street railway tracks."

When it is borne in mind that every one of the conditions referred to as "reasons," were, in 1895, when the Olmsted's first report was made, precisely the same as when this report was submitted—excepting that at the latter time the corporations were using their power to secure the avenue franchise, and thus prevent the parkway—both the text and tenor of this last report seems the more surprising. In other respects there had been, during the four intervening years, no change. The "serious inconvenience and hardship to the business and personal interests" were, in 1895, just as apparent, save the pecuniary interest of the traction company in the coveted franchise, as in 1899. The "financial limitations" of the commission were not so strained, with its new $1,500,000 appropriation, but that new and costly parkways, like the one in East Orange—which would have its southern parkway connection at Central avenue permanently destroyed by the abandonment of that avenue to the trolley interests—could, as recommended in the report, be extended. The plan "to extend Central avenue to the south end of Branch Brook Park" had never been officially considered; nor, so far as I know, had it ever been suggested in the plans for making Central avenue a parkway. Nor had the "ungraceful turns" or the short stretch of trolley tracks at the western part of the avenue ever before been deemed of serious importance, or matters that could not be readily, and with comparatively small expense, adequately and satisfactorily treated.

This Olmsted report was received and was before the Park Board for consideration on August 8, 1899. I am not aware that its contents have before this ever been made public. Soon after the report was received, and remained in secret in the Park Board archives, one of the traction company's representatives, with a smiling countenance, stated to me that the Park Commission had "an expert's report, which was decidedly against Central avenue." That the commission for some reason concluded it was not desirable to give out the report appears from the board's official action. At the meeting of March 5, 1901, in passing upon the matter for the annual report, it was agreed "that the Olmsted Brothers' report in regard to Park and Central avenues," should be included; and then, at the meeting of March 19, on motion of Commissioner Shepard, seconded by Mr. Murphy, the "motion of March 5, which included in the annual report the report of Olmsted Brothers in regard to Park and Central avenues," was rescinded, and a motion of Mr. Shepard, that that report be omitted, was then adopted.

A PARK BOARD HEARING.

When, during the latter part of 1899, and early in 1900, it was found that the Board of Freeholders was, on the parkway subject, immovable, an effort was made to secure from that board, if possible, its official approval of the transfer made by the East Orange authorities March 15, 1897, and thus have the full control of the East Orange portion of each of the avenues vested in the Park Commission. The Park Board gave a hearing, March 1, 1900, on this question. A large and representative delegation was present. The commission was reminded of "what were considered the promises to the East Orange committee three years before," and of "the condition of unrest that was growing out of the delay, in the absence of some action or earnest of its intention." This, it was urged, should obtain in a request to the freeholders to complete the East Orange transfer, so that that portion of the avenues could be improved. The commission complied, and, on March 20, 1900, adopted a suitable resolution toward carrying the desired object into effect.

On May 22 following, the Road Committee of the Board of Freeholders gave a hearing on the commissioners' request. About fifty persons were present. Able presentments for the parkways were made by Messrs. E. O. Stanley, A. P. Boller, F. H. Scott, H. Wallis, C. G. Kidder, G. F. Seward and others. W. Whittlesey and one other speaker openly favored a trolley on Central avenue. The opposition was, for the most part, however, under the usual cover. One of the speakers declared "there was nothing to show that the park commissioners were not willing for a trolley line to be constructed, should they take the avenue for a parkway." Another opponent was most solicitous about "ordinary traffic matters."

APPLICATION REFUSED.

The sequence of the meeting was, that the Road Committee, on the advice of Counsel Joseph L. Munn, reported to the full board adversely, and against granting the Park Board's application, notwithstanding the fact that a conference between that committee and the commission had been held with the object of coming to an understanding in the matter. Counsel Munn's opinion, as quoted by the committee, was that, "under the law, the Board of Freeholders had no right to make such a transfer;" but, "by the consent of all the municipalities through which the avenues ran, the board might make the transfer without leaving itself liable." The committee in turn gave as its reason for adverse action that the authority of the board "under the provisions of the park act, to take the action now requested is so far doubtful that such action should not be taken under the conditions referred to."

As the policy of that same freeholder's board had all

along been to obstruct the transfer and thus, to all appearances, serve the corporate interests desiring that object, the action of the full board at the July meeting, in sustaining the Road Committee's recommendation, caused little surprise. It was only another indication of the tenacious control the traction interests held over the proceedings of that board. The ostensible reasons for the action then taken were, as usual in such cases, specious and misleading. For four years the position of the freeholders in not taking any action favorable as to the parkways had been, that the municipal authorities should act first; while, for all that time, both in law and in fact, the entire control of, and jurisdiction over those county avenues, with the exception of very minor rights in the cross streets, were vested absolutely in that board. What logic or justification, therefore, could there be in the announced excuse for persistent inactivity, that the local boards, holding only these insignificant right, "must first make the transfer?": Then, years after East Orange had thus acted, in adding the farther excuse that "it was not good policy on the part of the Board of Freeholders at any time to relinquish control of a limited section of a county avenue"—which was the additional "reason" included in the report of this latter refusal of the Park Board's request.

The inconsistency of the other alleged reason, as to transfer, "that such avenues shall be permanently maintained in at least as good condition as heretofore," when the distinct object of the transfer was to improve them as parkways, is apparent. The Newark News of May 24, 1900, editorially gave the gist of the matter in a few words in commenting upon the hearing referred to, as follows: "It is not difficult to discern corporation influences behind the opposition to parkway development through the Oranges, that was manifested at the hearing before the Board of Freeholders' Road Committee on Monday."

In December, 1900, there was introduced into the Orange Common Council, for the third time, an avenues transfer ordinance. This document was carefully drawn with the view of removing every tangible objection that could be made against it. It provided that the commission should not restrict the ordinary uses of the avenues, or debar existing privileges; and that the avenues should not be widened, without consent being first obtained from the City Council of Orange.

On March 5, 1901, a copy of the ordinance was sent to the Park Commission by the city clerk with the inquiry as to whether that board "approved the ordinance." Under date of March 19, 1901, the board, on motion of Commissioner Shepard, replied:

"Since the request of the Essex County Park Commission for the transfer of those avenues was made to the Common Council of the city of Orange on November 13, 1896, circumstances have very greatly changed.

"The Park Commission, on the failure of their request, took up other work, and have expended and appropriated the funds at their command to such an extent that it is now impossible to undertake any improvement of said avenues.

"The Park Commission is giving very serious consideration to the question of completing the work already under contract and definitely planned, with means remaining at its disposal.

"It should, therefore, be understood that this commission cannot take up any improvement upon these avenues, and if they should be transferred to the commission they would necessarily remain in their present condition until funds should hereafter be provided by the Legislature for their improvement and maintenance.

"The ordinance, known as the Cuddy ordinance, is acceptable to the commission."

TRACTION COMPANY'S NEW MOVE.

Meanwhile, the traction company had become so much encouraged and emboldened by its success with the freeholders and the corporation's representatives in the Oranges, and the absence of any action by the Park Commission toward defending the parkways, that, on January 14, 1901, it filed a new application for a Central avenue franchise in East Orange. The application was received, as stated at the time, "with the understandîng that it was done simply to permit of a conference between the city authorities and the railroad representatives with the view of learning just what would be demanded on the one side, and what would be conceded on the other." No new property owners' consents were filed. James B. Dill and David Young were, as in 1896-7, the active sponsors for the new application.

Concurrently with its appearance were persistent rumors that the Park Commission had decided to abandon Central avenue for a parkway, and that the question of a railroad on the avenue was, therefore, before the East Orange authorities on its merits. On May 13, 1901, the City Council adopted the report of the railroad committee, favoring the drafting of a franchise ordinance.

At one of the meetings of this committee Counsel Munn was present. When he was asked if the Park Commission wanted Central avenue for a parkway he replied: "Not that I know of. Do what you please with the avenue."

By October the reports in regard to the Park Commission had become so unfavorable that an East Orange neighbor of Commissioner Shepard's wrote him on the subject, and, under date of October 14, 1901, received this answer:

"In reply to your favor of the 10th inst. The report that has come to you, viz., 'that the Essex County Park Commission were hoping to get rid of Central avenue by turning it over to the Consolidated Traction Company, and that possibly Park avenue might follow in time, in which case the crosstown parkway would be abandoned, except that portion nearly completed,' is untrue, and there is no shadow of a foundation for such a report. The Park Commission, acting on their adopted plans, and in accordance with the expression of the opinion of large delegations of citizens from the Oranges, asked from the freeholders and the authorities of Newark and the Oranges, for the care, custody, and control of Park avenue and a portion of Central avenue.

COMMISSION CAN DO NOTHING.

"The authorities of East Orange and West Orange granted this request, but the freeholders and the authorities of Orange and Newark have not yet granted this request, and until they take such action the Park Commission can do nothing further.

"In the matter of the East Orange Parkway, from Central avenue north to Watsessing Park, the Park Commission is waiting for the report of the Appraisal Commission, which was appointed by the court last spring, and which has been at work ever since. We are informed that they will probably present it to the court in November.

"I beg you will make public use of this letter, as it correctly states the present condition of the matter."

Directly this letter was made public the opposition set up the contention that it was a personal, not an official, communication, and hence of no effect as a binding document from the commission; that it was intended as a personal letter; that the board had not shown any very great anxiety over securing the parkway, and that, as Counsel Munn, in his official capacity, represented all the commissioners, his statements and representations should have precedence over those of any single commissioner.

At the meeting of the East Orange City Council, October 30, 1901, held in Commonwealth Hall, the new trolley franchise application was the special order of business. The hall was filled. Excitement at times ran high. J. B. Dill, with David Young, were the principal speakers for the street railway corporation. Henry G. Atwater, and other representative citizens, contended for the parkways.

The Park Commission was conspicuous by its absence. The chairman, Councilman William Cardwell, in opening the meeting, said: "At the request of the counsel the speeches will be limited to five minutes." Mr. Atwater said that he had made no such request. The rule was not enforced. All the old points in the controversy were gone over; a few new new-ones were brought out. Mr. Atwater protested against the consideration of the ordinance on the ground "that the statutory number of consents of property owners fronting on the avenue had not been filed." H. H. Hall, in addressing the City Council with much earnestness, said that it made his "blood boil, as a citizen of this town, to see the representatives of that corporation stand up here and snap the whip over you." The proceedings of the traction company are "a disgrace to the Christian State of New Jersey," he declared, and he said that he would "rather continue to walk twelve minutes to Main street, than to barter away the sacred rights of this city, and give away a perpetual franchise which, when your children read of your action, will make them hide their faces in shame." G. R. Howe said: "There is no possibility of parkways if we surrender the only two avenues left."

AS TO THE FRANCHISE.

Counsel James B. Dill held that "the gentlemen interested have had five years to build a parkway, but up to the present time we have only a verbal parkway." He denied that the perpetual franchise applied for was perpetual, or that there was anything properly in the way of using the old "consents." Arthur Baldwin, a lawyer, joined in this demagogic argument for class distinction, and, with much vehemence, asked: "Who is going to use these parkways? Will those who are away three months in the summer? How is the man who is compelled to stay at home to get the benefit of the parks? He must walk,"—thus perverting the fact that parkways, like the parks, are for all the people, the great majority of whom, remaining at home, all the more require such places for recreation.

No action was taken by the City Council that evening, but it was freely predicted that the members had, before the hearing, become fully converted to the interested corpora-

tion's way of thinking, both as to the "verbal parkway" and
as to the early needs of a railroad on the avenue instead.

The following letter is self-explanatory:

"East Orange, Nov. 18, 1901.
"Essex County Park Commission, Newark, N. J.:

"Gentlemen—We are advised that some members of the
East Orange City Council understand that your counsel,
Mr. Munn, has stated that the Park Board is really indif-
ferent to the proposed use of Central avenue as a parkway.
This belief on their part is doing much harm.

"We do not pretend to say what you may be disposed to
do under these circumstances, but, if it is possible, we think
it would be useful for you to give to us, or to the City Council, soon, a statement from Mr. Munn which would set at
rest the report in question.

"Mr. Munn must feel precluded by his duty as your
counsel from saying anything which tends to discredit the
good faith of your honorable body, and we cannot think
that he will in any way object to making it clear that he has
not intentionally said anything which, if properly understood, could mean what has been asserted.

"Respectfully and truly yours,
"George F. Seward, Frank H. Scott, Frederick W.
Kelsey, Henry W. Bulkley, Joel F. Freeman, William H.
Baker, Henry M. Ward, Executive Committee of the
Avenue Association."

PARK BOARD'S REPLY.

At the Park Board meeting the day following, November
19, on motion of Commissioner F. M. Shepard, the following reply was authorized transmitted by the secretary:

"The Park Commission holds that its attitude should be
judged by its official acts, and not by the expression of individual opinions of its individual members, or its officers.
The commission thinks it has, from the beginning, made its
attitude clear, and that it should not be asked to respond to
every suggestion or rumor or understanding that may be

found in circulation. The commission farther holds that the question now agitating the public in East Orange, should be decided by those immediately interested and residing in the locality affected. The counsel of the commission asserts that he has not undertaken to represent the views of the Park Commission or to speak for it, excepting when directed to appear in its behalf, and has at no time undertaken to express on behalf of the Park Commission any views differing from those set forth in its official acts."

The effect of this communication, even on the minds of the most loyal friends of the commission, was confusing. According to the board's own statement, its conception of the trust reposed in it by the Legislature, and by the people of the whole county, to make and execute its park and parkway plans, and create a great park system, was lowered behind the screen of the acts of another, and local board, which, at best, represented but a very limited part of the larger constituency, and which board, from the very circumstances of the case, was known to be especially susceptible to the enticing wiles of the corporate and combined political influences, which were being continuously exerted, through every possible channel and effort, to defeat the commission's own plans for the parkways. The difficulty in the practicable application of the commission's statement to the then existing conditions in the East Orange City Council was, that its own counsel, J. L. Munn, had preceded the letter, and the council members were so well satisfied to accept his interpretation of the commission's attitude, as to make, at the outset, any efforts for the parkways in that direction, hopelessly fruitless.

A PARKWAYS COMMITTEE.

The whole parkway subject was then taken up by the Joint Committee on Parkways. This committee was organized from three committees, one from the New England Society, one from the Avenue Association of the Oranges, and one from the East Orange Improvement Society. Each of these organizations had, in November or December, 1901, adopted resolutions favoring the parkways, and authorizing the appointment of special committees to co-operate with other organizations having a similar object in view. The following were the committees: From the New England Society, E. O. Stanley, Archer Brown, G. H. Austen, William J. Baer, H. G. Atwater, F. W. Baldwin, J. D. Everett, C. W. Baldwin, Ira A. Kip, Jr.; from the Avenue Association, F. W. Kelsey, D. S. Walton, F. H. Scott, J. F. Freeman, H. T. Ambrose, G. F. Seward, W. H. Baker, H. H. Ward; from the Town Improvement Society, H. H. Hall, G. R. Howe, Hugh Lamb, Alden Freeman, J. S. Richards. There were but few changes made in the committee other than the loss by death two or three years later of Archer Brown, Henry G. Atwater, John S. Richards, and Hugh Lamb. In March, 1904, W. H. Burges, G. W. Fortmeyer, B. F. Jones, A. C. Smith and T. A. Davis were added to the New England Society's committee.

From the time of its organization in 1901, the joint committee took an active and earnest interest in parkway affairs. Its direct purposes were to secure, if possible, the preservation of the parkways. It favored the lines of trolley extension west to the Orange Mountain, but contended that the routes should be located on parallel streets or through private property, if need be, outside the parkways. The committee was optimistic. It held, not only that a commission created by law with unusual powers and then solely entrusted with the expenditure of $4,000,000 of public funds, should have the ability for leadership and decisive action requisite with the great resource at its command; but also that such a board would or should respond to any co-operative effort toward completing the park system from an organization of the probity and standing of the committee. In conformity with this view the committee, early in March, 1902, wrote the commission:

"For some time past reports have been current through the Oranges that your board was indifferent to the present parkway situation and to the use of Central avenue as the great central parkway of the county accessible to the mass of people; indeed, it has been freely claimed by some that you are ready to abandon that feature of the parkway plans, and that the avenue should be given over to commercial traffic—in other words, to the trolley."

The letter then refers to the frequency and persistency of these reports; of the embarrassment of "the friends of the parks;" to how "the public at large, and, indeed, every one (excepting possibly the trolley managers)," had long before considered the parkway question "definitely settled;" and adding that as "representing a large constituency" the committee wished "to know at the earliest possible moment, whether there has been any change in your board on this question, and what position in the future interest of the parks and parkways should, under the circumstances, be taken;" also adding:

"We are quite aware that the board has now no money to use on the parkways. We equally appreciate the proposition that the park and parkway developments are of concern now, and will be in all the future. We are content with tentative steps. You will get further appropriations, and the plans already desired may be carried later. The avenues can be held indefinitely if your position remains firm in your adhesion to your own plans.

"We have stated to you briefly the conditions, and write thus frankly as we consider that you should know the facts, and have confidence that you will meet the situation in a way to warrant the continued support of all, who, like the undersigned and the organizations we represent, have been loyal to the county park and parkway project from its inception.

"Should one of your board, especially Mr. Shepard, appear before the East Orange City Council, reaffirming the position of the commission as to parkways, and thus set at rest the rumors and reports that are sapping public confidence in the movement, it would have a most excellent effect."

The following, under date of April 3, 1902, was the reply:

"At the meeting of the Park Commission held to-day the following resolution was passed:

'Resolved, That the secretary be instructed to inform the East Orange committee that the Park Commission has never taken any action looking to a withdrawal from its original position of desiring Park and Central avenues as parkways.' "

In commenting upon this statement, The Chronicle of April 12, 1902, said: "If the Park Commission, after all these official utterances, does not mean what it says, it cannot expect to retain either public confidence or support."

AN ACCOMMODATING COUNCIL.

Notwithstanding these assurances, progress with the railroad ordinance for Central avenue in East Orange was being constantly made. The City Council had, very accommodatingly to the traction company, held the application over for weeks in order to enable the company to obtain, if possible, the requisite property owners' consents. At the meeting of February 24, 1902, Councilman Thomas W. Jackson announced that "the trolley company had been too busy" to procure these consents. And that "Mr. Young had promised him that they would either file the additional consents at the next meeting, or withdraw the application."

The matter came up for action at the meeting of March 29. The council chamber was crowded. The atmosphere was surcharged with corporation influence. It was manifest that any discussion on the merits of the parkway or trolley proposition would be a waste of time. H. G. Atwater, who then appeared as counsel for some of the interested property owners, brought out the fact that the company did not have the necessary consents, hence, he said, the council was powerless to act. Councilman Jackson expressed his thanks "for the advice," and said that he was "tired of the business;" that it was not the duty of the council to act as a court; and suggested that "those opposed to the franchise should take the matter into the courts."

The Park Commission was not represented in any way at

the meeting. In view of the circumstances outlined in the joint committee's letter, above quoted, and the courteous suggestion there made as to clearing up the parkway situation before the East Orange authorities, the non-appearance of the commission, or of any one representing it, occasioned unfavorable comment. As the reply of April 3 had not then been received, no reference to the attitude of the Park Board at that time could be officially made. After a long and heated discussion the railroad ordinance was finally passed on first reading.

The public had not, however, long to wait before hearing further from at least one of the Park Commission's officials. On April 11, 1902, Counsel J. L. Munn's formal consent for a railroad on Central avenue was filed with the city clerk. It was for 337 28-100 feet frontage on the avenue in East Orange. At last the mask was thrown off. The traction company's representatives and lobbyists significantly referred to the "new consent" as unmistable evidence as to where the Park Board in reality stood on the parkway-railroad question.

"Actions speak plainer than words," they said, and "if that act doesn't represent what a majority of that board really want, why has Munn been retained all this time, when everybody knew, who knew anything, the interests he really represented in this matter?" And surely enough, why?

The publication almost concurrently, in April, 1902, of the "new statement" and of the "new consent" produced still further confusion and uncertainty.

The joint committee decided to go right forward, taking the commission at its word, and leaving the opposition and the coming events to demonstrate whether that confidence was justified by the facts. The avenue association committee acted as an executive body. On the passage of the railroad ordinance in East Orange, R. V. Lindabury was retained to test the case in the courts. The previous December (1901), the Court of Errors and Appeals had rendered a decision in the "Currie vs. Atlantic City" case, which, in effect, invalidated property owners' consents when once used by a governing body in considering a street railroad application, and determined that such "consents cannot be the basis of further municipal action upon a second application."

AMENDMENTS AGREED UPON.

These conditions were directly applicable to the East Orange franchise. The traction company decided that it would take its chances and have its completed ordinance in East Orange "delivered." It was accordingly gone over and some amendments were agreed upon at the council meeting April 14, 1902. On March 24 a committee, consisting of D. S. Walton, H. W. Bulkley, J. F. Freeman, H. H. Ward, G. F. Seward and W. H. Baker, had made a written request of the Mayor and Common Council "for a hearing, before any ordinance be introduced for locating a railroad on Central avenue to the permanent prevention of parkway improvement there." This request was denied. A similar request from the joint committee, April 14, fared the same fate. When these and many other well known citizens desired to speak at the meeting referred to, Councilman Jerome D. Gedney exclaimed: "If these gentlemen come here to oppose the trolley, I, for one, will listen to them with deaf ears." It was then announced that any "proposition or suggestions should be submitted in writing."

The council meeting for completing the franchise delivery to the traction company was held April 28, 1902. A great crowd, much excitement, and, at times, worse confusion were the features. Requests for a hearing by those favoring the parkways were again refused. "I think it only fair to all that the council hear nothing further," was the way Thomas W. Jackson, chairman of the Railroad Committee, put that decision before the meeting. Protests were drowned in the general hubbub that followed.

"I ask if the taxpayers have no rights here!" W. E. Scarrett in a loud voice demanded.

"The majority of the council object to hearing further a

discussion of the subject," replied Chairman William
Cardwell.

"The members of this City Council are our servants," was
Mr. Scarrett's answer.

"Yes, you have rights," said Mr. Cardwell.

"Then you decline to receive our protests. Are we not
permitted to speak?" again inquired Mr. Scarrett.

"It has been decided by a majority of the council that
you cannot," was the chairman's response. The city clerk,
in an almost inaudible, monotonous voice, then read the
written "suggestions" formulated by the full joint committee on parkways.

POINTS IN THE LETTER.

The communication cited the various official statements
of the Park Board regarding the parkways; referred to the
fact that a railroad on either of the avenues "would at once
and permanently prevent the eighteen acres of parkway improvements on that side of the city; would effectually destroy the continuous features of the crosstown parkway,
thereby preventing nearly one-half of all the park and parkway improvements possible in East Orange; and would disintegrate the park system past recovery. Whereas a trolley
road farther south would be a desirable improvement and
furnish convenient communication between that section and
Newark, and give us direct access to the parks."

Attention was also called to the ordinance before the
council as being "surprisingly defective in not properly safe-
guarding the interests of the city." It was also pointed out
that neither public opinion, nor the test of the future, nor
your unbiased judgment upon a fuller understanding of the
facts, can approve of the terms as now proposed in the franchise grant of any important street."

The facts as to the fabulous profits made out of the South
Orange avenue line (a parallel avenue) were then stated.
It was also shown how, on that perpetual franchise, and for
less than five miles of double track, $21,000,000 of securities
of the North Jersey Street Railway Company had been

issued, of a then selling or market value of $9,000,000; how this vast sum represented to the railway promoters and owners a clear profit of nearly $8,000,000, or an amount equal to about one-half of the entire real and personal ratables of East Orange.

The accuracy of these facts was not questioned or the correctness of the figures denied. They were elaborated upon by Milo R. Maltbie, the street railway expert, who offered indisputable evidence in support of the value of such franchises.

But the die was cast. It was evident that it had been cast for passing the ordinance before the meeting had convened. Facts and arguments were alike unavailing. The whip of the corporation, through the party machine, had been snapped. All the combined elements of good citizenship were there helpless. The roll was called. Down went the gavel. Again the curtain, with the lobbyists jubilant, the Park Commission unseen in the dim distance, and the forces that make for destruction in the cities of this country, for the third time, in the ascendency.

CHAPTER XV.

WITH the influences for the traction company in control of the freeholders and of the East Orange and Orange governing bodies, and the Park Commission as to the parkways nowhere in live evidence, those who had believed in and worked for practical parkway results, found themselves between the Scylla of doubt and the Charybdis of adverse condition. The decision, not to turn back, was soon rendered. On the morning of May 3, 1902, directly after the passage of the railroad ordinance in East Orange, William J. Baer, as secretary of the Joint Committee on Parkways, sent a written request to Mayor E. E. Bruen asking if he would "kindly indicate the time and place" for the conference, "agreeable to your conversation with Mr. D. S. Walton."

The Mayor had stated that he should take the full time allowed by law in acting on the measure. No reply was received. On May 6 the committee learned that the Mayor had gone to Boston the day, or day but one, following the passage of the ordinance, and that he had signed it before leaving East Orange.

There was public indignation. Charges of improper influences in the City Council were openly made in the local papers. The proceedings were referred to as "the gift of the Central avenue franchise," and much more vigorous language was freely used. A well known citizen who was present when the ordinance was "jammed through" declared: "It was the most disgraceful proceeding I ever witnessed, and worse than Tammany Hall."

The Park Commission was also severely criticised. "We should simply say, we don't propose to trust you any farther. We have had your promises and they don't pan out,"—was the way one East Orange resident paid his compliments to that board.

Other criticisms were aimed at the appointive commission, one that is "responsible to nobody and can do as it pleases." The East Orange parkway was referred as as a way "which begins nowhere and ends nowhere, and, for this, $175,000 has been expended."

The East Orange railroad ordinance for Central avenue came before the Board of Freeholders for action June 12, 1902. The announcement had been made that there would be a hearing by the board on the question. A large delegation of citizens and representatives of various organizations were present. Director Thomas McGowan said the meeting would be open only "for brief remarks." There was evidently no desire that any one should be heard. W. Ougheltree, chairman of the Road Committee, gave the cue to the proceedings by reporting the railroad franchise resolution favorably, with the statement that "it had always been the custom to concur in matters of this kind in the action of any municipality in the county, and the resolution for that reason should pass." This was stated with a sober countenance, notwithstanding the fact that precisely the reverse policy had been adopted, and for more than five years persistently followed by his own committee, and by that same board in refusing to concur in the action March 15, 1897, of East Orange, in the passage of the ordinance by unanimous vote of the representatives of that municipality transferring both of the avenues to the Park Commission.

COMMISSIONER SHEPARD'S LETTER.

H. M. Barrett, a lawyer, then announced that the trolley ordinance as passed in East Orange, relative to "the terms and conditions, was satisfactory to both sides." William J. Baer made an earnest plea for the parkways, and then read a letter from Commissioner Frederick M. Shepard containing some general expressions, and adding: "I am confident the Park Commission would be glad to carry out the original plan if the avenues and the money were put in their hands to do it. * * * I think that I have already done all that I can do to urge this result." A. P. Boller said that "future generations will call us blessed if we do our duty" in respect to the parkways. Archer Brown, Hugh Lamb, W. H. Baker and W. E. Kastendike all spoke in a similar vein. David Young, of the traction company, was present, but said little. It was perfectly evident that there was no need for him to urge favorable action for the company.

I had been requested as chairman of the Joint Committee to speak for that organization. There was immediate objection by Freeholder Wallace Ougheltree—"because he lives in Orange." Just why a resident of the second city of the county should be debarred from the "hearing" did not appear. The real reason soon became manifest. Reference was then made in my remarks to the fact that "the original request of the Park Commission, of November, 1896, for the avenues was still before the board unacted upon;" to the fact that "the parallelogram of the park system with the two avenues for the sides, and Branch Brook Park as the Newark terminus, and the mountain parks the other, with a railroad on Central avenue, would be forever destroyed;" and to the financial reasons, the munificent prospective profits, that impelled the corporations to insist on the franchise at the expense of the parkways. The favorable results of the development of park systems in other urban communities were also explained.

It was a receptive board on that 12th of June, 1902. All the members apparently listened to what was said. And then they did just what it was apparently understood they would do before they came there—passed the railroad franchise precisely as it was wanted by the traction company.

Before the vote was taken, a letter was read from the law firm of Lindabury, Depue & Faulks, stating that "two writs of certiorari had been taken out in the Supreme Court, one of them acting as a stay to prevent the carrying on of the work until the action of the East Orange Council had been reviewed." But what were court proceedings or court stays?

The demon of corporate greed was in the saddle, and the mandate had gone forth that the franchise should be granted. And so it was; and the case in the courts went on.

In the meanwhile the drift of public opinion was reflected in the press. On June 14, 1902, the Newark News, editorially, said: "Certainly it was not in response to any public sentiment that both the East Orange Council and the Board of Freeholders granted a franchise in perpetuity and upon the trolley company's own terms;" also, "It is now pretty well assured, however, that the park commissioners have practically abandoned the idea of embracing Central avenue in the park system."

The Orange Chronicle said: "Had the Essex County Board of Freeholders come out flatfooted before its meeting, last Thursday afternoon, and told the members of the Joint Committee on Parkways that it was not going to pay the slightest attention, any way, to whatever arguments might be brought against its concurrence in the action of the East Orange City Council, it would have won at least a reputation for honesty, if for nothing else. Happily the municipal and county authorities are not the court of last resort in this appeal." Individual criticism was even more caustic, both in the public prints and in private conversation.

The Park Board meeting of June 17 was devoted to parkways. The "counsel was requested to prepare a proper petition to the municipalities requesting the care, custody, and control of Park avenue, together with a statement of our position." The following day this communication was sent to the Board of Freeholders and the authorities of Orange:

"Newark, N. J., June 18, 1902.

"Gentlemen—The Essex County Park Commission, recognizing the need of at least one parkway located in a central part of the county, and running westerly from the city of Newark, renews its application to be permitted to make the avenue known as Park avenue into a parkway.

"This commission can, with the funds likely to be at its disposal for maintenance purposes, undertake the care of Park avenue, at least to the extent that it is cared for by the Board of Freeholders, and if the Park Commission shall, in the future, be provided with further funds, it will undertake to develop Park avenue for parkway purposes in a manner more commensurate with such purposes.

"Very respectfully,
"THE ESSEX COUNTY PARK COMMISSION."

As now read between the lines and measured at this distance of time, this communication seems to indicate clearly enough that the commission had quietly succumbed to the persuasive wiles of the traction syndicate and had, as predicted, "practically abandoned" Central avenue. Such reports were given wide publicity and were greatly accelerated by the statements of the trolley agents and attorneys. These reports were still more prejudicial to the commission. This latter request, for Park avenue only, contrasted with the board's prior statement of April 3, as quoted in the preceding chapter, was one of the alleged reasons.

The Chronicle of June 23, 1902, referred to the Park avenue request as "a surprising letter," and asked the Park Board for an explanation, adding: "Why has it been left to citizens to contend for the parkways? has been a question heard on every side with no satisfactory answer. The people gave their confidence, their support and vast appropriations of money, expecting the commission to be faithful to the trust reposed in it and carry out its own plans for the two connecting parkways free from political manipulation. While their words have been smooth, the best friends of the parks and of the commissioners have found it difficult to explain their action."

The Journal concluded that "the application of the Park Commission for permission to improve Park avenue as a parkway, is a pretty thorough justification of the position taken by The Journal that the Essex County Park Commission could not, and would not, develop Central avenue as a parkway."

PARK COMMISSION'S REITERATED STATEMENTS.

About this time the false rumors, put in circulation, as to the attitude of the public and the current unfavorable reports as to the Park Commission became so frequent that, on June 28, members of the joint committee wrote the commission as follows:

"The purpose and intent of those trying to make it appear that the people are behind a scheme to appropriate for private gain another enormously valuable county road franchise at the expense of one of the great connective features of the park system is becoming well understood, and both the conditions and the facts are so clear in this instance they cannot long be misconstrued.

"We have acted in confidence on your reiterated statements that you have not changed your position in desiring both avenues for parkways, and we will be glad either to confer with you, or submit further data regarding the subject."

On July 1, 1902, there was a conference between the Newark Board of Works and the Park Commission at the latter's office regarding the Park avenue transfer by the city of Newark. Commissioners Eugene Vanderpoel, Robert F. Ballantine, and William A. Brewer were appointed a committee on parkways. Commissioner Garrison, of the Newark board, favored the transfer.

On July 4, I went over the parkway situation quite fully with Commissioner F. M. Shepard. He assured me that "the commission had not changed its position as to the avenues" and suggested that I should "see Mr. Brewer." The day following I wrote Cyrus Peck as president:

"The proceedings in the East Orange City Council and the freeholders, and the way the deal to confiscate the avenue was carried through, have accentuated and materially enlarged the whole question to a point where it would seem that something must be done by the commission to clear up its past record and present attitude as to Central avenue.

"The counsel not only gives his own consent for a railroad, but both in word and action gives an entirely different view and statement from what Mr. Shepard informs me is still the attitude of the commission, and some of the county papers—clippings enclosed—accept editorially the counsel's view as representing the position of the commission."

A FREEHOLDER'S STATEMENT.

No reply to this letter was received. On July 15, 1902, by request of Commissioner Brewer, I wrote him officially; and as a member of the Joint Committee on Parkways, giving the statement of one of the freeholders, made to me in the presence of a witness in Branch Brook Park the day previous. This freeholder, as quoted in that letter, among other things, said, he "was favorably impressed by what was said in favor of keeping Central avenue for a parkway (the afternoon the trolley resolution was passed), and, wishing to know the present attitude of the commission before voting, went to Counsel Munn and asked him direct, 'Does the Park Commission want the avenue for a parkway?' Mr. Munn replied, 'No, not that I know of.' A similar inquiry was then made of 'Wally' Ougheltree, of East Orange, the chairman of the Road Committee, who replied: 'No. the railroad ordinance was before the East Orange City Council a long time, and no word of objection was ever received from the Park Commission, nor did any one appear there from the commission opposing its passage. Had they wanted the avenue they would have so stated to the East Orange authorities. The commission had made an indefinite statement some time ago, but their actions had not corroborated it.'"

"The statements quoted from Munn," I added, "are, as you will recollect, in entire accord with what members of the East Orange City Council positively stated and restated

Munn had said to them while the trolley ordinance was
before that body."

This letter was received by Commissioner William
Brewer, and a day or two later by the commission; but I
was never asked for further particulars. Counsel J. L.
Munn remained; and matters favorable to the traction company's obtaining Central avenue, went on as before.

FOR THE PARKWAYS AGAIN.

The Orange Republican City Convention of October 1,
1902, adopted in its platform a clean-cut and definitely expressed clause, declaring for Park and Central avenues for
parkways. The trend of public opinion was toward demanding that the City Council should take favorable action on
the Cuddy transfer ordinance as approved by the Park Commission months before, and which had been resting with the
Street Committee since its introduction on December 3,
1900. At the council meeting of October 13, 1902, the ordinance, then again offered as a new ordinance and approved
by the Street Committee, was passed on first reading by a
unanimous vote. The little discussion which followed was
all in favor of that action.

The ordinance (after the customary advertisement) was,
at the meeting November 10, again, under suspension of
the rules, in like manner, finally passed. It then went to
Mayor Henry Stetson for his action. In an interview in the
Newark papers just prior to this—and a few days before the
fall election—the Mayor had declared that he had "been
ready at all times to favor any action by the city authorities
which would further the parks and parkways," and "that,
whenever a proper ordinance shall be laid before me, I will
have no hesitation in approving it."

As the ordinance, as passed ten days after this statement
was made public, was drawn expressly to meet all the
objections the Mayor had made to the two previous transfer
ordinances, the statement was construed by the uninitiated
as a favorable omen, and tantamount to a promise of his intended action on the ordinance then before the council. He

was, however, very chary as to making any specific commitments. On November 11, 1902, he wrote the Park Commission to know if, "in the event of the ordinance's becoming effective, you intend to improve Central avenue west from Centre street, it having been rumored that, should the avenue be turned over to you, you would not improve it beyond the point mentioned; also is it your intention to open up the avenue, in a line from its present terminus at Valley road to the top of the mountain?"

The reply was equally elusive, although the commission had, in March, 1901, already formally approved a similar ordinance containing the same conditions. The substance of the response was that "the commission has not seen the proposed ordinance, and before making any statements concerning it would like to have a copy."

PEARLS, MINUS A STRING.

The sources of public opinion continued to reflect the general desire for favorable action on the parkway ordinance. This sentiment was well expressed in a published letter, written on November 2, 1902, by Monsignor G. H. Doane, in which, in referring to the Essex County parks, he said: "Little has been done as yet in the direction of parkways. We have the parks, but we want to connect them; we have the pearls, but we want to string them, and that is what the parkways would do.'

Mayor Stetson vetoed the ordinance. The message was received by the City Council December 1, 1902. This third "hold-up" of the action favored by the public, and as passed by the City Council, was, according to the veto, based on "two facts which became apparent; one, that your body has no power to make the proposed transfer, and, two, that the Park Board cannot consent to it. Ideally I think your proposed action would be very praiseworthy, were it practicable, but my opinion, as well as that of many other judicious people, is, that it is now impossible, for the reasons stated.

* * * The residents of these broad public avenues are entitled to have the most convenient means of access to business and church centres."

Who the "judicious people" were, who concurred in the Mayor's pseudo-legal decision, excepting the Park Board's counsel, J. L. Munn—who at once came to the rescue in a published interview December 4, expressing his "profound respect and consideration" for the Mayor's opinion—was never, to my knowledge, made public. City Counsel T. A. Davis, of Orange, in a written opinion to the Common Council of that place, on December 8, 1902, riddled the Mayor's legal contentions, and in an exhaustive statement cited ample authorities to show that the Mayor's position had no foundation in fact. Rev. H. P. Fleming, in a published letter of December 13, treated the veto message even more severely.

"I say that the Mayor is a traitor to the public welfare of this whole community, proven to be such by his pharisaical utterances," was the forceful way he expressed that view. This he did after ridiculing the points in the veto, and then appealed to the members of the City Council to override the veto.

Other criticisms were unsparing, alike of the Mayor's feelings and of the shallow pretense of his legal excuse. As in the case of the much "counseled counsel," the mask had at last been cast aside, and it was soon generally known, as some had known before, that the Mayor was for the railroad and against the parkway first, last, and all the time; and that, if one excuse should not avail, another would be readily found. Counsel Munn, in the interview referred to, endeavored to stem the adverse tide of public comment by declaring that "the Executive's view of the matter was radically strong, and that it should command the utmost attention." "There seems to be no question," said Munn, "that the legislation in regard to the avenues has put the scheme of transfer in a very perplexing position, for the present at least." And this public statement was made after he had for years officially, as the Park Board's counsel, advised that there was no legal obstacle in the way of the avenues' transfer.

Six members of the Orange City Council were evidently converted to the Stetson-Munn railroad side of the question. When the Mayor's veto came up for action before the council on December 15, 1902, five weeks after its unanimous passage there, these six new converts (?) voted the other way, and in support of the veto. And thus, for the third time, the parkway ordinance was killed in the house of its supposed friends. At once there were the usual charges and recriminations. "Under the eye of public scorn" was the caption of a drastic editorial in one of the leading papers in referring to the action of these six councilmen, who had shifted their votes; and "not a single soul of the group could or would explain his astounding action," was the way the article went on. And "the insidious influence of the trolley interests may, for a time, prevail, but we do not believe that those who have lent themselves to this scheme of interference, will, in the end, have to give away to a mercenary corporation a franchise for that which is the people's right," was the conclusion.

The News of December 17, said, editorially: "It is wonderful the number of obstacles that have been found to delay the transfer of these avenues to the Park Board. In this respect it almost equals the service of the local traction company."

December 9, 1902, I wrote the Park Commission as follows:

"The time has come for plain speaking and prompt action unless the commission wish to assume the task of carrying a load which will now rapidly become a staggering burden, I think, in the minds of all fair-minded men, certainly of the men well-informed on park matters throughout the Oranges.

"I want to say to you, in all kindness and with all earnestness, that the lines are now drawn, and the Park Commission, for its own credit and honor, must accept or repudiate the responsibility of an employe now so discredited in his own community as to make his retention in the Park Board a serious and growing menace."

And, on December 16, I wrote: "As the action of the Orange Council last evening will tend to accelerate rather than modify the situation you are placed in by the action of your counsel, I deem it just to you and to myself to state some of the causes leading up to the situation briefly indicated in my letter to you of the ninth instant." I then referred to the statements made by Counsel Munn to some of the members of the East Orange City Council while the railroad ordinance for Central avenue was there pending; quoted the statements of the freeholder in Branch Brook Park, as above mentioned; referred to the commission's "emphatic declarations" regarding the avenues for parkways, and to "their own counsel, whose statements and acts" had for months contradicted those declarations; and enclosed a copy of the statement of E. H. Snyder, of January 15, 1897, as quoted from at length in Chapter XII.

TRANSFER OF HIGHWAYS.

I was advised on December 24 that the communications "had been received and placed on file." And the plans of the traction company for appropriating the parkway continued to move directly forward, as before.

It may here be of interest to note, with what facility and readiness existing public highways, avenues, or streets may be transferred, and have been transferred under the Essex County Park Commission's charter, when such contemplated action on the part of the interested governing bodies is not subject to the demoralizing influences, which delayed for years and finally prevented the transfer of one of the two vitally important parkway avenues. Within ten days after the passage of the parkways resolution by the Park Board in November, 1896, H. H. Hart, then president of the South Orange Village Board of Trustees, called a special meeting of that board to act upon the question, and at the meeting of November 25, by unanimous vote, South Orange avenue, "from the westerly line of Ridgewood road, westerly to the western boundary of South Orange," was transferred to the commission "for the purpose of the park act." Owing to a modification of the Park Board plans, the avenue was never accepted, but the transfer on the part of the authorities was thus promptly effected.

The ordinance transferring the short end of Park and Central avenues in West Orange, was introduced at the Township Committee's November meeting, finally passed at the next meeting, and officially reported to the Park Board on November 20, 1897.

The application for Brookside avenue was not made until May, 1897, but the transfer was promptly made and accepted by the Park Commission September 11, 1897. In the board's official report for 1897 this reference (page 14) occurs: "The Brookside road, which has been transferred to the commission by the Millburn authorities, has been improved and is an excellent example of the way a neglected road can at slight expense be converted into a delightful pleasure drive. The entire drive of two miles has been drained, widened, graded and stoned at a cost of $3,000." Thus, from the Park Board's own standpoint this improvement was used as an illustration, and as an example of how existing avenues could be at comparatively slight expense converted into parkways. This, if important for a mountain roadway, how vastly more important was the practical application of the same principle to the two great connecting parkways so vital to the whole park system.

The transfer of Mt. Prospect avenue, West Orange, was not requested by the Park Board until March, 1898, but was made without delay or objection, the local authorities being anxious to co-operate with the Park Commission in securing parkway benefits for their localities, rather than opposing such improvements for years, under the blighting influence of the corporations, as in the case of Park and Central avenues.

On January 16, 1903, the Supreme Court rendered a de-

Central avenue as passed in East Orange, April 28, 1902.
The opinion was rendered by Justice Collins, who, prior to
his appointment on the bench, was a member of the law firm
of Collins & Corbin, and whose partner was a stockholder of
record of the North Jersey Street Railway Company.
Chandler W. Riker, and P. Woodruff, as also the counsel
for East Orange, appeared for the traction company, and
R. V. Lindabury made the argument for the property owner
plaintiffs. Although it was shown by the testimony that
Bishop J. J. O'Connor was not the owner of the cemetery
property on the avenue at the time he gave a written consent, and that that consent was necessary in order to constitute a majority of the frontage owners' consents, as
clearly provided by law, the court decided that, in this case,
"ecclesiastical polity" of the Catholic Church might be substituted for legally recorded ownership, and held that the
ordinance, based upon such consent, was accordingly valid.

APPEAL TO HIGHER COURT.

The case was at once appealed. The appeal acted in the
meantime as a stay or injunction against the traction company. Mr. Lindabury advised that, in his opinion, the
Supreme Court decision referred to could not be sustained
by the higher court. Efforts were then made to obtain from
the Park Commission some action or earnest of its repeated
assurances regarding the main parkways.

On April 9, 1903, the Joint Committee on Parkways had
adopted a resolution requesting "the Park Commission to
officially express to the East Orange City Council that
board's repeatedly expressed desire to secure the care, custody, and control of Central avenue,' and appointing a sub-
committee of three to present the resolution to the commission. This committee, consisting of H. G. Atwater, J.
F. Freeman and myself, made the presentment on April 12.
At that conference, the Park Board gave no suggestion or
intimation whatever that there had been any change in the
attitude of the commission respecting the avenue parkways.

It appears from the records, however, that at that same meeting, after the committee had left the board rooms, a resolution was, in executive session, offered by Commissioner John R. Hardin, and, at the next secret meeting of the Park Board adopted, that "the landscape architects be instructed to prepare, as soon as possible, a scheme of improvement for parkway purposes, of Central avenue from the East Orange parkway to the Orange line, assuming the avenue will not be widened, and that a double-track railway, with overhead wires, will be placed on the center line thereof; roadway twenty feet wide on each side of the tracks; lawn treatment, etc., shrubs and trees, and treated as a street for both business and pleasure; the landscape architects also to furnish estimates of cost."

NOT WORTH THE COST.

The report of Olmsted Brothers, of May 7 and May 16, following that resolution, advised that "the improvement in the manner indicated will not be worth the cost"; that it involved "a purely engineering affair without the slightest element of beauty or art;" if it should be adopted, the avenue should be widened from "the East Orange Parkway to the Orange line to at least 110 feet, and new building lines established." The estimated cost was then given at $119,384, with an annual maintenance account of $4,389.

Why this action of the Park Commission, in "assuming" as it did in the resolution quoted, that the question of a railroad on the avenue was then settled, and calling for a report combining a trolley and parkway project—which was at direct variance with the board's announced policy for years theretofore, in contending that a parkway and trolley way could not be properly made on a 100 feet wide highway —was kept secret and from the joint committee and the public, is to me now, as I make this record, in view of all the circumstances, unaccountable; and I pass from the subject without comment.

The request of the joint committee referred to, as to sending a communication to the East Orange authorities, was not complied with.

On June 15, 1903, committees of the Road Horse Association, the New England Society, and the Joint Committee, presented petitions and resolutions of these organizations urging that similar action be taken with Central avenue as had been recently taken with Park avenue. These resolutions referred to "the five hundred tax-paying citizens of the Road Horse Association" as recognizing "in Central avenue the natural parkway by reason of its width, level grade, and accessible location," and petitioned the commission "to immediately assume control of Central avenue, agreeable to the original plan of said commission." It was also set forth that this was "in no sense a local question," and that "neither are the local officials nor the public informed as to the need of convenient connecting parkways, as are you gentlemen, who have studied this question as affecting the whole county." J. B. Dusenberry stated that "the population of Newark south of Central avenue and east of Fourteenth street comprised seven-eighths of the total inhabitants, and there was no avenue directly connecting the mountain reservation and Orange parks possible for a parkway excepting that avenue."

Rev. Henry Rose, C. F. Lawrence, Alden Freeman, C. A. Dickson, W. J. Baer, and others were present and spoke. The commission was non-committal as to any future action. The reception of the delegates was not, however, enthusiastically cordial. The Newark News, in commenting upon the conference, said, on June 21, 1903: "Four influential organizations appeared, by their representatives, before the Park Commission last week and presented reasons why Central avenue should be made a parkway. The arguments they urged are incontrovertible."

The Daily Advertiser editorial of June 16 said:

"The Board of Freeholders cannot disregard this powerful sentiment at the behest of private corporate interests that have already been granted nearly all of the public highways; especially in view of the fact that the trolley extension can be built over another route which will just as well serve the public convenience. By utilizing existing avenues as parkways the cost of improvement is moderate."

The Orange Chronicle asked: "Why, then, should the Park Commissioners now remain silent in the matter of carrying out their own plans? Why should they not now, by their action, show a creditable desire to have the park system carried forward to a creditable completion?"

THE PUBLIC'S POSITION.

Another press comment was: "The absolute inertia of this 'better class' board has resulted in taxpayers going to great expense to contest the trolley grab; and, still worse, the very people who have been the stanchest supporters of the Park Commission find themselves obliged to organize in committees, and to almost demand of the Park Commission that its latest pre-election pledges be carried out."

Appeals were also made direct to the new management of the traction company. The Public Service Corporation had been organized, and had absorbed, by exchange of its stock and otherwise, all the leading traction, electric light, and gas companies of Northern New Jersey. Although the corporation was purely a "business" company, it consolidated and combined into one ownership the direct control of all the various financial pyramids that had been created with fictitiously watered capital, for the purpose of absorbing and retaining in the hands of the stockholders the millions of clear profits made out of the free franchises that had been mulcted from the county and local governing bodies. This scheme enabled a few men to thus concentrate vast financial and political power, to perpetuate, and, as far as might be possible, in the future, to control and hold the vast public privileges obtained, and to become an important, if not a controlling factor in shaping State and local legislation accordingly.

But the new ownership control was, under the new management, largely in the hands of Essex County institutions, and of men who, it was thought, could not be entirely

blinded to a situation so vitally affecting the Park Board
plans and so directly affecting, for all the future, the people
of the county.

With this view the joint committee on parkways on June
17, 1903, wrote President T. N. McCarter, referring to the
"drastic measures taken by the former management of the
traction interests to avoid insolvency," made necessary by
the unrestricted over-capitalization, get-rich-quick policy of
the various companies, and to the disposition theretofore
"to destroy the parkways"—a policy, the committee believed
"the continuation of which would not appear favorable,"
or appeal "to yourself and associates in the new management, either in the interest of your corporation or in the
public interest you now have the opportunity to serve acceptably."

The reply, as editorially interpreted by the News, was:
"Very beautiful and touching is the solicitude of the Public
Service Corporation for the good of the dear public. Mr.
McCarter is a firm believer in parkways so long as they do
not interfere with the plans 'of that corporation,' "—which
quotation gives, in a few words, the gist of the whole letter.
The attitude of the company was indicated in the concluding paragraph of this letter, as follows: "If the right of
the railway to extend its tracks on Central avenue be sustained, the question will then have to be determined by the
real needs of the people, to whom the duty of Public Service is paramount."

The East Orange railway ordinance case was yet before
the higher court, and the next move on the chessboard of
parkway affairs was the reintroduction, on October 5, 1903,
of the transfer ordinance in the Orange Common Council.
Since the action of the Republican City Committee the year
previous, and the continued public agitation in favor of the
parkways, the sentiment, outside of the limited circle of the
opposing Mayor and those especially friendly to the traction
company, appeared to consist of a general demand for favor-

able action by the authorities. The ordinance, which was a copy of the "Cuddy ordinance," passed November 10, 1902, and previously approved by the Park Commission, was, without opposition, passed on first reading at the council meeting October 5, and finally passed by a vote of 9 to 4 on November 9, 1903.

About this time a sufficient number of votes in the City Council were unequivocally pledged to pass the ordinance over the Mayor's veto, should the usual tactics of the executive be adopted in his action on this measure. The Mayor, presumably having a knowledge of what was going on, had previously begun to hedge and fence for position, so to speak. On May 15, 1903, he had written the Park Commission again, asking, in the event of the transfer ordinance becoming effective, did the board "intend to improve Central avenue west from Centre street."

The commission's reply of May 20, 1903, was as follows:

"Dear Sir—Your letter with regard to Park and Central avenues was laid before the commission at its meeting yesterday, and I was directed to say that the questions concerning Central avenue were thoroughly discussed in the last annual report of the commission, a copy of which I transmit under separate cover. Since that time questions relating to Central avenue have been and are now before the courts awaiting adjudication. The commission, therefore, has given no further consideration to that subject."

On November 10, the Mayor again wrote that he had before him "for approval or disapproval an ordinance providing for the transfer of Park and Central avenues"; that he enclosed a copy of the document, adding:

"Before acting upon the ordinance I desire to obtain the views of the Park Commission upon it, as to its acceptability in its present form, etc. I am also desirous of learning whether, in the event of the ordinances going into effect, the commission would improve Central avenue in this city west of Centre street."

The letter also asked for an early reply.

The Park Board's reply of November 12, after referring

to the enclosure of copies of the commission's letters of
June 18 and June 20, 1903, stated:

"The freeholders, acting under Chapter 234 of the laws
of 1903, have transferred to this commission the care, custody and control of Park avenue throughout its entire
length. Our views concerning Park avenue are fully expressed in our letter of June 18, 1903, and concerning
Central avenue in our letter of May 20, 1903."

To this communication the Mayor on November 14 made
answer:

"Gentlemen—I beg to acknowledge the receipt of yours
of the twelfth instant. Your letter does not give me all
that I requested. I would like to know whether the ordinance in relation to Park and Central avenues, of which
you have a copy, is acceptable to you in its present shape."

On November 24, 1903, the commission replied that "the
meeting that day was the first held since the receipt" of his
letter, and then this followed:

"The attitude of the Park Commission in regard to Park
and Central avenues is fully stated in the report of the
commission for 1901 on pages 15 et seq., as we have heretofore stated to your honor.

"It is unnecessary to discuss the form of the ordinance
transmitted to us by your honor, as we observe by the public
prints that your honor has vetoed it."

Mayor Stetson's veto was announced November 23, the
day previous. The alleged reasons, as stated in the message,
were, as before, that the Common Council had "no authority" to make the transfer; that the replies of the Park Commission to his inquiries had been "evasive and unsatisfactory"; that "it seems to me, so far as Central avenue is
concerned, the Park Commission does not particularly desire the care, custody, and control of the thoroughfore; and
that, in any event, it is not advisable to make a parkway
of Central avenue" on account of the heavy traffic there, etc.

It required two-thirds, or eleven of the sixteen votes, of
the City Council members to override the veto. The veto
message came before the council for action December 7,

1903. The eleven necessary votes were pledged. On roll call Councilman F. C. Read, who had each time voted for the ordinance on its passage, and had agreed to again vote for it, voted no. Two of his colleagues, Councilmen Frank Coughtry and E. S. Perry. stated that he had repledged each of them again after the council meeting was in session that same evening, to vote aye. Alderman Ira Williams, who had also previously voted for the ordinance, and had promised to vote for it on final passage, as suddenly "flopped," and voted with the minority of six to support the Mayor. No public reasons were ever given why those two votes were so suddenly changed. This action broke the requisite two-thirds line by one vote, and killed the parkway ordinance.

UNFAVORABLE TO THE PARK COMMISSION.

Thus, for the fourth time, the evil influences of corporate aggrandizement, following the courses and methods that morally irresponsible corporations know so well how, in legislative bodies, to use to best accomplish their purposes had prevailed, and again was the revolving wheel of parkway progress clogged. Both the Park Commission and the corporation representatives were publicly and privately severely criticized. The former was openly charged with "half-hearted" action, "and the impression has gained ground that the commission repents of its early stand and wishes to get rid of the problem lately grown out of the parkway business. Can the commission tell why it is that it does not want Central avenue now?" On every side were heard adverse comments over the traction company's proceedings. There were the usual castigations, where, as in many an American city, good citizenship finds, that, for the time being, it is bound hand and foot by an insidious lurking power, which robs the community of its birthright and good name at the same time that it sequestrates and appropriates to itself, as with perpetual utility franchises, the property of the citizens unto the farthest generations of those who shall come after.

But the agitation had been productive of good. It had
stripped off the mask of more of those who had officially
or personally masqueraded as standing for what they alleged was for the public good. It had aroused the public
conscience. It formed the incubator, and later became the
mainspring of the movement for limited franchises—which
issue, each of the leading political parties have since ar-
dently and assiduously claimed as their own. The irresistible power of public opinion, growing out of the parkways
discussion, had forced the corporations to abandon the
scheme for appropriating also Park avenue. And while
the Park Commission remained in silent inactivity, as
though stricken with official paralysis, or put to sleep by
corporate hypnotism, or led by the pernicious imp of pro-
crastination, the causes that were to create an awakening
of the people were, by the parkways' contest, well grounded,
and have since been rapidly extending. And if the apathy
of the good citizens of Essex County, and of the State—
the great lodestone of the present political and legislative
situation—can, through this or other agitations, be changed
to an active participation in public affairs, a repetition of the perpetual franchise-acquiring evils and the
corrupting, boss-ridden, and demoralizing conditions witnessed in the eight years' contest over the parkways, will
be impossible, and ample reward will have been made for
all the time, money, and effort thus expended.

PARK AVENUE SURRENDERED.

The surrender of Park avenue by the trolley interests
was decided upon early in June, 1903. No sooner had the
decision to allow the county and local governing boards to
transfer that avenue for a parkway been made, than those in
authority, apparently most anxious to do the corporation's
bidding, with alacrity responded. Although, as before
stated, the special request of the Park Commission for Park
avenue alone, when that board "recognized the need of at
least one parkway," after contending for nearly seven years
that two were necessary, was made June 19, 1902, that re-

quest had been allowed to rest in the pigeon-hole archives of both the Board of Freeholders and of the Orange City Council, without either report or favorable action all that time.

When, however, the Public Service Corporation managers recognized that, with the rising tide of public sentiment, should they continue to contend for both avenues, they "might fall backward and lose both," the yielding of one—the least valuable for either parkway or trolley way—was reluctantly agreed upon. Presto! The precedent of the freeholders, which, since 1896, had been promulgated as a principle, almost too sacred or too important to be waved or broken, viz., that the board should not, and could not, act on the avenue transfer question until after the local governing boards directly interested had taken action, was at once cast to the winds. The Orange authorities had not only failed to act favorably on Park avenue, but had then, three times, expressly declined to make the transfer of both avenues. Notwithstanding this action and the "precedent" mentioned, the Board of Freeholders promptly and formally transferred Park avenue June 11, 1903, and the formal acceptance "with thanks of the Park Commission" soon followed.

These acts and facts proved more clearly than words, that really nothing had stood in the way of the prompt transfer and parkway use of both avenues for years, excepting the baneful, hidden hand of the corporate giant, which was continuously pulling the strings behind the scenes, and manipulating the toy officials to do its bidding in thus thwarting the will of the people, and depriving them of both their parkways and franchise possessions.

CHAPTER XVI.

THE parkways movement culminated in 1904, as did likewise the plans for completing the remnants of the Essex County park system. On February 29 the Court of Errors and Appeals handed down a decision in the East Orange Central avenue trolley ordinance case. The decisions reversed the findings of the Supreme Court and declared the ordinance invalid. The case for the property owners and the Avenue Association was argued with great ability by their counsel, R. V. Lindabury.

The decision was reported as unanimous. It turned mainly on the point as to the validity of Bishop J: J. O'Connor's consent. The court was evidently convinced that ecclesiastical orders, or the internal regulations of a religious organization, could not be substituted for the well-established laws and precedents for determining realty ownership—the principle involved in the Supreme Court's decision of the same question. The action of the higher court cleared the parkways atmosphere.

Appeals were at once made to the Park Commission and to the Public Service Corporation. The former was reminded that "non-action by the Park Board is literally faith without works;" that "earnest, vigorous action would at once enlist the active support of press and public all over the county," and it was asked: "Will the Park Commission, with its great power, opportunities, and present privileges, lead or follow the movement?" It was also pointed out that "should one of your number appear before the freeholders, to state and explain to them your position and wishes, all doubts and misgivings on this question would

speedily disappear." One of the leading papers, on March
5, 1904, editorially reminded the commissioners that "the
time for standing upon their dignity and maintaining an
exasperating silence has, for the members of that body,
gone by." The New England Society, on the same date,
adopted by unanimous vote a resolution "unequivocally reaffirming its indorsement of the report of the special committee on parkways reported and unanimously approved
April, 1902," and authorizing "the appointment of five
additional members to act with the Joint Committee on
Parkways toward completing the transfer and improvement
of Central and Park avenues into parkways."

The commission announced on March 2, 1904, that it was
considering the parkway problem "very carefully, and when
they came to a conclusion on the matter" it would be com-
municated, and "they would use every effort to come to a
conclusion satisfactory to the citizens of the Oranges." A
legislative bill, prepared under the direction of the commission, was introduced at Trenton about this time by Assemblyman E. D. Duffield (Assembly 317), authorizing
county boards to transfer streets or avenues, in whole or
in part. The announcement was soon made that this bill
"would go through." A hearing was given upon it by the
Municipal Corporations Committee March 17. Notice of
the hearing was given in the Newark papers on March 16,
and the Joint Committee on Parkways received a special
notification. A number of citizens from Essex County were
in attendance and spoke for the bill. J. L. Munn and
others opposing the measure for the traction company were
present, but (publicly) said nothing. The Park Commission was in no way represented there. This caused much
unfavorable comment, and it was at once reported about
the State House that that board was indifferent as to the
fate of the bill. The lobby prevailed.

BILL IN THE LEGISLATURE.

One of the Assembly committeeman said he would do
nothing that would prevent the traction company from

extending its lines on Central avenue. The bill was pigeonholed. It was never heard of again. The Park Board's
secretary, Alonzo Church, afterward stated that he did not
know of the hearing on the bill. His partner, J. L. Munn,
was, however, present when the matter came up before the
committee.

The question as to whether the trolley extension should
be on Central avenue or by another route, and thus save the
parkway, was fully covered in the conferences and correspondence between the Public Service Corporation president and the joint committee, and extended over some
months. The situation was also quite fully presented to
Senator John F. Dryden in April, 1904. As one largely
interested in the Public Service and allied corporations,
and having advanced more than $300;000 for the organiza-
tion and early financing of the North Jersey Street Railway Company, which company had at that time become,
by exchange of its securities, one of the important con-
stituent parts of the Public Service Corporation, and having become active also in political and public affairs, it
was thought that Mr. Dryden's counsel and advice might
tend to prevent "the irreparable injury to this great county
improvement which means so much in cost and future welfare to all the people of the county, should the past policy
of the traction company be insisted upon by the present
management." The "responsibility and solution are alike
simplified from the fact that your company can select another route that will conserve all public requirements and
thus preserve the integrity of the park system, and thereby
end this controversy and the consequent antagonisms that
must continue to grow to larger proportions, now that the
underlying conditions are becoming better understood."

Mr. Dryden declined to exercise his good offices in the
direction indicated, advising that his "participation in the
management of the company does not extend to matters
of that kind." The practical response, or the result of the
correspondence with the Public Service Corporation, was,
on March 14, 1904, a new application from the Consolidated

Traction Company to the East Orange City Council for another Central avenue franchise.

ANOTHER CORPORATION MOVE.

The former defect in the "consents" had been made good by Bishop O'Connor's having signed a new consent for more than 900 feet of cemetery property fronting on the avenue, the deed of the property having in the meantime been transferred to him. This new railroad application brought the question squarely to an issue. It was generally believed, as indicated by public utterances and by the press, that much depended upon the attitude of the Park Commission, and that, if that board should enter an emphatic protest, the East Orange authorities would not again respond to the behest of the traction company, even under a repetition of the former methods of exercising its persuasion through the party "organization."

The pressure upon the Park Board to do something was continually being strengthened. On March 22 the commission issued a lengthy statement to the public, and a copy was sent to the freeholders. It was also published in full— pages 23 to 27 of the eighth annual report of the department, issued in August, 1904. The statement recited the "constant effort" that had been made "to obtain the avenue for a parkway"; that "whatever the commission could do in a proper and dignified manner" to that end "has been done"; that the action of the courts in setting aside the trolley grant in East Orange "does not alter the attitude of this board"; that it "was bound to respect the action of the Common Council and the Board of Chosen Freeholders" as "the direct representatives of the people"; and that "the Park Commission must decline to take a partisan stand" on the trolley question, although "it desires to obtain the avenue as a parkway, and has repeatedly said so, and its requests for the transfer are now on file with the East Orange Common Council."

The statement then refers to the Duffield bill, above mentioned, "introduced into the present Legislature to cure the new trouble," that "the board has been informed that it cannot pass," and again "positively declines, as it has repeatedly done before, to be drawn into a partisan quarrel between two factions of citizens, each of whom it represents, and for the interests of all of whom it is earnestly working."

As the two factions of citizens at "issue" on this particular question were, in reality, the general public, and supposedly the Park Commission on the one side, and the avaricious corporation octopus, with its widely extended tentacles on the other; and as the two interests were in this instance in direct and unavoidable opposition to each other, this statement tended to make the matter of the Park Board's previous uncertain attitude still more uncertain; and to enlarge, rather than curtail, the confusion that this "new straddle" occasioned.

The effect of the statement upon the Board of Freeholders was also, to all appearances, unfavorable. When the communication was read at the meeting of that board on April 14, 1904, Freeholder W. Ougheltree, referring to the condition of Park avenue, since its transfer, expressed his "surprise at the 'cheek' of the Park Commission in suggesting such a thing" as the transfer of another avenue. The Park Board's communication was then "placed on file."

The situation was also made interesting about this time by an informal conference between one of the former Park Commissioners and the Park Board over the avenue question. Four of the commissioners were present. They were appealed to to state definitely and conclusively: First, if they still believed that Central avenue should be secured as a parkway; and, second, did they "consider it a necessity" in properly carrying out their plans? Each of the four commissioners gave an affirmative response to each of these questions. On March 22 this ex-commissioner wrote the commission at length on the subject, concluding the letter as follows:

PLAIN STATEMENT WANTED.

"To offset the adverse influence now applied at Trenton, in the councils of Orange and East Orange, and in the

Board of Freeholders, a plain, unmistakable public expression of their desires by the Park Commissioners will be effective, and will certainly bring good cheer to those public-minded citizens who have been, and are, contributing their efforts, as they believe, in furthering the purposes of the Park Commission."

In furtherance of this conference and correspondence, the sub-committee of the Joint Committee on Parkways attended the Park Board meeting of April 13, 1904. This committee consisted, as at the previous conference meeting with the board, of H. G. Atwater, J. F. Freeman, and myself, as chairman of the committee. As the commission had informally given the assurances as above quoted privately, the committee went to this meeting to petition and request that a representative of the commission should go before the City Council of East Orange, or in such other manner as the board might deem best, by or before the following Monday night, when the new franchise application was to be considered, and make a similar, unqualified statement as to the position of the commission regarding the Central avenue parkway. The committee urged that the commission could, in its opinion, "as trustees of the people of the county, consistently, and very properly, defend both the parks and the parkways"; that "many believed this to be an obligation under the trust imposed and accepted by the commission under the law for establishing the park system," and under their oath of office, which prescribed that they were to "preserve and care for, lay out and improve, any such parks and places," as provided in their charter; "and that the appropriations voted by the people had been made with the expectation that the commission would preserve as well as create the desired parks and designated parkways."

The commission was, as it had been theretofore, wholly non-committal. No assurance was given the committee, other than that the request would have "due consideration."

The following day the published reports of the conference were so entirely misleading—putting words in the mouths of both the commissioners and members of the committee that had never been uttered, and placing the whole subject in such a false light—that the committee at once wrote the president of the commission referring to the facts, and adding: "Whatever views yourself and your associates may entertain on those matters, the giving out for publication of such a misleading statement as the one in question would seem to call for prompt action and correction, due alike to the public, to you, to the conferees, the joint committee and the organizations they represent. Both the tone and erroneous statements of the article make manifest a purpose for giving out such a statement, the tone and meaning of which should be gratifying to those opposing Central avenue for a parkway and making special efforts to obtain the use of the avenue for commercial purposes."

COMMITTEE'S LETTER IGNORED.

No acknowledgment or reply to that communication was received by the committee, although the commission's attention was again called to the matter April 25, in which letter of inquiry was added: "You no doubt noticed the response of those interests to whom the boquet referred to was thrown, viz.: in the billingsgate of abuse of the commission from the Public Service attorney, at the meeting in East Orange last Monday evening."

The correction of the false report referred to was never made. No representative of the commission appeared before the East Orange City Council. No communication from the Park Board was received when, at the meeting April 18, 1904, the new trolley ordinance came up for action there. That meeting was a lively one. For nearly four hours the contest over the avenue was waged. Matters were at high tension. Preparations for the struggle had been going on for weeks. The meeting was in Commonwealth Hall. Lawyers A. J. Baldwin, F. W. Fort and L. D. H. Gilmour represented the traction company. G. S.

Hulbert, Gardiner Colby and other representative citizens, with Attorney F. H. Sommer, spoke for the parkways. These arguments covered the usual wide range, including a suggestion by Mr. Hulbert for the appointment of a "commission to investigate the whole subject and report." The corporation attorneys made the usual meaningless promises and defined "curbing the gutters, laying brick pavements, paving the roadway as desired, planting grass between the rails, keeping it watered and cut," as "parkway treatment."

The usual tactics of the traction company's representatives were followed, when Lawyer A. J. Baldwin exclaimed: "The Essex County Park Commission never kept a promise made to East Orange, and never made a promise!"

The final struggle over the franchise was postponed. On May 16 the limited franchise question was officially injected into the situation on Councilman Farnham Yardley's motion to limit the terms of that ordinance to twenty years. This was unanimously agreed to. The public was excluded. The executive sessions doors of the Council Chamber were opened just wide enough to admit E. W. Hine and Attorney Baldwin, of the traction company. This gave the interested corporation the "secret session" secrets and the opportunity of watching and "checking up" their own representatives at that important juncture of their franchise affairs.

The trolley agents said the company would not accept a limited franchise; would not allow the city more than $1,000 a year compensation; or make any more favorable terms than the perpetual franchise adjustable at the end of fifty years, the same as the franchise of two years before. That settled the question, apparently to the satisfaction of six of the councilmen, who continued to espouse the trolley company's cause to the last.

The test came at the council meeting May 23. The ordinance was then passed on first reading. Every amendment offered by Councilmen Lloyd, Brownell and Yardley for the protection of the city, was, by "the six," voted down. The matter of transfers, limit of franchise, even of decent compensation and other important restrictions, all went by the board as fast as the votes could be taken, and against the earnest protests of the minority members. They openly charged that the ordinance had been drawn by, and for, and in the interests of the traction company. The charge was not denied. It also transpired that the Railroad Committee, Councilman T. W. Jackson chairman, had, "without any right or authority" from the council, eliminated the twenty-year term limit to the franchise previously agreed upon.

On June 13, 1904, the ordinance was before the East Orange City Council for final action. The council room was packed to suffocation. The exciting scenes of the previous meeting were repeated. It was a repetition of the old, old story of the conflict between popular rights and the exercise of mercenary corporate power wielded by the few. For six hours, until nearly two o'clock in the morning, the struggle went on. Neither the logic of facts, entreaty nor appeal to protect the city availed. When the committee of 100 found it useless to consider the parkways matter, and that every indication pointed to an agreement having been made before the meeting to pass the ordinance on the corporation's own terms, G. S. Hulbert, in speaking for the committee, after reminding the council that not a single organization representing public opinion had favored the railroad, while the reverse was true as to the parkway, urged that the experience of other cities, in limiting franchises and securing fair compensation,, be considered before action be taken. The official records, showing the suicidal policy of giving away a perpetual franchise, such as the one under consideration, were quoted from at length. Expert estimates were also given as to the present cash value of the Central avenue franchise, which a majority of the city representatives (?) then evidently proposed to grant for the insignificant (compared with its value) sum of $1,000 per year. "Solemn protests" were entered by a number of citizens. About midnight a motion to postpone consideration of the subject until June 27 was defeated. The majority were manifestly determined to deliver the franchise that night—or, rather, before daylight the next morning.

The "six" had evidently come to the meeting invisibly tagged, and mentally labeled, by the same power and influences that had insidiously and surreptitiously "held up" the parkways and advanced the railroad interest in defiance of public opinion for the preceding eight years. The "deal" was to be put through then. As a legislative proceeding the whole meeting was therefore a travesty, both upon parliamentary rules and deliberate assembly procedure. The rules were, under the ruling of Chairman William Cardwell, finally suspended, and against the protest of the minority, the ordinance, long after midnight, was passed. The excitement was intense: And out of this meeting, and the franchise agitation that had grown out of this struggle over the Central avenue parkway, rapidly grew the agitation for limiting utility franchises. This movement, locally, had its culmination in Orange a few months later, when the traction company, under the usual methods, made another attempt to secure a perpetual franchise there. The public conscience was by this time thoroughly aroused, and, as expressed in a massmeeting of citizens of all shades of opinion (December, 1904), swept everything before it.

Two days after the passage of the railroad ordinance in East Orange, June 16, 1904, G. S. Hulbert, H. G. Atwater, A. P. Boller and J. Colter, as a sub-committee on behalf of the committee of 100, had a conference with Mayor E. E. Bruen. The committee submitted in writing the concessions it was deemed imperative that the city should secure before any such valuable franchise could be properly granted. Mr. Boller said that, should the Mayor sign the ordinance, "he would betray a public trust."

"This is not a defensible franchise, either before the public, on the platform, or before the people at the polls," declared Mr. Atwater. The Mayor argued at length for the traction company. It was expected that he would sign the ordinance. It was currently reported that he had agreed to do so weeks before its passage. His signature was soon attached to that document.

The goal of the traction company for Central avenue in East Orange was now reached, save for the approval of the franchise grant from the freeholders. The pro-corporation proclivities of a majority of that board were well known. So well, indeed, was this condition understood, that none of the civic organizations which had been deeply interested in the parkway-trolley question deemed it worth while to attend the August meeting, when the matter was to come up before the freeholders for action. This understanding of the board's position grew out of its previous adverse action at various meetings, as already described, in acting on the parkways in the interest of the traction company; and the indifference or contempt with which Director Thomas McGowan and a majority of the board had treated the citizens at the previous "hearing," as though presentments favoring the parkways and protesting against the encroachment of the corporations on the parkway reservations were not worthy of the slightest consideration.

TRACTION MEN'S BOAST.

The traction company's officials had also boasted of their power over the county and local governing boards. When the attention of one of the head officials of the Public Service Corporation was called to the possibility of trouble growing out of the agitation over the parkway-trolley contest in the Oranges, his reply, in referring to the franchise, in language more forcible than polite, was: "We've already got it; it's all set to music to go through." This view was evidently shared by the corporation managers generally, for early in August, 1904, before the application for Central avenue in Orange had even been considered by the City Council, and before any action had been taken by the freeholders on the East Orange ordinance, the company distributed rails for quite a distance on both sides of the avenue in Orange.

These events cast their shadows before, and no surprise was therefore occasioned when, on August 11, 1904, the Board of Freeholders danced to the "organization" music and put through, without a hitch, the Central avenue franchise just as had been done in East Orange—on the corporation's own terms.

Before the passage of the ordinance a communication, which, on behalf of the Joint Committee on Parkways, I had prepared, was read. This letter called attention to the inconsistent position of the board in now doing for the trolley company—in ignoring the non-action of the Orange authorities—just what for years they had declined to do for the Park Commission and the public; referred to the vast sums being expended in other growing urban communities for parkways to unify their park systems, instead of destroying the available parkways, as would result in granting the avenue franchise; and cited numerous instances showing these conditions; also the favorable results of restrictive franchises, and the inimical effects to the public of such a franchise as that formerly granted for South Orange avenue. In the letter it was also pointed out that the passage of the Central avenue franchise "under its present terms, will, if not otherwise prevented, destroy the parkway and hand over to the traction company at least hundreds of thousands of dollars—the property of the people of the county, as much as the courthouse, the hospitals, asylums, or any other county property."

Soon after the freeholders had passed the franchise the case was again taken into court. The property-owning plaintiffs were handicapped from the outset by the care exercised by the corporation attorneys in avoiding legal defects, as a result of the failure of the previous ordinance; but more from the fact that they found nearly every conspicuous lawyer in the State retained, or in some other way under the direction of, or indirect obligation to, the Public Service, or its allied corporations. R. V. Lindabury, having been retained by the Public Service Corporation on the announcement of the Court of Errors and Appeals' decision in the East Orange case the year before, was unable to continue as counsel.

Alan Strong and F. H. Sommer made the argument before Judge W. S. Gummere on the application for a suit for certiorari to review the proceedings. Frank Bergen and R. H. McCarter represented the company. Judge Gummere, on apparently the merest technicalities, denied the application. The case was ended. The final scene of the last act in the "Public Service" (?) parkways drama was over. The corporation had won;—though a very costly victory it has been. The power conferred by the people, to be used for their benefit and to protect and preserve their interests, had been, by their own representatives and through the manipulation of special interests and the party "machine," turned against them. The experience, as it has been in Philadelphia and other cities, was costly—the object lesson most valuable. And out of the loss of that parkway there may continue to grow a spirit of civic pride, of interest and devotion to local, State, and public affairs, that will make a repetition of such an experience in the future impossible, and the lesson in civic and political affairs well worth all it has cost.

EAST ORANGE PARKWAY.

The improvement of the East Orange parkway, extending only from Park avenue to Central avenue, has dragged along for years. Even now (December, 1905) it is in a chaotic and unfinished condition for about half the distance—the portion south of Main street. Although a "crosstown boulevard or speedway" in East Orange was one of the first matters brought to the attention of the Park Board in 1895-6, and from the first persistently advocated by Commissioner F. M. Shepard, it was not until April 13, 1897, that tentative plans and estimates of cost between Bloomfield avenue and Central avenue were from the landscape architects and engineers authorized. This report, covering the section between Park and Central avenues only, was submitted, and land options authorized, on May 18 following. During 1898-9 the crossing of the Delaware, Lackawanna and Western Railroad tracks and of Main street were, for many months, undetermined problems.

The expense of the costly stone bridge for elevating the railroad over the parkway was borne by the commission. As a suitable subway under Main street and the trolley tracks there, as favored by Commissioner Shepard, was estimated to cost $93,271, the grade crossing at Main street was finally determined upon. By these matters, together with the complications over condemnation proceedings in acquiring some of the land for the parkway, and the controversy between the commission and the city authorities over the drainage, this shortest and smallest of all the acquirements now in the control of the Park Commission, has been proportionately the most expensive, and the time in making the improvements the longest drawn out. This, notwithstanding, deeds for much of the land were given to the commission. The larger owners, whose lands were located on the line of, and mostly on both sides of the parkway, and their frontage there were respectively as follows:

Frederick M. Shepard, 2,361 feet; Rockwell estate, 531 feet; Randall estate 454 feet; David S. Walton, 1,462 feet.

The contest over the drainage matter is yet unsettled, although the commission on June 18, 1901, paid $11,000 toward the expense of drainage for the short portion of the parkway north of Main street. The contract for the first construction, amounting to $24,018, was not let until November 13, 1900, and for the section between Park avenue and William street not until the autumn of 1903.

Owing to the uncompleted condition of this parkway, its short length, and the fact that within this small distance it crosses one double trolley trunk line at Main street, and that, since Central avenue has been given over to the trolley, the southern terminus is directly on another double track railroad there, the parkway is but little used. It is thus a constant reminder of the landscape architect's report, already quoted, which advised that if Central avenue could not be used to form a continuous parkway "this East Orange parkway will hardly be worth to the people what it will cost."

The land for the East Orange parkway, outside of that donated, has cost about $100,000, and the improvements, including the bridge for changing the grade of the Lackawanna tracks, completed some years ago, nearly as much more. What the cost would have been had this parkway been extended from Bloomfield avenue to Weequahic, or to the West Side Park, and from Watsessing Park to Irvington, as was at one time proposed, it would now be difficult to estimate.

Why there should have been for years such apathy and official indifference as to securing the two great east and west parkways, which, save surface embellishment, were mainly ready for use, and this, too, on the lines connecting the most important by far of the country parks, and in the direction of the greatest tide of travel; and at the same time a new, costly and untried cross section parkway was preferably sought, connecting only a parkway at one end and now a railroad at the other end—is a question, which, as time goes on, and the more it is studied, the more difficult a sufficient or satisfactory answer will appear. It is a policy which, to say the least, is not in conformity with the plan and policy upon which the Essex County Park Commission was originally established and approved by the people.

RÉSUMÉ AS TO PARKWAYS.

The question finally arises, what have the people of the county obtained for the five millions of dollars contributed, and has the Park Commission accomplished all that could have been done to make the park system a great success? It is manifestly evident that the park system is incomplete, because the Park Commission has failed to secure a system of parkways to connect the existing parks.

While the parks themselves have been, for the most part,

well selected, also good work done in securing park lands, and the parks made beautiful and satisfactory to the people, yet there has been no system of parkways established to connect the several parks, and the commission has failed to improve its opportunity in accomplishing this result.

In every extended park system in the country one of the first duties of the commissioners has been to secure the requisite parkways. The impotent and ineffectual action of the Essex County Park Board, for years, after asking for the control of Central, Park, and other avenues for parkways, appears from every standpoint unjustifiable. If the commission had followed up the application for the main parkways, with earnest work, as have other park commissions, and made the fact appear that without them no real park system could be established, the commission would, without doubt, have been successful.

As a result of this non-action and of these adverse influences, the Central Avenue Parkway was forever lost, with no possible avenue to take its place, as the great cost of land for such a parkway makes it prohibitory.

Park avenue will, when improved, make an excellent parkway, although lacking in accessibility to the people of the county in the convenient and central location and easy grades of Central avenue.

CHAPTER XVII.

THERE are but few matters remaining for reference or record in this volume. Although it has been my purpose in compiling this history of park events, to omit trivial or minor incidents, and note only the potential facts, it has already transcended the space intended. Only a brief account or mention of other topics will, in conclusion, be given.

One of the interesting events which occurred after the second commission was organized in 1895 was the action of the old Newark Park Commission of 1867, in turning over to the new County Park Board all the maps, plans and other papers in the possession of the survivors of the former commission. At a meeting held in Mayor J. A. Lebkuecher's office, Newark, in June, 1895, Messrs. D. F. Tompkins, W. A. Righter, T. T. Kinney, W. H. Burnet, Francis Mackin, D. Meyers and Thomas Sealy, former commissioners, were present, and formal resolutions authorizing the transfer of the papers, etc., to be held by the new commission, "for the public," were passed. Before final adjournment there was an informal conference, and pleasant reminiscences were exchanged between members of the two boards at a meeting held at the commission's rooms, 800 Broad street, Newark.

Another interesting event, was the inspection of the Boston and metropolitan park systems by the commission, landscape architects, counsel and secretary August 5 and 6, 1896. While many features of interest were noted and others commended in those extended park and reservation grounds, it was found that there was little, in the various kinds of improvements there, that appeared to be applicable to the park problem in Essex.

Reference has already been made in the preceding chapters to the petitions of citizens, and hearings given by the Park Board to numerous delegations from various parts of the county. Perhaps one of the most interesting and commendable communications was the circular letter of the South Orange citizens' committee of December 6, 1895. The committee proposed "a plan of self-assessment" of from forty cents to one dollar per front foot on property fronting on the streets more especially affected by the local park, which "it was desired should be established, extending from the Orange Triangle Park, by and including the Montrose tennis grounds, to South Orange avenue." This letter, or petition, I had before me, or in mind, when at the Park Board meeting March 2, 1896, I offered the resolution authorizing the preparation by the landscape architects and engineers of an official "map of a connecting parkway along, or adjacent to, Mosswood avenue, from Warwick avenue via Tremont avenue to the triangle tract," as mentioned in Chapter VIII.

With Central avenue as a parkway, as planned at that time, this extension by the tennis grounds to South Orange, would, in time, have made a park and parkway route direct from Branch Brook Park, Sussex avenue, Ninth avenue, Grove street or Sixteenth street, Central avenue and the Orange Park, one of the most attractive park system features to be found in this country.

On May 6, 1898, the landscape architects and engineers, Messrs. Barrett and Bogart, made a report to the commission on the subject of a parkway on the lines of Mosswood avenue, the plan to include a proposed gift of land just previously offered by Sidney M. Colgate. No action, however, was taken.

August 20, 1898, a delegation of citizens from Belleville petitioned for a parkway from the Second River northerly to the county line. The district was deemed too sparsely populated, and too lacking in objective and connective points to warrant favorable consideration.

The largest petition for any one improvement which I think was ever received by the commission was that urging a parkway location along the Passaic River. Attached to this document were more than 3,000 names, and with it was also presented a resolution from the Newark Board of Trade of similar purport. While the first park commission had looked with favor upon the west bank of the river as a desirable parkway for the future, the condition of the stream has, from that time to the present, precluded favorable consideration for any kind of park treatment there.

On May 29, 1900, a delegation of Roseville citizens advocated the acquirement from the Newark city authorities and the extension and improvement of Second avenue as a parkway from Branch Brook Park to the East Orange parkway. Other delegations from Bloomfield, Montclair, the Oranges and the various wards of Newark have at different times waited upon the commission to urge park or parkway improvements in their locality. On April 4, 1905, a committee representing the South Orange Improvement Society—Messrs. H. S. Underhill, Ira Kip, Jr., Spencer Miller, S. M. Colgate and E. E. Clapp—appeared to again urge parkway improvement from the Orange Park to South Orange avenue, and offering to donate the entire right of way. On June 19, 1905, a committee from Montclair—W. B. Dickson, E. O. Bradley and D. M. Sawyer—advocated more small parks for that locality. Likewise on the same day delegations of Newark citizens from the Fifth and Twelfth wards urged that a small park be established in the northern section of the "Down Neck" part, or "Ironbound District" of the city.

The chief engineer formally called the attention of the commission on December 12, 1899, to the fact that "the sidewalks fronting the parks were in many instances disfigured by trolley, telegraph and telephone poles." These poles had been in some instances erected without permission or a shadow of authority. The special attention of the Park Board was also called to this fact. The poles still remain.

COSTLY NEGLIGENCE.

On June 2, 1903, about the time of the transfer of Park avenue by the freeholders to the commission, a delegation from the citizens' committee of Roseville was given a hearing. The committee protested against the execution of the plans for the proposed Park avenue bridge over the Lackawanna tracks at Thirteenth street, which, it was declared, would "disfigure an approach to Branch Brook Park and would prove dangerous to drivers and pedestrians." The bridge as then planned was to narrow the roadway down to a width of only forty feet. A conference with the railroad officials was, by the commission, requested. The company at once took the ground that as the specifications with the freeholders and the Newark and East Orange authorities had been agreed upon, the charge in widening the bridge to the requisite width must be borne by the commission.

In the seventh annual report of the Park Department, reference is made to the "negotiations with the railroad authorities in the endeavor to have the bridge, which is to cross the tracks, as much in conformity with park design as possible," but, as the railroad had "secured the proper consents, whatever is done toward altering them (the plans) must be at the expense of the county."

As early as February 24, 1902, the Newark Board of Works had asked for a conference with the East Orange authorities regarding this bridge. At the time, in 1903, the specifications were agreed to, it was well known to those interested that the traction company had capitulated as to surrendering Park avenue—as evidenced by the expressed willingness of the freeholders to transfer that avenue to the Park Commission—and that it was to be a parkway.

Why, therefore, no attention was given to the requisite

width of the bridge before the specifications were agreed to by the freeholders, or what the "much-counseled" counsel was doing, entrusted as he was with the legal matters of, and drawing a salary from, both the Board of Freeholders and the Park Board, in approving those specifications, which were sure to throw upon the taxpayers of the county the entire fifteen or twenty thousand dollars' expense for making the necessary changes afterward, is a matter regarding which I do not think any satisfactory explanation has ever been attempted.

SMALLER PARKS.

Besides the parks now under the control of the Park Board and already referred to, there were two small areas, transferred by local authorities, which have received park treatment, or are in process of improvement by the commission. Early in 1898 the authorities of East Orange decided to turn over to the permanent care of the commission the land comprising about fifteen acres on the border line of Bloomfield, which tract had been formerly used in connection with the local sewerage system as disposal works. The proposition was to transfer the land without cost to the county on condition that it should be made a park. The matter was afterward submitted to a vote of the city electorate and approved by a liberal majority. The tender was accepted by the commission December 10. On October 23, 1900, $5,000 was appropriated for improvements. The grounds have been laid out and planted and now constitute Watsessing Park.

It was also at the same time proposed to transfer the small unimproved tract in the southern part of East Orange, known as Elmwood Park, and an ordinance was drawn for that purpose. The commission, however, did not accept it.

At the Park Board meeting of August 15, 1902, the commission voted to accept the thirteen acres of park land which had been presented to Montclair Township by C. W. Anderson, and which, in turn, had been offered the commission on condition that the tract be improved and maintained as one of the county parks. The formal transfer was made June 23, 1903. This tract, like the Watsessing Park, is isolated from the other and larger parks and both must remain in future, as now, local parks, outside of any connective features of the county park system.

One of the local attractions in Branch Brook Park is the fountain in the old city reservoir. Its construction was authorized June 30, 1903, "Not to cost more than $2,000." The water is supplied from the Newark supply mains without charge. The four-inch centre pipe throws the water about fifty feet in height, and the circular outlets fill the sides and diameter to a corresponding height and width. The fountain in summer is always a most attractive feature. The same may be said of the boating in that park, of the flower shows during the season, of the skating in winter; and of the band concerts in all the Newark parks and the Orange Park during July and August, which have become an established and popular feature each year.

On May 23, 1904, an interesting event occurred in Branch Brook Park in the unveiling of a bronze bust of Mendelssohn, a gift from the United Singers of Newark.

In 1902 two very important matters, vitally affecting the parks, were disposed of—the question of a maintenance fund, and another million-dollar appropriation "for completing the parks." Up to that time there had been no separate provision for maintenance, the cost having been provided out of the available funds derived from the sale of "park bonds." Three times—January 15, September 11 and November 26, 1901—the commission had ordered prepared by the counsel, for introduction into the Legislature, a maintenance bill, but, with the usual delay and want of attention, the matter was not attended to and it was February, 1902, before the bill made its appearance in the Senate at Trenton.

The bill provided for a mandatory insertion by the freeholders, in the county tax levy each year, of "not less than one-half of one mill on the dollar, nor more than three-fourths of a mill on the dollar, of the assessed valuation of the taxable property and ratables of the said county," the "amount to be paid over to and expended by the commission;" unless the "Park Commission shall certify to the Board of Chosen Freeholders that a less amount is needed for the maintenance of the park system during that year," etc. The measure met with active opposition. The Republican county organization was up in arms directly. Carl Lentz, at the Lincoln Day dinner in East Orange, the evening of February 12, 1902, took advantage of the opportunity accorded him of speaking by giving a tedious argument against the bill, interspersed with the usual specious plea of home rule. Some of the newspapers lined up with "the organization" in disfavoring the bill.

The measure passed the Legislature, was approved, and thus became the law, on March 28, 1902. The act contained a referendum clause and was submitted to the voters of the country at the fall election, November 2. Only 28,467 votes were cast—16,379 for and 12,088 against the bill, making the majority but 4,291 for the entire county. In November, 1902, the Park Board made a requisition for $100,000 for maintenance account, under the provisions of this law. The amount provided for maintenance for the current year (1905) is $118,586.25.

ANOTHER MILLION DOLLAR APPROPRIATION.

Long before 1902 it was known to the commissioners that additional funds would be asked, by another issue of park bonds, notwithstanding the pledges made in 1898, when the last $1,500,000 were called for, that that amount would "be sufficient to leave the county in possession of a park system, properly connected with parkways, second to none in the country," as previously quoted. At the board meeting of November 26, 1901, the commissioners had the subject of, and estimates for, another appropriation for-

mally before them. The question at that time was whether
they should ask for one, one and a half, or two millions
of dollars. On March 18, 1902, Senator J. H. Bacheller
introduced in the Senate a bill of similar text to the previous appropriation act, but fixing the amount of bonds to
be issued at $1,000,000. The bill was rushed through two
readings in the Senate the same day. The Park Commission, the New England Society, and, I believe, one or two
other civic organizations, favored the bill. The general
public sentiment, as it appeared reflected in the press, was
mainly unfavorable.

The objections to an appointive commission were again
forcibly brought out. There were few, if any, arguments
put forward in the bill's favor. It contained, as had the
previous bills, a referendum clause. Before the November
election there was much outspoken comment and severe
criticism. The Newark News of October 16, 1902, said,
editorially: "As to increasing the bonded debt of the county
another million of dollars for the improvement of the
parks, the News believes the decision of the voters will be,
and should be, in the negative." The Call said: "Give the
people a rest." The Daily Advertiser, while the bill was
before the Legislature, March 21, paid its respects to the
proposed law in these words: "The most audacious demand made recently upon the people of this community
is that of the Park Commission for $1,000,000, with which
to complete its park system." Reference is then made in
the article to the first commission's "promise to complete
for $2,500,000, when the commission was instituted sev-
eral years ago." Later the commission came before the
people and said, in effect: "We have spent all of your
money in such a manner that it will be necessary to spend
$1,500,000 more for you to get any good out of a large
part of the park system."

The bill passed the Legislature, and was also approved
March 28, 1902. The comparatively small majority and
the large adverse vote on November 2 reflected the lack of
sympathy and support of the people of the county in the

undertaking. There were only 15,888 votes cast for the bill, and 12,248 against it, or a total majority of only 3,640.

The question as to the constitutionality of the law as related to the appointive commission feature was brought forward by the refusal of Judge John A. Blair, of Hudson County, to appoint a park commission for that county under a law similar to the Essex County park act, and applicable to Hudson County, having been passed by the Legislature about this time. The Hudson County act, however, provided for the appointment of the commissioners by the presiding judge of the Court of Common Pleas, and divided the party participation in the management, by making the number of commissioners four—two to be chosen from each of the leading political parties.

Both the Supreme Court, and later, the Court of Errors and Appeals, June 15, 1903, upheld the appointive feature of the park charters as being constitutional.

On October 1, 1903, $500,000 of the four per cent gold bonds, authorized by the last appropriation law, were sold by the freeholders to the Mutual Benefit Life Insurance Company at the (to the company) favorable price of a 103 per cent basis. On October 12 the proceeds and the small premium received for the bonds were paid over to the Park Commission. On January 31, 1905, a requisition was made for the balance of the $1,000,000 appropriated, and, on February 3, the remaining $500,000 of bonds were sold to J. D. Everett & Co. and Farson, Leach & Co. on their joint bid of $107,273. The $536,375 proceeds were soon afterward received by the commission.

On March 28 the commission took up the consideration of estimates and data, as previously prepared, for the expenditure of this last $500,000. The matter is still under consideration. On July 1, 1905, there was in round numbers about $700,000 on hand, but against this amount there were liabilities and commitments to quite an amount, and more being from time to time determined.

CHAPTER XVIII.

SINCE this history of the Essex County parks was begun, I have received various inquiries and requests, if I would not, in a concluding chapter, indicate, from my intimate knowledge of park affairs, such changes as might be made, in the interest of the public and for the good of the parks.

As this record deals principally with the past, and the line is therefore drawn on the course of events mainly to the present, I will make here but a brief reference to the points covered in these inquiries. I do not, however, hesitate to express the conviction that there are changes which I believe most important, which demand early attention, and that should soon be made.

First;—Restrictions and further safeguards by statute should, in my judgment, be thrown around the present method of selecting park commissioners. When the present plan of leaving the appointment of commissioners entirely to the presiding justice of the Supreme Court was adopted, it was confidently expected that the selections from year to year to fill this responsible position would be made for reasons of special "fitness," and that other influences in the determination of that question would be thus effectually eliminated.

That a different result has obtained, and that this method of creating park commissions has been, in its practical workings in Essex County, a disappointment to the public, is not, I believe, a question of the slightest doubt in the mind of any well-informed person on the subject.

The manifest tendency of the present system, where the

absolute power of appointment is conferred upon one court official, and an appointive official at that, has been to create conditions akin to those of a close corporation. This result was never intended nor contemplated by those who originally suggested this plan. Under the usages of this system a park commissioner may be repeatedly chosen from reasons of personal or political favoritism, or by the desire of corporate or special interests to perpetuate appointments and conditions inimical to the public interests, and thus tend to continue in authority those neither competent nor well qualified to fill the position, and to nullify the original intent, and to undermine the fundamental structure upon which this plan of creating and continuing county park boards was based.

The plan was cordially approved by the people and by the Legislature in 1894-5, because the objects sought strongly appealed to the press, the electorate and the public generally. Were the questions involved, in the light of experience, again submitted to the Legislature and to the people of Essex County, there can be little doubt that the verdict would be emphatically against the continuation of the present system.

Experience in all such matters is an excellent teacher, and it may be of interest to note here the methods of selecting park commissioners and the result in other places where large public park undertakings are well established.

OTHER LARGE PARK SYSTEMS.

In most instances the control of the parks is treated as a municipal function, similar to other city departments, with commissioners either appointed by the Mayor or the City Council, or elected the same as other officials at the regular elections. Some of the States, like Massachusetts, have a general park act, providing for the selection and appointment of park commissioners by the mayors in cities, and for their election in the usual manner in the towns.

The Metropolitan Park Commission of that State consists of three members, appointed by the Governor, "by and with the consent of the Council." In this combined State and municipal great park enterprise the plan appears to have worked out thus far very well. The Park Board of Boston has also three members appointed by the Mayor, "with the approval of the City Council." As Boston has usually had good mayors, the appointments and work of the commission there have been generally acceptable to the people.

In New York the charter for the greater city provides for a Park Commission of three members. The appointments are made by the Mayor. No confirmation by the Aldermen is required. Each of the Commissioners have administrative jurisdiction in the boroughs of Manhattan and Richmond, the Bronx, and in Brooklyn and Queens, respectively. While the members meet weekly as a board for the whole city, in practical workings there is a single-headed commission for each of the three boroughs mentioned. As New York has had a varied experience in the kind of mayors chosen, and political influences not infrequently form an important factor in the selection of Park Commissioners there, the personnel of that board has usually reflected the predominating qualities of the chief executive and the conditions determining the appointments. Since the location of Central and Prospect parks and the park system of the Bronx, many years ago, there have been many excellent and public-spirited men who have served as Commissioners there.

The Fairmount Park Commission of Philadelphia is composed of sixteen members: Five are appointed by the District Court, five by the Court of Common Pleas, and six members of the city government—the Mayor, presidents of the Select and Common Councils, Commissioner of City Property, the Chief Engineer and the Chief Water Works Engineer—are members ex-officio. While the appointees have usually been prominent citizens, there has been adverse criticism from the partisan character of the board, and the number of complex elements in the Commission have apparently made it difficult to carry out a progressive park policy for the city as a whole.

In Chicago the five Commissioners in control of the South Park system are chosen by the several Circuit Court judges of that district. Since the acquirement of the first South Side parks, in 1869, these court officials have agreed upon appointments which have been free from political interference, and the appointees being men of standing, and devoted to the parks, they have retained the confidence and support of the public to a marked degree.

The North Side, or Lincoln Park Board, and the Commission in charge of the West Side park system of that city, are both appointed by the Governor. There have been good men from time to time appointed on each board, but each in turn has for years, under different administrations, been subject to partisan uses, or under the influence of practical politics.

The Park Commissions of Baltimore, Buffalo, Cincinnati, New Orleans, Omaha, Providence, San Francisco, St. Louis and St. Paul, are parts of the city governments, respectively, either appointed by the Mayor or elected by the City Council.

In Washington the comprehensive plan for the capital as prepared in 1791 by the great landscape architect and city builder, Peter C. L'Enfant, has been only partially carried out. The city parks and squares are now under the control of a local officer of the War Department; the effectively planted avenues and streets, of the Parking Commission; and Rock Creek Park of still another commission, composed of District officials or officers of the general government.

Cleveland and Detroit are both experimenting with single-headed commissions, the former park boards having been abolished by the general city charter legislation of Ohio a few years ago, and the so-called "ripper" bills of Michigan in 1901. In both instances the Park Department is a branch of the city government.

AN ELECTIVE PARK BOARD.

From the time of the establishment of the Minneapolis parks, in 1887-9, the Park Board has been an elective body, and perhaps one of the most successful and satisfactory commissions in the country. There are fifteen members of the board, twelve of whom are elected the same as other city officials. Four of these members are elected every two years, to serve for a term of six years. The Mayor, and the chairman of the Committee on Public Grounds, and of Roads and Bridges, are members ex-officio. While Minneapolis does not claim the distinction of having always chosen ideal mayors, good men for the Park Board have almost invariably been elected, and that system has apparently given excellent satisfaction to the people of the city. Mr. C. M. Loring, one of the original Commissioners, now a member of the Commission, and one of the most earnest public park exponents, states that "in twenty-two years there have been but three adjournments for want of a quorum." With the divided responsibility and diversified interests of such a board of fifteen members—a number many municipal experts deem unwieldy—this record alone indicates the care with which the selection of candidates for the office has been made.

Another Commission which was organized and has since continued on somewhat different lines, but with results which have proven most satisfactory, is the one at Hartford, Conn. Under that plan the Park Commission itself makes the nomination for the new member, one vacancy occurring by expiration of the term of office each year. The Mayor is an ex-officio member and presides at the meetings when a nomination is to be made. The ten original Commissioners were named in the charter. The nomination to fill the place of a retiring member is subject to the approval or rejection of the Board of Aldermen. If rejected, the Commission then nominates another candidate, and so continues until the nomination is confirmed. This method of attaching a direct responsibility both upon the Commissioners and the chosen representatives of the people has given that city a "model" Park Board, and a park system, for its size, perhaps second to none. Both in Minneapolis and Hartford the comparatively large Commissions were evidently created with the view that in numbers there is safety, and with the belief that the combined judgment of many is preferable in such important matters to the decision of the few.

In most of the instances above cited, as in most American and foreign cities, the office and position of park commissioner is an honorary one, the members serving during their term of office without compensation. The notable exceptions are the single-headed commissions, where, as a rule, a salary is paid in conformity with the scale of salaries in the other city departments. In New York the three Commissioners are paid $5,000 per year each.

INQUIRIES AND RECOMMENDATIONS.

In response to the direct inquiry as to my conviction or recommendation as to changes in the law affecting Essex County park matters: I favor an elective commission. I believe, as I did when the amendments to the park charter were under consideration in 1895 (as described in Chapter III), that "the people can be trusted on the issue." The recent popular uprising, here as elsewhere, all over the country for better municipal and legislative conditions, again vindicates the sound principle upon which our elective system is founded, and creates a new condition favorable to enlarged opportunities for the selection of such officials directly by the electorate, without the intervention or assistance of the courts. Under an elective system, the taxpayers, who foot the bills for public parks, have the opportunity of directly expressing their confidence in the men who are to spend their money. In the appointive system, as now in force in Essex County, no such opportunity exists, and to establish official responsibility to the people is a roundabout course, and an uncertain determination of conclusion to reach. If the court appointive plan is to continue, I should favor the substitution of at least three judges for the one now exercising that authority, as under the present system. The addition of the judges of the Circuit Court, and of the Court of Common Pleas, to the present appointing power, the Supreme Court justice, and making the concurrence of two of those judges as to any selection for a park commissioner imperative, would be an added safeguard and remove the one-man-power objection, and condition heretofore exercised and still existing. Such a change, however, would be merely in method —collateral, not fundamental. The people contribute directly in their taxes practically all of the money for the parks; why should they not be entrusted to elect the men to care for and maintain their pleasure grounds, the same as they select their other executive and legislative representatives.

The more the comparison between the appointive and elective systems are studied, the more decided, I believe, will be the conclusion averse to. the appointive plan, and that at least in Essex County this method should soon be a thing of the past.

EXECUTIVE SESSIONS.

The second change it seems in every way desirable should be made is;—

That all regular meetings of the Park Board should be held in open session, and that all public records and documents in the possession of the Commission should at all times be open to examination by any taxpayer and reputable citizen of the county. I believe a law should be passed by the next Legislature making this principle of transacting public business compulsory on every board expending public funds throughout the State.

The executive-session-close-corporation method which has for years been in vogue here is not congenial to American ideals, and I believe should have no place in any republic, nor should it find lodgment, continuance or encouragement in any State, county, municipality or the smallest borough or hamlet, concurrently with republican institutions.

Such conditions of continuous secret sessions in exercising the control and expenditure of vast amounts of public funds and the transaction of public business generally, are, to my mind, not only un-American and contrary to the principle upon which our system of government rests, but they constitute a wrong upon every citizen and taxpayer, who is entitled to the services of the best men who can be selected for filling important positions of public trust, and who should have the unquestioned right at all times to know how the business for which he is contributing both the cash capital and the power conferred is being conducted.

Perhaps one of the most effective remedies for correcting errors or defects in such matters is publicity; and for continued star chamber proceedings of public boards, more publicity.

FOR PARK MAINTENANCE.

Third;—In return for the millions of dollars in free franchises heretofore granted in Essex County, a plan might well be enacted into law, which would, by a sufficient tax on gross receipts, provide for the entire cost of the care and maintenance of the parks.

In Baltimore the charters of the street railway companies originally provided for a six-cent fare, one cent of which was paid over to the city for park funds. On reduction of the fare to five cents the proportion to be paid to the city was reduced to nine per cent of the gross receipts. This payment is rapidly increasing and now amounts to about $400,000 per year. The city has excellent street-car service, and the franchises have proven enormously profitable to the companies.

A similar law applicable to Essex and Hudson counties would not only provide for the entire cost of maintenance of all the public parks, but the revenue would be constantly increasing, and provide funds for the enlarged acquirement of land and for needed improvements.

This suggestion will, of course, be promptly met by the interested corporations, and perhaps others, with the plea that, as many of the most valuable franchises have already been granted, and the New Jersey courts having rendered decisions against municipalities recovering rights and added compensation for privileges heretofore granted, such a law is not practicable, nor would its legality be sustained.

Perhaps the best answer to this contention, may be found in the decisions of the United States Supreme Court defining the rights of municipalities in dealing with franchise values; also of several of the State courts, not only in rendering similar decisions, but, in some instances, declaring emphatically against the right of any municipal grants for the use of the public streets, as public property, in perpetuity. The recent popular movement for limited utility franchises is merely the advance step in a forward movement by which, through the regularly constituted channels, the people will again come into the possession, by tax or otherwise, of at least a fair portion of their own; and some of the great values wrongfully taken from them by this perpetual franchise process restored.

If the courts have not yet discovered a way that this can be done under the present law, new legislation and other courts may discern a new light to that result, as the recent illumination of the franchise value question has already opened new avenues of action toward better things, both in State, County and Municipal affairs.

FIELD HOUSES FOR PARKS.

Fourth;—As public parks are created and maintained by, and for, all the people, there should be enlarged opportunities and extended conveniences for their enjoyment by the general public. These pleasure grounds should not only be attractive to the eye in their natural and aesthetic adornment, but should also provide every possible feature for rest, recreation and benefit, that is consistent with public administration. The plan recently adopted by the South Park Commission, Chicago, in introducing in ten of the fifteen new parks of that system "Neighborhood-Center Buildings," or "field houses," is, I believe, most commendable and a practical move in the right direction.

In these recreation houses are assembly halls, for district meetings, lectures, etc.; a branch of the public library, clubrooms, refectories, gymnasiums, swimming pools, etc. All have running tracks, and an outdoor gymnasium for additional service in summer, wading pools and sand pits for children, swings, giant strides, and other athletic paraphernalia, all under the supervision of a gymnasium director, and all free to any person conducting himself or herself properly.

Although these field houses were opened for the first time in the past summer (1905), they have been patronized by hundreds of thousands of people, and beyond the expectations of those advocating their construction in the parks. The "Public thus receives a continuous and ample return on its investment—daily dividends in health, happiness and progress."

While this plan for the enlarged use of public parks is something of an innovation, it combines, with the "park beautiful," the park practical, and vastly increases for the mass of people the usefulness of their pleasure grounds throughout the year. That the present trend of activity and agitation for more playgrounds in all centers of population will gradually develop into some such enlarged use of the parks, is, I believe, inevitable. And the sooner the people of Essex County are enabled to enjoy increased benefits and extended opportunity for recreation, in return for their generous appropriations for the parks here, the better. While the park system has been irretrievably injured by the loss of one of the vitally important parkways, the parks are susceptible of great possibilities for the future. The 3,600 acres of park lands are forever dedicated to park uses. A portion of this area is already embellished with the best of modern park improvements. Other attractive features and utilitarian conveniences will from time to time be added.

When it is remembered that the public parks of to-day have all had their inception and development within the past fifty years, what is in store for the future and for the coming generations of the rapidly growing population of this country, with the proper care and management of the parks, it is difficult now to predict.

When the Essex County parks shall provide the greatest beneficent opportunities possible, concurrently with their aesthetical adornment, they will best serve the purpose for which they have been created.

THE END